STANDING on the ROCK

Central Pennsylvania's First African-American Radio Station Owner Shares His Life Story and Tackles the Issues of Religion and Race-Card Politics

JOSEPH GREEN

TownhallPress

Standing on the Rock

Chapters 1 to 14 Copyright © 2012 by Joseph L. Green

Chapters 15 to 21 Copyright © 2012 by Joseph L. Green
and Impact Communications

ISBN: 978-1-62419-342-2

All rights reserved solely by the author. The author guarantees all contents are original and do not infringe upon the legal rights of any other person or work. No part of this book may be reproduced in any form without the permission of the author except for brief quotations in critical reviews or articles.

To book Joseph Green, e-mail:
info@icinc.info

Cover concept and interior layout by Impact Communications

Unless otherwise noted, Bible quotations are from
The Holy Bible, King James Version

As a part of Salem Communications Corporation, Townhall Press is on-demand book publishing for conservative authors and Townhall.com is the leading internet source for conservative news and political commentary and analysis.

www.Townhall.com

Contents

ACKNOWLEDGEMENTS 5

INTRODUCTION 7

SECTION 1   MY BEGINNINGS

Chapter 1	My Early Life 11
Chapter 2	Growing Up With Nana & Pop Pop 17
Chapter 3	High School Days & Hormones Gone Wild 23
Chapter 4	The College Years 30
Chapter 5	Chasing Dreams. 40
Chapter 6	Living the Married Life? 51
Chapter 7	Virginia Beach Living 65
Chapter 8	Deep, Troubled Waters 73

SECTION 2   MY LIFE ON THE DARK SIDE

| Chapter 9 | Life on the Run . . . . .81 |
| Chapter 10 | Full-Time Dealer . . . . .94 |

SECTION 3   RETURNING TO THE LIGHT

| Chapter 11 | The Path to Repentance . . . . .107 |
| Chapter 12 | A New Life Brings Change . . . . .118 |

SECTION 4	THE CALLING	
Chapter 13	Recognizing & Accepting the Call of God	135
Chapter 14	Growing in the Wisdom & Freedom of God	147

SECTION 5	THE BUSINESS OF RELIGION AND RACE-CARD POLITICS	
Chapter 15	Evaluating the Obama Phenomenon	159
Chapter 16	The Issue of Life	176
Chapter 17	Murder in the Black Community	186
Chapter 18	Justice Is the Main Issue	197
Chapter 19	The Startling Truth About Democrats & Republicans	215
Chapter 20	Is There a Case for Polarized Politics?	224
Chapter 21	Your Call to Action	239

ABOUT THE AUTHOR 247

Acknowledgements

I want to first and foremost thank Jesus Christ. He is my Lord, my savior, my friend! He chose me before I was even born and then he purposed me, empowered me, and separated me for the destiny He called me to.

I want to thank God for all of my wonderful children and for my wife Gwen; she is my partner and my friend. No one is perfect but she is the perfect wife for me. She helps me to be the man that God has called me to be. She keeps me and the family in order and focused on the things that are important.

I want to thank my mom, Elma Scott. She has always been supportive of me; she has always told me that I could be whatever I wanted to be. When I was being chastened by the Lord, she was there to give me a place to live.

I want to thank the late Dean Lebo, who allowed God to use him to move me into my destiny.

I want to thank my pastor, Earl L. Harris. He helped start my quest to understand the Bible as the living Word, not just a book of stories and catchy sayings.

I want to thank Sister Audrey Jackson, who told me about the power of fasting. Fasting is a powerful tool that helped to accelerate my spiritual growth. Once I started living a fasted life, the Word of God was opened up to me in a miraculous way.

I am also very thankful for my ghostwriter who prefers to remain a "ghost" and was instrumental in providing most of the dynamic research in the "Religion and Race-Card Politics" section of this book. With my approval, my ghostwriter actually wrote a few chapters entirely, acting as my alter ego due to our parallel thinking regarding these very polarizing issues.

Introduction

I want to begin this book by saying that everything I do and everything I will ever become is by the grace of my Lord and Savior Jesus Christ. I've read many books in which the authors go through many trials and tribulations to ultimately overcome their circumstances. Those writings cause us to want to give the authors accolades and to celebrate their perseverance and determination. I don't want this book to be anything of the sort. As children of the Most High God, it is important that we recognize that only by the grace of God can any of us do anything of any significance. God must always get the glory in all that we do.

At the time that I am writing this book, I'm at the precipice of something big. God has been working on me for the last several years, and I can see that he is about to do some really big things in my life. To me, the next step in my life does not seem like that great of an accomplishment, but I believe that for several reasons. First and foremost, when you look at the endless possibilities that could have caused me not to have made it to where I am today, I cannot get too excited about myself. Secondly, I feel that this is just the beginning of some major things for the Kingdom of God. I am looking to the bigger and better things of God, and so again I am not going to get overcome with excitement about my accomplishments to date. I will say that I feel privileged that God has chosen me to be used as his servant to help to build his Kingdom here on earth. I am very grateful for this. My writing is in obedience to the spirit of God that has been leading me to write this book—not for my own glory but to glorify Him for how He has and is using me as a part of the Body of Christ.

—Joseph L. Green

Section 1
MY BEGINNINGS

Chapter 1

My Early Life

Without question, God is real and He is amazing! My life is living proof of His miracle-working power and ability to take what is shattered and bring it full circle to a place of healing, order, and completion.

I was raised by my mother and my great aunt and uncle, who I called my Nana and Pop Pop. I was a relatively good child, very strong minded, and I usually stayed out of trouble. As a child I was very active in many different things. I had a lot of interests, and I always wanted to participate in new activities, ranging from being a Boy Scout to a crossing guard in school.

I grew up regularly attending a Baptist church and all the activities that the church offered. I loved going to Sunday school, the morning service, and the youth events. When I was baptized at the age of nine, I was fully aware of what it meant. I knew that I was saved by accepting Jesus as the Lord of my life, and that now, as a child of God, I was responsible for my actions. It was my understanding that bad people went to hell, and the only way to avoid this was to accept Jesus and follow the Ten Commandments.

Without question, my devotion to God was sincere. I believed what I learned at church and had a deep awareness that God was watching everything I did. I didn't know it then, but I was actually operating in the *fear of the Lord*, which is the beginning of wisdom (see Psalm 111:10). Of course, we are not called to be *afraid* of God, but we are to have reverence and respect for Him and His unchanging Word. Once someone fails to have a reverential fear of the Lord, that person can become very dangerous.

Thankfully, I made a lot of *right* choices while growing up. Ironically, at that time I believed *I* was the one calling all the shots and making choices based on my *own* knowledge and desires. But now I know better. As Psalm 37:23 reveals, "The steps of a [good] man are directed and established *by the Lord...*" (AMP). So while I thought it was me doing such a great job, it was really God working with me all along. Interestingly, the older I get and the more I know, the more I know *I don't know*. We really know nothing in comparison to our omniscient God!

Big Dreams

As a child, I prayed just about every night. I still remember some of the things I asked God for on a regular basis. I prayed to be liked by others, to know the truth, and to be a good person. Truly I had a heart for the Lord, and through it all, I believe God faithfully answered my prayers.

I also remember some of the other requests that I made to God, such as praying to one day own a radio station. Back in the '70s, radio was big. Most cars didn't have high-tech stereo systems like they do now. A few had eight-track tape players, but for most lower-middle-class families, the radio was the way to go.

I really admired the local radio personalities and still do. They seem to have the personal touch and special ability to connect with people from all walks of life, telling them the local happenings in a way they can relate to. Whenever you want to know what is going on in a city, all you have to do is scan a couple of the most popular stations in that area. Of course, in this day and age with Internet and satellite radio, the local radio personalities have less of a following. But I do not believe that they will ever die off any more than cable television will kill the local newscaster.

When I look back, I wonder if my dream to own a radio station was something that I prayed for based on my own wants, or if God Himself had instilled in me the desire. In John 15:16, Jesus says, "You have not chosen Me, but I have chosen you and I have appointed you [I have planted you], that you might go and bear fruit and keep on bearing, and that your fruit may be lasting [that it may remain, abide], so that whatever you ask the Father in My Name [as presenting all that I AM], He may give it to you." Little did I know that my prayer request to own a radio station *would* be answered many years later. Indeed, it was answered and it is bearing good, lasting fruit today.

Pursuing My Passions—Music & Sports

Throughout the majority of my school years, the two things I enjoyed most were *music* and *sports*. Music has always been a love of mine, and I have always had a good ear for it. My mother played the piano, which was a very intriguing instrument to me. Normally, you had to be at least six in order to begin taking lessons, but because I was advanced for my age, I began practicing and playing at the age of five. As I grew, I tried many instruments, including the clarinet, the bass, the baritone, and the drums.

I quickly caught on and was able to do well when I practiced, but when things came too easy for me, I usually lost interest. Eventually, practicing became tiresome because it required staying inside, and as a young man of that era, the streets were always calling me. I loved being outside, and all I could think of was running and playing with my friends. Ultimately, my love of sports won out over my love of music, and consequently, my future as a musician took a back seat to my desire to be an athlete.

Aside from school, family, and the time I spent in church, sports took up the rest of my life. When I wasn't playing sports or watching sports, I was reading about them. I loved studying biographies about great athletes and how they made it to the top of their playing field. When I came across someone who had achieved greatness, I didn't just admire him as a great ballplayer; I also looked to learn from his experiences and one day surpass his level of success. In fact, I have never looked at another person's accomplishments as something out of reach. In my mind, if another human being did it, I could do it too.

Participating in sports taught me many things, including the importance of commitment and the discipline of daily practicing. Team sports also helped me to develop accountability and cooperation, and witness firsthand the rewards of hard work and determination. If I ever came up against an opponent who was better than me, I knew I just had to work harder than he did. Learning how to win and lose was also a very important part of my development. Even in defeat, I learned how to express myself in a healthy way.

All in all, I'm grateful to God that He gave me such a passion for sports. It kept me out of a lot of trouble. When I look at the music industry, I see how many musicians get caught up in drugs, sex, and other dangerous vices. This is not to say that athletes don't get caught up in some of the same things, but athletes by nature are called to live a more health-conscious lifestyle. In order to perform at a high level physically, they are required to get plenty of rest, eat right, and utilize their energy to play or practice their game. I would strongly encourage parents to consider getting their children involved in sports at an early age.

Like Father, Like Son

To understand my personality, it is important to understand my father. He was a large man who could have very easily been an offensive lineman in the NFL. He had a presence about him whenever he entered a room, always giving people the impression that he was very important. He didn't necessarily do this on purpose; he, like others, just had that way about him. Basically he was a good man who would never intentionally harm anyone, including me. The harm he inflicted usually resulted from not taking responsibility for his actions or considering their effects on those close to him.

My father's charisma and charm made him a very likable person; he loved to party and he loved women. He came from a large family in South Carolina and grew up on a farm. He was a relatively hard worker, but having a good time usually took precedence over perseverance and building for the future. Over the years, he held many different jobs, and like myself, experienced a certain level of success in many fields. He spent the last fourteen years as a nightclub manager before retiring to Cheraw, SC, with his third wife.

I believe my father would have been great at anything he put his heart into. With his abundant charisma and his convincing speaking ability, I think he would have made a great politician or been a great addition to the Kingdom of God. But he chose to use his gifts for his personal benefit. Indeed, "God's gifts and His call are *irrevocable*. [He never withdraws them when once they are given, and He does not change His mind about those to whom He gives His grace or to whom He sends His call]" (Romans 11:29).

Made in Their Image

In Jeremiah 1:5 God says, "Before I formed you in the womb I *knew* and *approved* of you [as My chosen instrument], and before you were born I separated and set you apart, consecrating you; [and] I appointed you as a prophet to the nations." In other words, you and I are no accident. God knows all about us even before we are born, including who our parents are going to be.

I used to wonder why I was born to my mother and father. They met back in the late '60s in Washington, DC, while she attended Cortez-Peters Business College and were only together for about three years. He was the "older man" who had the gift of gab and knew how to show her a good time. She quickly fell for him head over heels. At the age of nineteen, my mom got pregnant and gave birth to me. She and my dad, who was twenty-eight at the time, then got married and lived together for a short period. Unfortunately, it didn't work out, mainly because of my father's love of partying and womanizing. Out of great frustration, they separated and my mother returned to Harrisburg, PA. But God was working His plan.

It is important to understand that genetically we are made up of two distinct parts—we get our DNA from both our mother and father. When I look at my parents' strengths and weaknesses, God's plan for my life begins to unfold and make sense. One of the greatest blessings I received from my mother was a humble spirit. Actually, most of my Mom's relatives are very conservative in nature, emotionally calm and not easily excited. They have also had lasting marriages and long employment records, staying at the same job for twenty to thirty years until retirement.

From my father, I can also see the gifts I inherited. Because God has called me to preach His Word, He gave me my father's outspokenness and charismatic personality. Another quality found among those on my father's side is that most of them are fighters by nature. This is not to say that my father and his relatives went around picking fights with people. It just means they were not wimpy, nor were they quitters.

All of these traits from my mother and father were necessary ingredients to make me the man God planned for me to be. Isn't it amazing how two people who have a chance encounter can come together and form a life that impacts the lives of so many others, and I am not just talking about myself. When you take into consideration how easy it is to conceive a child, the influence that that life can have on the world is mind-boggling. I truly believe that God created each of us intentionally with our purpose and destiny locked up inside our DNA, and when we submit to Him, the Holy Spirit unlocks those gifts to be used for the glory of the kingdom of God!

Pro-abortion advocates often try to *deny* that life begins at conception. They take this position in an attempt to justify the murder of innocent babies. But as we read in Jeremiah, it is clear that God knew you even *before* you were born. In Psalm 139:13-16 NKJV King David declares:

> For You formed my inward parts; You covered me in my mother's womb. I will praise You, for **I am fearfully and wonderfully made**; marvelous are Your works, and that my soul knows well. My frame was not hidden from You, when I was made in secret, and skillfully wrought in the lowest parts of the earth. Your eyes saw my substance, being yet unformed. And in Your book they all were written, the days fashioned for me, when as yet there were none of them.

Amazingly, God has already set aside a plan and purpose for you and every other person born on earth. This included His elect—those who humbly accept Jesus into their lives as Lord and Savior. Understanding this has helped me to realize why certain people come together to conceive a child.

The reason I feel it is important to go into detail about my family background is to help you understand why I made some of the decisions I made and ended up in the places I did. The truth is by understanding our genetic makeup, we can better understand why we react the way we do in the situations we face. Even though our DNA definitely has a big impact on our lives, thankfully, we are not slaves to it. I believe that no matter what your makeup is and no matter what type of environment you grew up in, once you have repented of your sins and been washed with the blood of the Lamb, you can choose to be whomever God has called you to be!

Chapter 2

Growing Up with Nana & Pop Pop

I thank God for the people He placed in my life. As I mentioned, not only was I raised by my mother but also my Nana and Pop Pop. As a child, my mother had a special attachment to them, and they had a special attachment to her, especially because Nana was unable to have children. As a result, they asked her to stay with them quite often, and eventually she moved in with them and they raised her as their own daughter. Although she remained close to her natural mother and father, she considered Nana and Pop Pop her parents. This is why she returned to their house when she and my father separated and I was born. I believe Pop Pop was about 55 at the time.

Nana and Pop Pop provided a very peaceful home where I was pretty much the center of attention. Although Pop Pop worked a lot, he always seemed to make time for me. Likewise, Nana only worked part-time at the church, and since we lived within a few blocks, she was usually available when I needed her. My mother was a hard worker as well. Like many others in Harrisburg, she worked for the state government since it is the state capital. She didn't make a lot of money, but the benefits were good. With Nana and Pop Pop around to supplement her income, I usually had whatever I needed or wanted. All in all, I would say that I had a very good childhood.

Pop Pop's Roots

Pop Pop was born in a small country town in Georgia in 1912. Like the majority of small towns in that area, it was predominantly a farming community. Most black families had many children, and the children were usually expected to work on the family farm. There wasn't much need for schooling because most of the family's income and food came from the ground. As a rule, people in those days made a living with their bodies, *not* their minds. Those who did not work on the farm usually worked in a factory or mill or at some other type of job involving physical labor.

Because of his obligation to his family, Pop Pop only went to school until the third grade, and he never really learned how to read or write. This was very common for that time and place. He was one of the older boys of a family of twelve children. His father died while he was a teenager, and as a result, he had to go to work full time to help support his family. In spite of his limited education, he carried himself with great dignity and class. So much so that I often forgot that he could barely read and write. Sadly, his story was not the exception but more so the rule of his day.

In our school history class, I remember studying how bad things were during The Great Depression of 1929. We heard that many people lost everything they had, and some of them even committed suicide. I remember going home and asking Pop Pop about it. Interestingly, he said, "We were so poor that we didn't even hear anything about the Depression until years later." When you are as poor as Pop Pop's family, the financial impact of the depression wasn't that great.

All in all, Pop Pop was an easy going man who never really let anything ruffle his feathers. For instance, when he started first grade, his teacher asked him what his name was. He told her *Judge*, which was his real name (I thought it was Jerge because that was the way it sounded when people with a heavy Georgian accent pronounced it). Well, his teacher didn't believe him and in a matter-of-fact way, she told him that *Judge* was not a name but a title and that he needed to go home and choose another name. She suggested Jerry, which Pop Pop didn't like, and then Joseph. He didn't mind Joseph, and it just so happened that his older sister, Mary, had a boyfriend named Joseph. So that clinched it; from that point on, Judge became Joseph. All his friends and relatives still called him Judge, but for everyone else it was now Joseph.

As I said, Pop Pop didn't let things shake him, which is a vital quality for a true disciple of Christ. He learned the importance of not sweating the small stuff and persevering through both good and bad times. He used to say that he could spend a year in hell if he knew that it would mean an eternity in paradise. This statement would become one of the strongest philosophies upon which I approached life.

An Inspiring Work Ethic

One major mind-set that Pop Pop instilled in me while growing up was a diligent work ethic. He started working in a brickyard in Milledgeville, GA, at the age of fourteen. He was a hard worker his entire life, all the way up until his early eighties when he became physically unable to work. I always felt sad for men like him because he didn't have any hobbies—all he knew was work.

Pop Pop came up during a time when blacks were treated as second-class citizens and segregation was deeply ingrained as the law of the land. There were no equal opportunity employment laws or affirmative action laws to ensure that minorities received equal treatment. However, Pop Pop never grumbled or complained, and I never heard him say that the "white man" was trying to hold him down. He just worked hard and did what he needed to do to provide for his family.

In the 1940s, there was a large exodus of African-Americans from many parts of the south, especially Georgia. This was when Pop Pop came to Harrisburg, PA, and soon afterwards other family members followed, including my biological grandfather. Many moved north in search of employment opportunities. The fact that there were more inside factory jobs free from the effects of the weather was very appealing. Furthermore, from what I understand, many workers were also able to receive benefits from northern employers, such as health insurance, dental care, and a retirement plan.

The other factor motivating the massive exodus of blacks from the south was a desire to get away from the overt racism that was very prevalent in the southern U.S. Most of the whites in the north kept their prejudice below the surface. It was not as politically correct to express racist views in that part of the country. Consequently, this made for a more peaceful environment to work, live, and raise a family.

For most of his life, Pop Pop worked three jobs to provide for his family. Even though he was not a well-educated man, he didn't use it as an excuse. Through his example, he taught me that you either win or lose in life—the reason is not important. If you do *not* reach your goals, you lose, but when you reach them, you win. Through his actions, more than his words, he demonstrated that no matter who wronged you or what circumstances hindered you, you should not focus on it.

I look at all the excuses people use today and it bothers me greatly. So many people have countless opportunities to achieve great things, yet they let their excuses hold them hostage. God used Pop Pop's life to instill in me a powerful perspective: If an uneducated man from the Deep South facing the challenges he faced was able to achieve what he achieved, what excuse could I possibly have not to succeed in life?

Pop Pop & Nana's Relationship

Now Pop Pop had two children from a previous relationship, and from the day he and my Nana got married, she was very bitter over it. Consequently, she never really accepted them. To make matters worse, Nana was unable to have a child of her own and had suffered at least one miscarriage. Sadly, she carried deep grief and growing resentment in her heart that only fueled the fire of anger toward Pop Pop's two children. The one good thing in all of this is that Nana took a real liking to my mom and, as I mentioned, she and Pop Pop eventually took her in as their very own.

The tension and animosity between Nana and Pop Pop remained until her death in 1982. Although I very rarely perceived them as being a happily married couple, they did, nevertheless, share one major high point in their married life: They enjoyed spending time with family. Family was always very important to them. All eight of my grandfather's children were very close to Pop Pop. He always had a pleasant demeanor and a pocket full of candy to give out. Needless to say, all the children of the family loved visiting him. With his ever-present smile and loving personality, He was a joy to be around indeed.

THE *POP POP* — *GRAND POP* CONNECTION

My biological grandfather, who I affectionately call "Grand Pop," was my Pop Pop's brother. He was about ten years younger than Pop Pop and they were very close. Actually, Grand Pop looked to him as a father because their Dad had passed away when he was very young. As best he could, Pop Pop functioned as his parent in spite of the fact that he was only a teenager.

I remember Pop Pop telling me about the last spanking he gave my grandfather. Grand Pop was around thirteen years old and had matured rather quickly for his age. He had grown to be a strapping, 6'2" young man. Pop Pop, although very strong physically from many years of hard work, was only about 5'8". Needless to say, he had reservations about issuing corporal discipline to Grand Pop because he was so much bigger.

What had happened was, Pop Pop had made homemade wine for the holidays as was his tradition even though he never drank. Grand Pop evidently wanted to taste some of it, and when Pop Pop discovered that some was missing, he felt compelled to discipline Grand Pop. With extreme reluctance, my grandfather accepted his spanking, but he made it very clear that it would be the last. I am sure that the conversation they had was not quite as neat and clean as this, but I believe that you get the picture.

Time passed and Grand Pop grew, becoming a diligent worker and fathering eight children. He later retired from Bethlehem Steel Mill and lived a lower middle class lifestyle. Unfortunately, his interest in liquor didn't diminish. Unlike Pop Pop who never drank, my grandfather often went on drinking binges around the holidays that lasted for a couple of days. Yet, aside from his struggles with alcohol, he was a very friendly person that got along with most people. Even when he was on an alcohol binge, his bark was worst than his bite. I don't ever recall him being violent in any way. Through it all, he was a hard worker and a good provider for his family.

Disciplined in Love

Nana and Pop Pop had a strict but traditional home environment. Character was very important and emphasized often. At times, I openly expressed my opinions about things, but never disrespectfully. I was taught to honor and obey my elders and that whoever was in authority could discipline us—from the adults in the neighborhood to the principal at school. When I got into trouble, I was afraid to let Nana and Pop Pop know. I loved and respected them so much that I was actually more concerned about what they thought of me than the actual punishment I received. I believe this healthy motivation kept me out of a lot of trouble. To take this away from young people is dangerous and tends to produce children who don't care about the consequences of their behavior.

Pop Pop came from a family of disciplinarians where the line was clearly drawn between children and adults. As a child, you might overhear an adult conversation, but you had better not attempt to add anything to it. The old adage that children should be "seen and not heard" prevailed. I was not allowed to use words like "Shoot!" or "Darn!" because when used in the right context, they sounded too much like a cuss word. Saying things like this would usually result in a slap on the mouth. And when I was told to do something, I was not allowed to act as though I wasn't going to do it.

Don't get me wrong... Although I was raised in a strict environment, there was also plenty of love to go around. In fact, there was never a time when I did not feel loved by my family. Of course, when discipline was applied, I didn't like it and I thought all kinds of bad thoughts about the disciplinarians. But they were passing thoughts that lasted about as long as the sting of the strap used to apply the punishment.

The Bible is full of scriptures declaring the importance of discipline, especially the book of Proverbs. Proverbs 13:24 says, "He who spares his rod [of discipline] hates his son, but he who loves him disciplines diligently and punishes him early." Proverbs 22:15 states, "Foolishness is bound up in the heart of a child, but the rod of discipline will drive it far from him." Proverbs 23:13,14 instructs, "Withhold not discipline from the child; for if you strike and punish him with the [reedlike] rod, he will not die. You shall whip him with the rod and deliver his life from Sheol

(Hades, the place of the dead)." And Proverbs 29:15 proclaims, "The rod and reproof give wisdom, but a child left undisciplined brings his mother to shame." (Scriptures taken from the Amplified Bible.)

Scriptures like these and others are very important when raising children. Now, I am not suggesting that raising children is just about discipline, but it is a very vital part of it, as my family will attest. When a foundation of discipline, love, and structure is laid in the home, children are raised in a healthy, balanced way and equipped for a productive life.

A Lasting Impression

I think by now you can see that the influence of my Pop Pop was *immeasurable*. I know that without God placing him in my life, I would have been a totally different person, and *not* for the better. I learned so much wisdom from sitting and listening to him talk. To me, Pop Pop was one of the most Christ-like men I have ever been around in my life. No, he was not perfect, but to me his flaws were very minor.

As we get deeper into the story of my life, you will see just how far I strayed from the path of my upbringing. Certainly, I veered from the road of righteousness. But thankfully, every time I got close to the edge of disaster, the Spirit of God brought back to my remembrance of where I came from. If it were not for the direction that I had been given in my formative years, I would have gone a lot farther down the path of destruction.

Clearly, when you raise children in an environment where God is the *center* of everything, then you have laid a foundation they will never forget. Even if they stray from the path of righteousness, realize that God is still in control. Looking back over my life, I can see that surrendering myself to Jesus at a very young age is what kept me, even when I wasn't aware of it. Indeed, when we "Train up a child in the way he should go… when he is old he will not depart from it" (Proverbs 22:6 NKJV).

CHAPTER 3

HIGH SCHOOL DAYS & HORMONES GONE WILD

High school was an eye-opening time in my life. As a student, I excelled academically. As a result, I was always placed in a special program designed for advanced learners and separated from a lot of the other students. When I was not in school, I was usually practicing some sport, which also kept me guarded from many bad influences in life. While children with a lot of free time were out doing mischief, I was usually doing something constructive. In most cases, I believe it was better *not* to know the things that I was being guarded from, especially when you are too young the handle the consequences.

CRAVING NEW EXPERIENCES

I remember having a conversation early in high school with a fellow athlete in which we both agreed that if we had a choice between playing ball and chasing women, we would choose sports every time. Well, as time passed, that changed and I developed a growing desire to experience the world. High school became a chance to explore the things that I had never been exposed to before. I wanted to encounter the intimacy of a woman (preferably without actually performing the act of sex). I wanted to know what it was like to hang out and be a rebel. Don't get me wrong. I didn't really want to do bad things. Excelling in sports and going to college were still top priority. But the enticement of the world was quickly gaining momentum.

Somehow I had bought into the phony philosophy that by experiencing things, I would gain knowledge and be better equipped to deal with life and fit into the world. I believed the false notion that if I "sowed my wild oats," I would get them out of my system. Well, I can tell you first hand that the more you indulge in sin, the more enticing and rooted sin becomes. Like a drug addict or an alcoholic, the more you "use," the more you want to "use." So this philosophy of getting things out of our system is a major tool of the devil that appeals to our carnal mind and sensual cravings.

Hormones Heat Up

With each passing day, my perspectives on life continued to change. I still had my same interests but they now had to share time with my overwhelming attraction to the opposite sex. As with most young men, the hormones coursing through my veins became a very powerful influence in my life. I had always been attracted to girls, but when puberty hit me at full force, women took center stage on the consciousness of my mind. There are certain strongholds that I believe we all have in our lives. For some, it is an obsession with money. For others, it is drugs, alcohol, or their career. For me, however, it seemed to be my attraction to the opposite sex.

All of us are born with a natural, innate desire for the opposite sex. But through movies, music, molestation and the like, Satan has perverted it. Sexual sins that are not dealt with turn into *generational curses* passed on to future family members. Personally, I believe that one of the major reasons I faced overwhelming sexual temptation was because I was a recipient of the "sins of my fathers." When I say the *sins of my fathers*, I am not just talking about my biological Dad; I am also referring to the sins of my family line, going back to the third and fourth generation (see Exodus 20:5). Over the years, I heard many stories of the sexual sins of past generations that cause me to believe this to be true.

Even though I knew that sex was only to be realized between a husband and wife, I couldn't escape the alluring temptation of lust. I fought it all throughout my high school years, but the urge was just overwhelming. This would turn out to be one of the hardest things for me to overcome in my life. Giving in to my sexual desires proved to be the start of my downward spiral away from God.

Based on what the Word of God says and what life has shown me, purity and holiness are not a suggestion but a *must* for all who follow Christ (see 1 Thessalonians 4:3-7). Once I was headed down the path of fornication, my overall direction in life became very much skewed. I still had the same goals, but a spirit of lust seemed to always be lurking in the background, whispering in my ear and looking for opportunities to gain ground in my life. Little by little, I became more and more obsessed as I gave in to the sexual urges in my mind.

Doorway of the Mind

The main avenue through which Satan works to trap us in a life of sexual sin is our **mind**. Unfortunately, many people never truly grasp this—they fail to see that *physical* sin begins with impure *mental* images and thoughts. I now know that part of my problem was constantly fantasizing about the girls I went to school with. During the day, I spent most of my time daydreaming about them, and during the evening I spent my time talking to them on the phone or trying to show up where they were meeting. To make matters worse, I was developing physically, which earned me extra attention from the girls my age. Indeed, Satan truly had free reign of my mind when it came to women.

Jesus cautions us along these lines in Matthew 5:28 saying "...that everyone who so much as *looks* at a woman with evil desire for her has already committed adultery with her in his heart" (AMP). Just as it is sinful to actually perform the act of sex outside of marriage, it is also sinful in God's eyes to harbor lustful thoughts in your mind. Now, I am not suggesting that just because you have lustful thoughts about a woman in your mind that you should go ahead and act on them. What I am saying is that you must take control of these thoughts before they gain entrance into your heart. This is the powerful principle found in 2 Corinthians 10:5: "Casting down *imaginations*, and every *high thing* that exalts itself against the knowledge of God, and **bringing into captivity** every *thought* to the obedience of Christ" (KJV).

I believe one of the greatest ways Satan has been able to develop such a *stronghold* of influence in our churches and keep many of the saints discouraged, ineffective, and powerless is through a yoke of sexual sin. Many Christians have not understood that as long as we entertain sexual thoughts, we are opening the door for the enemy. Sadly, it is reported by some hotel chains that the amount of pornography ordered by guests during Christian conventions is very high. The truth is, we can't watch sexually charged movies and TV shows and listen to sexually suggestive songs and expect it not to affect us and our families. Fornication, adultery, and homosexuality are now running rampant in our modern churches, and we are paying the price for the seeds we have sown.

The Way It Was Meant to Be

God made men and women to enjoy each other both physically and emotionally within the holy institution of marriage. In fact, the attraction between husband and wife is the closest and strongest bond two humans can share. It is a symbolic of Jesus' relationship with every member of the Church, which is also known as the Bride of Christ (see Ephesians 5:22-32). Look at how the Bible records the first marriage:

> And the Lord God caused a deep sleep to fall on Adam, and he slept; and He took one of his ribs, and closed up the flesh in its place. Then the rib which the Lord God had taken from man He made into a woman, and brought her to the man. And Adam said: 'This is now bone of my bones, and flesh of my flesh; she shall be called Woman, because she was taken out of Man.' Therefore shall a man leave his father and his mother and be joined to his wife, and they shall become one flesh. And they were both naked, the man and his wife, and were not ashamed.
> **—Genesis 2:21-25 NKJV**

The sexual relationship between a husband and wife is a beautiful gift that God has given to us. It gives us pleasure without guilt or shame. It brings us closer together and enables us to procreate and replenish the earth. When we act out sexually in any way other than the God-ordained relationship of marriage, we muddy the purity and wholesomeness that God intended to be enjoyed between a man and a woman. This is what I did through all the impure images I saw, the fantasizing in my mind, and the eventual acting out with women. I came to the place where, I, like many others, allowed myself to think that everything short of intercourse was acceptable. By the end of my senior year, this too would change, and I would give in to what Satan had been driving me toward for many years.

All the Way

By the time I was a high school senior, I was no longer playing organized sports. I was young, good looking, athletic, intelligent and well-liked by my peers. In my mind, I had done pretty well for myself up to that point. I knew God was with me and that Jesus was my Savior, but I decided to only use Him in case of emergencies. My life became one big party. If not for the grace of God and the momentum I had built up in the previous years, I would have never graduated on time in 1985. As it was, I barely escaped with my high school diploma.

Just before graduating, I traveled to the University of Pittsburgh (Pitt) to check out the campus and all the school had to offer. While I was visiting, I received the news that I had been accepted to the college. To celebrate,

I smoked marijuana with a couple of Pitt's football stars—one of which eventually went on to the pros—and I experienced my first real sexual encounter. Ironically, it happened in the university dorm with a young lady I knew from my home town.

Like a person's first cigarette or drink of alcohol, my first experience of sexual intercourse was not at all what I expected. I know that it was largely due to my inexperience, and the fact that we were both high didn't help matters. My partner, of course, did not know that it was my first time. As awkward as it was, I knew I wanted to do it again. This experience put me over the edge and allowed me to begin justifying in my mind that fornication was not a big deal.

At that point, I had completely lost focus of my goals for college and playing ball. After I had finally broken the virginity barrier and moved from heavy petting to actually having sex, I was like a child with a new toy. My mind began to race to several women that I had not gone all the way with. In my estimation, I had made it to "third base," which is doing everything short of the act of sex. At third base, I had undressed women of their tops and bras, and sometimes taken off everything but their underpants. Of course my intent *then* was not to have sex with them, and I had justified in my mind that I was not sinning because there was no penetration involved. But now with the barrier broken, it was a whole new ball game.

THE SUMMER OF '85

The summer before college was my time of transition from teenager to adult. It was July of 1985, I had just turned eighteen, and I was a few weeks away from leaving for Pitt. I had just quit my part-time job and the world was my oyster! I looked forward to living life to the fullest. The last few months of my senior year and the months leading up to my freshman year of college were spent the same way—honing my basketball skills, chasing women and hanging out with the boys. I wanted to get all the partying out of my system before going to college. I worked hard on my game—both on the court and even harder with the women. Pop Pop was still working three jobs, so I had a lot of freedom at the house. By this time, my strained relationship with my mom and stepdad had caused me to move out of her house and into Pop's. Many times I had uninterrupted encounters with women while no one was home. At the time I thought it was no big deal. Regretfully, I now look back on what I did with great remorse. I had disrespected and dishonored my Pop Pop and his house, and I needed to repent.

The night before I was to leave for college the fellows and I were having a going-away party, and the celebration was anything but common. Two of the new things I discovered that summer were malt liquor and hanging out on the corner—the legendary location everyone in my neighborhood called *the Beaumont*. It was about two blocks from my house, and it was the happening hangout passed down from previous generations. I have no idea where it got its name, but I used to see the old "heads" hang out there when I was a youngster, getting high and "talking trash" as we called back then. I remember standing around the older guys and listening to them tell their hood stories of the fights they had, the women they slept with, and all the acts of rebellion they committed. To a young man growing up in my neighborhood, this was the ultimate show of your blackness and macho independence—it was a way for someone to make a name for himself and build his self-worth.

This particular summer, I felt honored because I was the premiere topic of conversation on the Beaumont. I was big, strong, handsome, intelligent and going places. I felt like I was unstoppable, and to top it all off, I not only had the "full package" but also my father's gift of gab to go with it. In my mind, there were few areas in which I was not superior when it came to interaction on the Beaumont. Ironically, I found out years later that of all the people who bragged about doing things, I was one of the few who actually did them. It appears that everyone else was just talking. That was the thing in my community; everyone always seemed to be doing more than they really were.

As strange as it may seem, I believed all the trash talk I heard. I was the type of person that valued my words, so I assumed that everyone else did so too. Only later in life was I able to discern the difference between trash talk and *real dialogue*. Some would say that I was a bit naïve as a young man, but I truly felt that you should say what you mean and mean what you say.

Most of the guys in the hood use words very frivolously and do not realize their power. The Bible tells us that *life* and *death* are in the power of the tongue (see Proverbs 18:21). Unknowingly, people often curse and speak death to each other, especially in the black community. I even hear young black people call themselves all kinds of negative things in jest. We must begin to understand the power of the tongue and learn from the compelling examples found in Scripture. The more we understand the concept of blessings and curses, the more we will guard our words.

A Closing Thought

Even though I had every intention on waiting until I was married to engage in sexual intercourse, I was unable to carry it out because I didn't understand God's principles on sexual purity and grace. It is one thing to *say* "Just don't do it," but it is another thing to actually *live* it. I can now understand why God set up a standard of sexual intimacy within marriage between one man and one woman only. I can also see why we are not to lust after others in our mind or look at sexually suggestive material. Truly, couples who remain virgins until they marry are blessed. I have always admired them, and I always will. It is also important for us to instill sexual purity into our young people; it is God's will and it should be our standard as well.

I want to make it very clear that I am sparing the more graphic details of my encounters because of the inappropriateness of sharing them. I do, however, believe that in order to truly help people with my testimony, I must be somewhat transparent and not try to cover up things under the guise of being holy and righteous. Indeed, the only way to truly give God the credit for how much He has done in our lives is to give a clear picture of the depths from which he has brought us. If I were to use very vague terms, then it would be unclear as to what I am talking about, and I may not communicate the true meaning of the message I am trying to deliver. In other words, I am **not** telling these secrets of my life to glorify fornication. On the contrary, I tell them to reveal just how far God has truly brought me. We give God the glory for the heights He has brought us to by revealing the depths to which our own choices had taken us.

Chapter 4

The College Years

My college experience started off much the same way that my high school years had ended. I continued to be more and more promiscuous. Sex went from being a novelty to virtually a necessity like food or shelter, and the guilt from my sin lessened with each encounter. Like any sin, the more you do it, the easier it is to transgress the laws of God.

At the same time, I was full of self-confidence. I had spent all summer in training, and I was in great shape to walk on Pitt's basketball team. I had big dreams and aspirations of becoming a professional basketball player and was confident I had the ability to do it. I was at the top of my game, and I felt unstoppable. If it had not been for my preoccupation with chasing women, I am sure that I would have made an excellent college basketball player. But my lack of focus made me very inconsistent—not only on the court but also in the classroom.

Setbacks Steal the Show

Unfortunately, my career at Pitt never got off the ground even though the buzz had gotten around campus. By the time I figured everything out, it was too late in my freshman year to walk on. So I switched my attention to using the extra year to bring my game up to the college level.

Pitt had a good team that played in a great conference. It was a part of the Big East, which was arguably the premiere basketball conference in the country. It included such teams as Georgetown, St. John's, Syracuse, Seton Hall and Connecticut. Pitt was on the rise and becoming one of the better teams in the country. I had positioned myself to make the team in my sophomore year, and with that accomplished, the pros would have been within my reach. As a player on a nationally-ranked team, I would have many opportunities to be seen by the entire country, which meant many pro scouts would have gotten familiar with my name. Things were really looking up for me.

However, there were several other things that happened my first two years of college that changed the course of my life and ultimately caused me not to realize my dream. The first was a serious foot injury I sustained during my freshman year. While playing a pickup game, I was running for a loose ball and I hit my left foot extremely hard on the floor. Looking back, I believe that I probably broke a bone, but at the time I thought it was just a very bad jam. Consequently, I never got it x-rayed and continued to play through the pain, pushing towards my goal of making the team. It took almost a year before I was able to play at my previous level, and even to this day, some twenty years later, I can still feel a twinge of pain at times when I step on it wrong.

By the time my sophomore year rolled around, I had gotten all my affairs in order in time to make an official tryout. I had played all summer with the scholarship players, most of which were confident I could make a positive contribution to the team. However, during my conditioning phase of training, one thing became very evident: I lacked discipline, which made it much more difficult for me to play. Oh, I practiced my game a lot and was very good. I had no problems competing with others, and I even had the opportunity to go up against several players that had successful NBA careers.

What I did *not* have was a consistent training regimen. In other words, I didn't commit myself to doing the drills that the other players were doing. I also didn't play the game the way the coaches wanted. My rebellious and prideful attitude had me training myself the way *I* thought was best. There are many players who play this type of improvised game, but very few coaches accept them. For most of the preseason, it actually looked as though I would become a member of the Pitt basketball team. I survived all the cuts up until the last one. Just before the official start of the basketball season, I was let go. Actually, there were two scholarship football players that had been promised a spot on the roster. So right before the season started, the coach made room for them and I was cut from the team. As a result of these circumstances and my choices, I failed to make the team in my sophomore year, which brought on many repercussions.

Throughout the entire time, my grades were suffering as a result of the extended hours of basketball practice. To make matters worse, I had not chosen a major, which only further reduced my desire to invest any energy into my academic studies. Aside from being a basketball player, I had no career in mind that I wanted to pursue. Needless to say, these first two years of college were a vicious cycle.

With all that was going on, I began to feel a sense of depression and emptiness creeping into my life. You would think that by this point I would have turned back to God for help, but I didn't. I was totally blind to my spiritual condition. I was clueless to the fact that we are all designed with a hole in our spirit that only God Himself can fill. I, like others, tried to fill the void with many different things from basketball to partying to more sexual encounters with women. But nothing would suffice. I can tell you from personal experience that there is **no** substitute for a relationship with the true and living God—*nothing*.

The Pain of a Strain

In addition to being depressed over my poor grades and not making the team, I was also dealing with a strained relationship between my Mom and me. This had actually been going on for several years. When I was around thirteen, my Mom remarried. At the time, we didn't live far from Pop Pop's. But the man she married I did not respect. As a matter of fact, I hated him. I thought his wild lifestyle was terrible, and I couldn't stand the disrespectful way he treated my mother. Later in this book I will share how the power of forgiveness marvelously changed my relationship with my stepfather for the better. But before I came to Christ, we had a very tumultuous relationship.

The main reason I hated him was not so much because of the way he treated me but because of the way he treated my mom. I have a deep disgust for men, especially black men, who mistreat and disrespect their women, especially black women. The only reason I make this distinction is because of that fact that it really hits home with me. I also feel this way because of all the negative stereotypes that have been passed down through the years concerning black men. I believe we owe it to our women and children to live our lives with decency and respect. More importantly, we need to respect the women in our lives and be an example to young men regarding how to respect and treat women.

Needless to say, my stepdad and I did not get along, which in turn affected my relationship with my mom. She felt her relationship with him was more important than her relationship with me, which in one sense was true. The Bible does say that a man shall leave his father and mother and they shall cleave to each other. However, it does *not* negate a parent's responsibility to her children. In my mind, I believed my mom should have chosen a better man and given me a more positive male role model to be my stepfather, and because she didn't, I deeply resented her.

To me, Pop Pop was the ultimate example of a godly man who was worthy of honor and respect. He represented what was *right* with men. He came from a generation where it was more important to do what was right than to do what felt good. I watched him sacrifice himself many times to provide for his family. In spite of his inability to read and write or his lowly position as a janitor for a health care company for thirty years, he carried himself with the dignity of a king.

My stepfather, on the other hand, was in many ways just the opposite. He represented many of the *negative* stereotypes we see in our communities. He was very carnal and more interested in doing what was satisfying to him than to do what is right. He was raised in the north during a time when blacks were fighting for their rights. It was no longer socially acceptable to call African-Americans the "N" word and get away with it. Blacks were standing up for themselves, and more and more laws were being passed to guarantee that they had equal rights under the law. Minorities also had increased access to education, and in many state schools in the north, financial assistance was given away to black students in order to increase diversity. Indeed, this was a time in which the tide was turning, and black consciousness was at an all-time high. Black America had made some of its largest strides during this period in our country's history.

In spite of all these opportunities, I find that many blacks insist on using racism as the main reason why they can't get ahead. This kind of thinking has always bothered me, especially when I see what Pop Pop and many others were able to accomplish with all the odds that were against them. Even when I have failed to accomplish my goals in life, I have always looked back to see what else I could have done to achieve them. Although many black people were, and at times still are, treated unfairly due to racism, it is still no excuse for failure as my stepfather claimed.

Ironically, when I look back on my thoughts and feelings about my stepfather now, I can definitely see a hint of hypocrisy in my life. As it turns out, I was also being disrespectful to the women I was involved with by dishonoring their bodies and having sex with them while not being married. Of course, in the natural world I was just being a man, but to God my sin was just as bad as my stepfather's.

I share all these things to give you an indication of what was going on during this time of my life. My strained relationship with my mother caused a deep depression in me that was hard to overcome. College is not easy, but it's even harder without emotional support. My mother never seemed overly concerned with how I was doing. When I needed money and called her, she always told me she didn't have it. What hurt even worse were the times she said, "I never told you to go to college in the first place." Needless to say, this built an even bigger wedge between us. Thankfully, I was living with Pop Pop at the time, and he was there for me whenever I needed him. If I got in a jam, he did whatever he could to help. With this in mind, I tried to call him only when I didn't have any other place to turn.

Homegrown Love

After my second year of college, I began seeing a young lady from my hometown. Her name was "Kathy," and she was a year ahead of me in school. She was a friend I had known since I was a sophomore in high school, but we had never gotten serious with each other. I always thought of her as just someone to hang out and to have fun with, but as time passed, we began seeing each other regularly and developed a very serious relationship. This was very convenient because we were both from the same area, had socialized in the same circles, and knew each other's family. It seemed like a perfect fit, but more importantly, the relationship gave me a level of stability in my life I desperately needed.

One thing I learned through my relationship with Kathy is how vital love is to our makeup as human beings. There was a study that examined two groups of infants. Some of the infants were born in a dysfunctional family environment, and they did not receive regular physical affection. The other group of children lived in an environment in which they were held and shown regular affection by the nurses in the hospital. Both groups of babies were given milk when they needed it and were wrapped in warm blankets. But the infants that were placed in the adoption agency did not receive the caring embrace of the nurses. Even though both groups received the necessities of life, the group that was given affection cried less, contracted less sickness and developed intellectually and emotionally better than the group of infants without loving physical touch. Indeed, if we do not receive physical touch and affection, we will wither and fail to develop correctly.

Without question, the love and affection I was receiving from Kathy had a definite impact on my life. I could not see it at the time, but God was using her to put many things in my life in motion. She helped to fill a lot of gaps I had, especially the need for a woman's love that had been missing due to the rift between my mother and me. She also helped give me the motivation I needed to buckle down and get serious about the direction of my life. Before this point, I was spending most of my time playing basketball and chasing an empty way of life that I thought would bring me happiness. But meeting Kathy caused me to turn away from my promiscuous lifestyle and begin living a more conservative one—one that better reflected how I was raised.

As time passed, we became more and more serious with each other and even began talking about marriage. By the time I turned twenty, I believed that Kathy was going to be a permanent part of my future. I still had aspirations of becoming a pro basketball player, but that goal began to take a back seat to love. My main focus now changed to finishing school and pursuing a career and a family.

Cracks in the Foundation

Kathy and I grew very close, and we did just about everything together. Unfortunately, because it was my first real experience with being in love, I didn't understand my role in the relationship. Consequently, I became what many consider *henpecked*. I understood the basic premise of trying to please your woman, but I didn't have any real example to go by. As good as my Pop Pop was, his relationship with Nana always seemed full of tension and strife. And my stepfather was very dysfunctional in his approach to treating a woman; he was definitely not a good example to follow. He also did not fulfill the traditional role model of a breadwinner or the man of the house. He, like many other men, only got half the story. He saw the man as the king of his castle, but what he failed to realize is that in order for man to be king, he must treat his woman like a queen and provide her with respect and financial support.

Kathy was a very strong, opinionated woman who had been spoiled by her parents. Like many relationships that start out good but end up bad, the things that seemed cute in the beginning of our relationship ended up being its demise. Because of the absence of my mother's involvement in my life, Kathy's overbearing ways were somewhat of a substitute for her. Later in our relationship, as I matured into a man, I began to resent the very trait that I once loved.

As I said, Kathy was a year ahead of me in school, and she was studying communications with plans of going to law school. I was a psychology major with plans on being a psychiatrist. Halfway through Kathy's senior year at Pitt, she received the news that she had been accepted to law school in Maryland. Even though I knew it meant we would be separated for awhile, I was very happy for her. I was willing to go through the time apart because as Pop Pop always said, "I could spend a year in hell if I knew that it would mean an eternity in Heaven." In other words, I could endure the heartache of being apart as long as I knew it would benefit us in the long run.

Major Change

As Kathy began to prepare for law school, I began to entertain the thought of going to law school too. I was always very articulate, and I had a gift for getting people to believe what I wanted. Law school seemed like the perfect fit for me. So at the end of my second year of college, I changed my major from psychology to communications. It didn't seem like a big deal at the time, but later in my life I would clearly see God's hand in the decision.

So there I was—at the end of my second year of college and the beginning of my third. Once I changed direction regarding my major, I decided to take some time off. In addition to my academic struggles, the cost of college was more than I had anticipated. Before this time, I thought that I would have been on a full sports scholarship, so I didn't really pay attention to the cost of tuition, housing, etc. In retrospect, it was a good thing that I didn't look at it because if I would have, I would have never decided to go to Pitt.

My decision to sit out a semester was one that Kathy did not agree with. As our relationship grew closer and closer and as we were making plans for the future, sitting out a semester didn't seem like a good idea to her. Through a series of long talks, I assured Kathy that it would only be for one semester and that I would come to see her as often as I could. Our time apart confirmed just how deep my feelings for her had become. It also confirmed that I needed to stay in college and to complete my degree.

Reality Check

Summer had arrived, and many companies were offering good-paying jobs for college students. It was 1987, and I landed a job with a public utility company paying over $10 an hour. At the time, minimum wage was $3.35 an hour, so this job was a great opportunity to make some good money. They also gave us a lot of overtime, which allowed me to bring home checks totaling over $600 to $700 a week. For a poor college student, this was a huge amount of money.

When summer was over, however, things changed drastically. Most of the companies that offer summer jobs for college students end them when school resumes. This makes a college student like me, with only a handful of credits and seeking employment, just like any other person looking for a job. Every time I proudly proclaimed to a potential employer that I had two year's worth of credits from Pitt, they usually responded, "Do you have your degree?" Apparently, forty-eight college credits are no more useful than a high school diploma to most companies.

True to form, I worked two or three jobs during my semester off, and none of them were special. However, it was a reality check that really put things in perspective. Hard work was never a problem for me, but the drudgery of some of the mindless jobs I did was just too much for me to bear. I don't knock anyone who makes a living working in a factory or on an assembly line, but I knew that I could not do it. The summer before, I worked at UPS, which was one of my favorite jobs. I loved the physical challenge of competing with other employees to see who could unload their truck the fastest. I didn't mind getting sweaty while unloading the large, heavy boxes from the back of a trailer. It gave me a real manly feel about myself at the end of the day. The only problem I had with it was the thought of doing it for the next twenty years. That was not very appealing.

Deep inside, I desired to make a difference and leave a positive mark on the world around me. For instance, I have always had a desire to have a library with my name on it. Not just to show off my accomplishments, but to be able to donate enough money to an organization, a college, or a community that would really help make a difference in the lives of people. In my mind, unloading boxes at UPS or working at one of the other blue-collar jobs I had during my semester off would not help me accomplish this goal.

My experience in the work force gave me a taste of what life would be like *without* the proper education. This, along with Kathy, my new found love, helped me become motivated to do my best in school. Oh, I still played basketball, but nowhere near the amount of hours as before.

GETTING THE "WORD'S" EYE-VIEW OF WEALTH

One thing I have always believed is that someday I would be rich. I never wanted to be rich just for the sake of having an exorbitant amount of money or material possessions. I wanted to be wealthy for the freedom it brings and the ability it provides to bless others.

Think about some of the great patriarchs of the Bible, like Abraham, David, and Solomon. They were all wealthy and left a lasting imprint on the lives of others. Likewise, when the children of Israel left Egypt, God forced the Egyptians to give them gold, cattle, and many other precious possessions. Again and again, we see examples in Scripture of God providing material wealth for his children. As Psalm 35:27 says, God "... takes *pleasure* in the prosperity of His servant" (AMP).

So God is okay with us having wealth; He just doesn't want wealth to have us. When Jesus spoke to the rich young ruler (see Mark 10:17-30; Luke 18:18-23), He knew that the man valued his riches more than anything else, including his relationship with the Lord. And because of that, Jesus could not use him in the extraordinary way He wanted to. God does not want us to put anything before Him because when we do, we limit His ability to use us.

He desires to bless us because He loves us, but more importantly, He wants to bless us so that we can use His blessings to build His kingdom here on earth. Just think about how many lives you could change for the better if you had the financial means to feed the hungry, clothe the naked, and to house the homeless. These are things that Jesus expects for us to do.

In all my years of growing up and studying Scripture, I have come to realize that poverty is a curse—one of the curses that came upon us as a result of sin. Most families that pass down poverty from generation to generation share many of the same philosophies about money and life in general. The Bible says that Jesus became poor so that we could be rich (see 2 Corinthians 8:9). Money in itself is not evil; it is the *love of money* that causes evil (see 1 Timothy 6:10). When we love money too much, then money becomes our God (see Matthew 6:24).

We as believers have to realize that God has called us to be stewards of the wealth and resources He has given us. He wants to bless us with material wealth but it is for *His* glory and *His* purposes, not ours. His ways are always right. If we will "…seek (aim at and strive after) first of all His kingdom and His righteousness (His way of doing and being right)…then all these things taken together will be given you besides" (Matthew 6:33 AMP). This means that if we pursue a close relationship with God, He will put all the rest of the things in our life in order.

For many years I wondered why God did not grant me material wealth and great success when I was younger. I believe I was talented enough to have been a pro athlete, a successful businessman, or even an actor. I understand now that God did not bless me with great wealth or success because I could not have handled it. Indeed, 1 Corinthians 10:13 confirms that He will not give us more than we can handle. He loves us too much to give us anything that will destroy us. I believe He kept me from great success because I had not put Him at the center of my life. Likewise, if I had been allowed to attain wealth and fame *without* God being the center of my life, I would have gone even further down the path of death and destruction.

Many people cannot handle material wealth or great success, and I was one of them. When I look back on how badly I acted with the small amount of material wealth and success I had, I can just imagine what my life would have become if I had earned millions. I am sure that if I would have achieved great wealth, fame, and success *without* the life lessons God has taught me, I would have ruined my life. I also believe that God orchestrated my life as an answer to my childhood prayer to be a "good" person. He was preparing me for what He had prepared for me.

A Chance for a Fresh Start

The time finally came for Kathy to leave for law school in Maryland. The thought of being four hours away from the woman I loved bothered me, but I quickly adjusted my mind-set and went on. Kathy, on the other hand, seemed to have a much harder time with the change. So by the end of her first year, I made plans to transfer to school in Maryland to be with her.

As much as I hated leaving Pittsburgh, I felt it was a chance to make a fresh start. At Pitt, I had failed at making the team, I had almost failed out of college, and I had initiated many short-term relationships with women strictly for physical fulfillment. These meaningless sexual encounters felt good for the moment, but soon afterward I returned to the emptiness that was there all along. The move would give me an opportunity to leave behind negative experiences like these and carve out a new identity for myself.

Amazingly, through all I experienced, I never took my failures to heart. Although I was far from God in the way I lived, I believe He was always with me, even in my lowest moments. This theme would become more and more real and meaningful as the years passed. Somehow I maintained a hope that I would have a successful life; I just needed to find out what my calling was. There were times when I would go into a minor depression and I didn't feel like being around anyone. It was during these times that I sat and reflected upon my past mistakes. Again and again, I received valuable revelation and wisdom concerning my life and the things I had been through.

Looking back, I believe God was speaking to me at these times, but I just never realized it. I always credited the insights I received to my own wisdom. Isn't it funny how we can deceive ourselves into believing that we can do anything in our own power? I know now that a lot of the wisdom I received came from the Bible verses I had learned in Sunday school, as well as the hundreds of services I sat in as a child and a teenager. Even though I wasn't always paying attention, I believe that God's Word was somehow absorbed by my spirit.

Chapter 5

Chasing Dreams

My move to Maryland was successful and invigorating. Kathy and I were now living together, which felt good and seemed to be the best thing for both of us at the time. I was getting a fresh start academically, and the job market in Maryland looked a lot more promising for blacks. It seemed as though a whole new world of possibilities was opening up for me.

A Tale of Two Cities

Immediately, the contrast between Pittsburgh, Pennsylvania, and Towson, Maryland, became quite evident. Pittsburgh was more dark and dank. Both the buildings and even the sky were still stained with residue from years of billowing black smoke spewing from the smoke stacks of the now abandoned steel mills. While Pittsburgh was one of the top corporate cities in America, the old, empty buildings left over from the failing steel industry gave me the feeling of a ghost town every time I rode past them. Although a new and more modern world was beginning to emerge there in 1989, the transition from the old, blue-collar mentality into the new was a gradual one. The residue of the old still bled over into the emergence of the new.

Pitt's university area was basically concrete, three-lane streets, a bus lane and the Original Hot Dog Shop (affectionately known to those familiar with Pittsburgh as the Dirty O). It consisted of a number of marked buildings intertwined within the landscape of Oakland, a section of Pittsburgh that was more of a college town than not.

Towson University, on the other hand, was beautiful. Located just outside of Baltimore, Towson had a *real* campus with a mixture of older, more classical buildings and some very modern state-of-the-art facilities. The people there seemed much more pleasant, and the campus itself was a tight community. Maryland itself was a state with loads of nice roads and lush green trees. What a picture perfect place to start afresh.

Even the communications departments at Pitt and Towson were very different. At Pitt, communications focused on dialectic and rhetoric and had a greater emphasis on philosophy. We studied some of the ancient Greeks like Aristotle and how they used language. In contrast, Towson focused on mass communications, featuring classes geared toward advertising, public relations, radio and television. At the time, I had no real future interest in using my radio classes; they were just a lot of fun. I had a little bit of a background as a DJ, making tapes and deejaying at some parties and wedding receptions. I even received credits for working in the radio lab, helping other students with their assignments. This experience would prove to be invaluable for the work God had for my future. The overall change in my academic backdrop was just another way God was putting me in position for what he had in store for my life.

Towson's "new" campus feeling fit like a glove with the place I was at in life. I was now more dedicated to achieving academic success and graduating from school. I had pushed my dream of playing basketball to the background and was also looking forward to having a career. As I prepared academically, I also had the goal of starting a family in mind. I believed I had finally found my direction in life.

Acting Out

Another new world opened up to me while in Maryland—the world of the theatre. I have always had a heart for acting, and one of my elective classes for communications was theatre. In the back of my mind, I felt that if basketball didn't work out, I could always be an actor. During one of my classes, the professor told me about a movie being filmed in Baltimore that he thought I should audition for. The name of it was *Cry-Baby*, and it starred an up-and-coming actor by the name of Johnny Depp. The director was John Waters, a man with somewhat of a "cult" following, for lack of a better word. He had made a number of "B" movies, such as *Hairspray* and *Serial Mom*. These films were very popular but not considered good quality. This didn't matter to me. I was just excited about the possibility of being in a real movie.

As it turned out, I was cast as an extra after auditioning, but because I was not actually an actor; the weight of the opportunity didn't really hit me. There were many stars featured in the film, including Ricki Lake, Traci Lords, Iggy Pop, Polly Bergen, David Nelson (Ozzie Nelson's son), and others. Much to my amazement, I was placed in three scenes and had the chance to meet some really big names. Through it all, I learned that making movies is a lot of hard work. Even when I wasn't filming, I was on the set for twelve hours or more. Although *Cry-Baby* was not a box office hit, it did have a definite following. After it left the big screen, it played dozens of times on HBO, USA network, and even regular TV. Even if I never act again in another movie, I am grateful for the experience.

Managing the Problems of Monotony & Money

Life seemed to be going well for me. Kathy was in her second year of law school, and I was working two jobs and going to school full-time. Before long, however, the monotony and the pressure of the situation began to be unbearable. Occasionally, I was going to church and praying, but I was far from living a life of commitment to Christ. I didn't know it then, but that fact that Jesus was not at the center of my life was my biggest problem. As I searched for answers, my thinking began to wander and deviate from the right path. It seemed as though the genetic makeup of my father, who loved to party and run wild in the streets, began to gain influence in my life once again.

So there I was at a very young age beginning to feel the effects of burnout. The little bit of free time I had was spent doing the 'family thing,' which basically meant Kathy and I did the things she wanted to do. In addition to burnout, I was also feeling discouraged over a lack of money. Most of the people I went to college with seemed to come from families that were either financially well-off or that had made provisions for their education ahead of time. At Pitt, I knew a handful of people that came from wealthy backgrounds, but they were few are far between.

Many of my college classmates at Towson had BMWs, and their parents paid their tuition in full by check when they registered for class. I, on the other hand, depended on student loans and financial aid to pay my tuition. My bill usually didn't get paid in full until about half way through the semester. My mother could not afford to provide much help, and I didn't like to bother Pop Pop with my financial woes. Thankfully, I can look back and see that God was there every step of the way. Somehow, someway my tuition always got paid, I always had a roof over my head, and I usually had something to eat—even though it was far from being a gourmet meal.

I'll never forget the summer after my freshman year at Pitt. Money was tight then too, and I stayed at my apartment near the campus in Oakland to take a couple of classes. My two roommates were not scheduled to come back to school until September. I arrived on a Sunday evening a few days before classes were to start. Being only eighteen, I had failed to get my utilities turned on or to buy any groceries. To top it off, the previous tenants had left food in the refrigerator, and for five weeks the heat had caused the food to spoil. The horrible smell took months to go away. Needless to say, my first night that June was a very memorable one, but not in a good way. I had no lights, no air conditioning, and the apartment smelled like rancid meat. All I had to eat was a box of oatmeal cream pies, which was all I ate for the next two days. In spite of it all, I was never worried or felt despair. Again, I can look back and see that the Comforter was with me. Even when I wasn't serving Him, He kept His promise to never leave me or forsake me (see Hebrews 13:5).

Not having a lot of money during my college years was not a new thing. The same thing was true when I was a child growing up in Harrisburg. My Pop Pop was very frugal, and he basically only spent money on necessities. Yet, even though we lived a pretty meager lifestyle, I always had what I needed. I always had the toys I wanted, and when I got my driver's license, he bought me a Ford Escort. He made the payments, which were about $150 a month, and he paid for my insurance. I paid for everything else. By the time I got to high school, I had a part-time job that allowed me to have spending money for pretty much anything I needed. Other than basketball sneakers, school clothes, and an occasional movie, I really didn't have many expenses in life.

Of course my life in Maryland was drastically different. My expenses were greater, and I always seemed to be financially strapped. Most of Kathy's friends from law school that we hung out with were from well-to-do families or were working in the corporate world. As a result, they had the means to do things like eat at expensive restaurants and go on fancy vacations. Even Kathy's parents made sure that she had enough money to do these things. I, on the other hand, was barely getting by.

The pressure began to mount, and I felt I needed to begin making more money in order to be able to live the happy lifestyle Kathy and I wanted... the type of life that she was used to. Again, I was twenty-one years old, in college, working two low-paying jobs, and believing I needed to be making a lot of money—and right away. Before this point, I thought that I would have been going to school on a scholarship and well on my way to being a pro ball player. Once I realized this was not in my immediate future, I began to search for a way to make a substantial amount of money right away. Going to law school was still a consideration, but without a large influx of funds, this would have to be put on hold.

ACCEPTING AN APPEALING INVITATION

When I first moved to Maryland, I had thought about selling real estate. But after the person I interviewed with informed me that even if I sold a house right away it would probably take months before I would see any money from it, real estate was no longer an option. I just could not afford to work for free. Then I heard about A. L. Williams, a multi-level insurance company that promised a potentially unlimited amount of income in a short amount of time.

I was first introduced to A. L. Williams (now called Primerica) during the summer before my senior year of college. Someone invited me to one of their business seminars with the promise of an opportunity to change my financial future. Obviously, this was very appealing at the time, so I went. The business concepts presented were sound and made a lot of sense, and the people who spoke were very motivating. With great energy and enthusiasm, they talked about how the company had changed their lives. Some of the company's top leaders wrote big numbers on a board and began outlining the ease with which a person could become financially independent in a short period of time. One of the senior vice presidents was reportedly making $20,000 a month. He even showed us one of the checks that he had received from the company. Without question, this caught my attention!

The other thing that struck a nerve with me were the terms *average* and *ordinary*—words they used to describe some of the people who were *not* A. L. Williams agents. Now, these were two words that I would never use to describe myself. I have always believed that I was destined to be something special, never just a part of the crowd. The speakers went on to outline a plan that would provide me with residual income, which is income that you receive even when you are not working.

Basically, the main philosophy of the company is to encourage customers to cash in or cancel their whole or universal life insurance policy from the company they are presently with and buy a term life insurance policy with A. L. Williams. Term insurance is cheaper than whole or universal because you are just paying for a death benefit, which in my opinion, is really all life insurance should be about. The other portion of a whole or universal policy goes toward building up savings.

All in all, A. L. Williams does have a good concept, which makes it even easier to sell than many other multi-level business products. In most people's minds, life insurance is something they need—especially if they have a family depending on them. Armed with this mind-set, A. L. Williams' members march forward like soldiers fighting for a worthy cause. We were pitted as a small company of "rag-tag wannabes," or warriors, fighting the large, "evil empire" of the insurance industry.

After being adequately informed, I felt very strongly that this was something I could excel in, so I dove in to it full force. I began working my business with the same passion and a desire with which I had pursued sports. I understood very well from years of playing that the more effort you put into something, the more you get back, which is basically the law of sowing and reaping. I also knew that with any new business, you usually don't see any profits in the beginning. It takes time for you to lay the foundation, build your clientele, and then reap the rewards.

Nevertheless, I became totally sold out for the cause and very effective. My biggest problem, however, was I didn't have Kathy's support. Additionally, my school work began to suffer because most of my time and energy was being put towards the new business. I was traveling back and forth between Maryland and Harrisburg (about 70 miles one way) two or three times a week. Lucky for me gas was pretty cheap, so I was able to afford it. I had maintained one of my jobs for income, but I was heavily banking on striking it rich through the A. L. Williams system of business.

A Cloud with *No* Silver Lining

Well, in a short period of time, I moved up the ladder by selling policies and signing up new agents to sell the products. Before long, I advanced to become a regional vice president with the company. At the annual awards ceremony I cleaned up, taking home four or five different awards, including Team MVP and Rookie of the Year. The only problem: *I was still broke*. This didn't mean the system didn't work; it just meant that I hadn't begun to reap what I had sown yet. Wanting instant results is a huge obstacle people face in life. As a result, they don't hold on long enough to see the benefits of their efforts. Often, the person that comes along behind the one who quits walks right in and receives the rewards the previous person worked so hard for. It is like putting money into a slot machine. You sit there for hours pumping money into it; you get discouraged and walk away, and then the next person walks right up and puts in one coin and hits the jackpot. In a similar way, this is what happens many times when we don't persevere quite long enough to reap the benefits of our hard labor!

Another big drawback I discovered with a business of this nature (or anything that we get emotionally involved with) is that we can make a god out of it. The truth is, many of the A. L. Williams' business meetings were more like testimony time at a church service. Again and again, I watched as people stepped to the microphone and shared how poor they were *before* joining the company, and how their life was totally changed *afterward*—they even had a new Mercedes to prove it. The main purpose of people sharing was to encourage others sitting in the audience not to get discouraged or to give up. Speakers would say things like, "It takes time to build a business," and "Your friends will probably not understand what you are doing, and if they aren't rich, how can they tell you how to get rich?" Indeed, seeing and hearing someone on the stage that reminds you of yourself is very motivating. It makes you think, *If they can make something out of their life, so can I!*

In the midst of it all, an even more critical issue developed. As a result of all the time I had been spending building my business, a real strain developed in my relationship with Kathy. It probably wouldn't have been as bad as it was if I would have been bringing home the big checks I had been promised. People talked to Kathy about how great a job I was doing, but none of my efforts had turned into substantial money—all I had to show for it were awards and praises from my peers.

In spite of it all, I pushed even harder to develop my business. I have always been a very strong minded person, and when I make up my mind on an issue, I stand firm on it. I felt that since I had sacrificed by moving to Maryland while Kathy pursued *her* career goals, she should have been more supportive of my business pursuits. But she didn't feel the same way, and eventually we ended up separating on the issue. Of course, there were other problems we were dealing with, but this one was the final straw. I felt strongly that I needed a partner who supported me; without one, I could not be effective.

Shortly after, I participated in what would be my last business function with A. L. Williams. It was a national convention in New Orleans. This was their big event of the year, and it usually lived up to what it was billed as. Of course, there were excellent speakers and some very exciting testimonials from some of the company's big success stories, which I always loved to hear. Clearly, I can see how hard it is for someone to *not* get caught up in all the hype. But at that point, I had already been sold on the concept; I just hadn't made any money. The whole thing forced me to do a lot of thinking, and by the end of the trip I decided I was *not* going to continue in the business.

A Time of Reflection

Upon leaving A. L. Williams and separating from Kathy, I once again entered a time of deep reflection in my life. Some people may call it depression, but I didn't see it that way. I truly believe God was the one who sat me down and ministered to me about my life. I began to look back over the preceding years and tried to determine why I was where I was. I took the good that I did and hung on to it, and I took the bad and tried to think of how I could change it. Unfortunately, during those times I was still not focusing on God or meditating on His Word. Even though they helped me, the help always remained incomplete because I had not given God His place of pre-eminence. Consequently, instead of my introspection bringing me closer to God, it gave me a false sense of pride—thinking that I was figuring out life by myself.

During this particular time of reflection, however, I did make a few major discoveries and decisions. First, I decided I needed to focus on finishing school and getting my degree. I only had a few classes left, and my time with A. L. Williams had almost caused me to forsake this endeavor altogether. Pop Pop, my mother, and the rest of my family had always instilled in me that education was vitally important. Whenever I asked the meaning or spelling of a word as a young child, I was always told to "look it up". This meant getting a dictionary or an encyclopedia and finding the information myself. Truly, this was one of the best lessons I ever learned. Later in life, I would use this same concept in my quest for knowledge concerning my relationship with God. I never wanted to simply know about God based on someone else's relationship with Him. I needed to "check Him out" for myself.

The second thing I decided during my time of reflection was that I needed to seek more specific skills in order to be better equipped and make myself more marketable. Deep down, I knew I would one day own my own business; I just didn't know what it would be at the time. Looking back, I believe God purposely hid from me the business I would eventually own in order to send me on the journey that I needed to take to fulfill His calling.

The third revelation I received was that I needed to be married because I did not have the gift of celibacy. God says in Genesis 2:18 that it is not good for man to be alone, and I wholeheartedly agree. During the times when I was *not* in a monogamous, stable relationship, I usually lost focus on my life goals. But when I was in a monogamous, stable relationship, the opposite was true. This third revelation paved the way for Kathy and me to eventually mend our relationship. At first, we were still seeing other people, but when I received the news that she was pregnant, my plans changed dramatically.

The Quest to be a Better Parent & Find Better Employment

No matter how irresponsible I had been in my life, I always viewed parenthood differently. My father was absent from my life while growing up, and as a result of this pain, I never wanted to have a child experience the same void. Consequently, when I first became sexually active and a girl I was seeing told me she was pregnant, her words gave me an intense empty feeling in the pit of my stomach. I knew in my heart that I would have to spend a lot of time with her because she was carrying my child. But the thought of this made me miserable because I *didn't* love her. You can imagine how relieved I was to find out she had made it up. Thankfully, I didn't feel the same way about Kathy. I really wanted to do right by her—especially in the area of being a good provider.

At the time, I was working at MCI in Maryland as a telemarketer. The Federal Trade Commission had taken away some of AT&T's power by breaking up their monopoly and allowing other companies to come in and compete for business; MCI was one of them. Telemarketing really tested a person's selling ability, and I was very good at it. I sat for hours in front of a computer screen, hitting a button, and letting the computer dial the number. When a person answered, their name came up on the screen, and I went into my spiel. Of course, my supervisors encouraged us to personalize our script as much as possible. This I did with ease, thanks to my Dad's gift of gab. Before long, my boss promised me that I would be able to move up to corporate sales in a reasonably short amount of time, which I was looking forward to. But once I found out Kathy was pregnant, I knew I had to get another job. The position at MCI was only an entry level one, and in order to support a family, I would need higher pay and benefits.

I learned from a friend that Bally's Health and Fitness, a company that owns health clubs all over the country, was paying more and that a person could also earn a large amount of money on commissions. With this in mind, I left MCI and took a job at Bally's. Although the position was in collections instead of sales, I believed that I could somehow use my proven sales techniques to make money from the other side.

Meanwhile, things were going relatively smoothly as Kathy and I were working together on our relationship and planning our wedding. She was also finishing up her last year of law school, and at the same time, I was preparing for fatherhood. I attended all the prenatal and Lamaze classes with her, learning all the breathing techniques I could. I desperately wanted to be the best father I could possibly be.

In spite of all the wonderful things happening on the "family side" of my life, I still wasn't happy with the direction my career was taking. Although my job at Bally's paid well, I didn't see much room for advancement. I was working as a bill collector, and it just wasn't the job I saw myself doing for very long. As time passed, I began to feel a growing pressure to secure a stable, long-term career. All of my friends and Kathy's friends had already become professionals, and she was just on the brink of becoming a lawyer. More and more, I began to feel inadequate. I also began resenting Kathy because I had put *my* career goals on hold for *hers* as well as for our relationship. I just knew I needed to step to the plate and deliver.

As my mind once again began to race for a new avenue of revenue, I remembered taking the PSAT test in my junior year of high school. Because I had scored fairly well, I received materials from many schools all over the country. One of these schools was the U.S. Naval Academy in Annapolis, MD. Initially, I seriously considered attending the school, but I ultimately decided against it because of the strictness of the program. I wanted to go to a school where I could party and explore the things in life that I thought I had missed out on. Consequently, I never applied.

However, now that I was going to be a family man, my interest in the military was rekindled. The discipline, the reputation, and the thought of being a military man became more and more intriguing. (I think watching a lot of Rambo movies also made military life seem romantic.) With all this swirling inside me, I finally decided I wanted to be a Navy pilot. I believed it would provide a good living for me and my family, and at the same time, enable me to travel and give me status as it had for many presidents. Now, I didn't necessarily have aspirations of becoming president, but I felt like this would be a good career move for me. So I began to research the steps necessary to enlist.

Labor & Delivery

During my last semester at Towson, there were some major events taking place in my life. I was wearing myself thin by laboring at two jobs and trying to secure the last few credits I needed to graduate. At the same time, I was also preparing to marry my college sweetheart, be a father, and start the process of becoming a military pilot. As a result of the extreme intensity of my schedule, I ended up dropping one of my college classes, which made me three credits short of getting my degree.

Again I wrestled with resentment and despair. Even though things seemed to be going in the right direction with regards to having a family, I was still not satisfied. I knew that I needed more, but I didn't know what it was. Jesus was the answer, and I had access to Him all the time. Unfortunately, I still did not turn to Him.

In May of Kathy's senior year of law school, she went into labor. I was so excited! I wanted to experience all that I could about being a father, so I willingly stayed there throughout the fifteen hours of labor. I also helped Kathy with her breathing and pushing, and when the baby was born, I had the honor of cutting the cord. My heart melted... She was a beautiful baby girl. The first time I looked at her, she immediately had my heart. She was so vulnerable...so dependent on me. I would have willingly given my life for her.

To me, holding a newborn baby in your arms is the closest thing to feeling God's *agape love* for us. Agape love is *unconditional* love that is not based on anything we do. Romans 5:8 declares, "God shows and clearly proves His [own] love for us by the fact that while we were still sinners, Christ (the Messiah, the Anointed One) died for us" (AMP). God loves us so much and wanted to be back in relationship with us so much that there was nothing He wouldn't do for us—even die for us. Holding "Danielle" in my arms that day really gave me a glimpse of how much God truly loves us!

Chapter 6

Living the Married Life?

Soon after Kathy graduated from law school, we moved back to Harrisburg so that she could prepare for our wedding and study for the bar exam. Again, I relocated myself for her convenience, and subconsciously it was really beginning to affect me. To make matters worse, we moved in with her parents so that we could save some money. Don't get me wrong; it did help financially, and their willingness to babysit while I worked and Kathy studied for the bar was great. But mentally, it was taking its toll.

It was during this time that the devil began to relentlessly attack my mind. My feelings of inadequacy really began to grow deep, and all the negative emotions I was experiencing began to affect my thinking. More and more, I began to harbor feelings of resentment toward Kathy for *my* decision to put my career on hold and relocate back to Harrisburg. I had to do something fast, but I didn't know what to do.

A "Friend" of the Family?

One afternoon I was hanging out with someone close to me and having some drinks. He gave me an idea that would change my life forever, but not for the better. For the sake of the story, we'll call him "Paul." Paul and I used to get together and talk about many things, and he was always very open about his experiences. I had never really been through a lot of the things Paul talked about. The extent of my wild days up until that point was mainly partying, drinking, and chasing women.

On this particular day, the conversation started out normal, but it didn't end up that way. Paul had recently gotten out of jail after serving time for a drug offense, and he began to explain the events that caused him to be incarcerated. He elaborately described a lifestyle of drug use, women, and *lots of money*. Out of all that he said, the thought of having a lot of money appealed to me most. So, I asked him to tell me more. Keep in mind, I was engaged to be married and I was a father. So the part about chasing women wasn't really an option for me. But the idea of easy money…that was very enticing.

The devil knows what our strongest temptation is, and he likes to test us on it every chance he gets. For me, it was money, and at that point in my life I had made a couple of attempts at becoming rich, but they did not pan out. To make matters worse, I had been working a couple of dead-end jobs which, although I knew they were temporary, were adding to my frustrations. I had also put Navy flight school on hold, in order to give Kathy adequate time to study for her bar exam. So once again, my career and future were up in the air. The thought of making fast money sounded very good. The driving desire to make more money was to support my family so that we could move out of my in-law's house and start a life of our own. Indeed, it was an admirable cause, but the methods I was considering were shameful.

The time this took place was the early '90s, and the cocaine epidemic in America was full blown. Movies like *New Jack City* and *King of New York* painted a picture of high-profile drug dealers that had a seemingly unlimited supply of wealth through the drug trade. Paul described to me what seemed like a foolproof plan that he had used to make money. He explained how easy it was to flip money through buying and selling "coke." He would buy an ounce off the street in New York, and then sell it in the Harrisburg area for about twice the price he paid. I quickly did the math, and with dollar signs dancing in my eyes, I made the wrong decision that drug dealing was worth the risk.

It's important to realize that if you are a child of God, the devil can only present thoughts to you—he can't make you take them. He has no control over a child of God. When he presents wrong thoughts to us, we must choose not to receive them. Even though I accepted Satan's thoughts and my life was about to take a turn for the worse, God was still with me. He never intended for me to do the bad things I did, but regardless of what happened, it would all eventually be used to fulfill his plan for my life. As Romans 8:28 proclaims, "We know that all things work together for good to those who love God, to those who are the called according to his purpose" (NKJV).

My First Time

The first time Paul and I traveled to New York to buy drugs, I was more nervous than I had ever been in my life. At times I could feel myself shaking almost uncontrollably, but for some reason I pushed past it. It was late one evening and I had downed a couple of drinks to calm my nerves. This was the first of many trips I would make up I-81 North to buy coke.

As we entered the city, I remember marveling at the New York skyline. I had been there before, but this time was different. My nervousness gave way to the thoughts of all the money I was going to make on the deal. The most ironic part about it was, I kept telling myself I was doing it for my family. I believe that buying into the deception is the only thing that enabled me to overcome the bouts of uncontrollable shaking that welled up in me from time to time.

Once we arrived in Manhattan, Paul quickly directed me through the bustling streets of the city. There was a section of Manhattan that was well known for drugs, and Paul informed me that it would be very easy to "pick up" or "cop" some coke. While we were still driving, he instructed me to always look calm and to let him take the lead. I was so nervous at that time that there was really no need to mention that last point. Following Paul's instructions, I parked my car a block or two off the main strip so that the out-of-state tags would not draw attention to us. Even though New York consistently has a large number of out of state visitors, out-of-state tags at 1:00 a.m. in a high drug traffic area was always a red flag.

At our first stop, which was 160th and Broadway, we were quickly greeted by a couple of young males from the Dominican Republic who were very eager to do business with us. This was my first experience with people from the Dominican Republic, and for the most part it was hard to tell that they weren't African-Americans until they began to speak in their native tongue. Now, whenever you did business with the Dominicans, you had to use some of the drugs in front of them before you could buy them. Their policy was always, "If you don't sniff it or smoke it, we won't sell it to you." I guess there is a law that says a cop cannot use drugs while making an arrest.

At the time, Paul was on parole and had some jail time still hanging over his head. He was regularly subjected to drug testing, so he couldn't touch any drugs. As a result, I was the one who had to sample the product. Paul gave me a small pebble-sized amount of cocaine powder and told me to put it in my mouth. The coke had a bitter aspirin taste, and it immediately got my mouth numb. The potency was so strong it felt like the bottom of my jaw was filled with Novocain. If that weren't enough, I also had to snort some of the coke in order to prove that I wasn't a cop. Looking back, I believe that the Dominicans must have known I was a novice coke user, because they gave me a larger than normal amount to snort. Immediately, I got a "freeze," which is exactly what it sounds like. Right away, I could understand why it was so appealing to millions of people, even though it is so destructive. This was my first time using a hard core drug. Up until that point the only drugs I had used were alcohol and marijuana.

I was really amazed at how easy it was to pick up drugs off the streets of New York in the early '90s. There were literally dozens of dealers that would approach you once you got into the hot zone. "Do you want to check my scales?" was one of the code phrases for buying coke. This is what the dealer would say to you, and usually you would respond by saying something like, "Yeah, what you got?" This made my initial trip into the drug world a short one. I would say that within forty-five minutes from hitting the street, we had already made the transaction and were headed back down I-81 with two ounces of very high-quality powdered cocaine.

Ironically, although I did make some money, my inexperience and lack of ruthlessness proved to be my downfall. I was still trying to be a family man while dealing drugs. I was trying to hide the fact that I was now a drug dealer from the people around me. Undoubtedly, this attempt at secrecy limited my ability to be successful in my new hustle. By this point in my life, I knew that in order to truly be successful in any endeavor, you have to put all your effort into it. I was trying to be an upstanding citizen during the day and a drug dealer at night, and it just did not work.

I had been covering my tracks pretty well and giving Kathy money every week, so it didn't seem to be a problem. However, as time went on, there were a lot of inconsistencies and blocks of time that I could not account for, and this led Kathy to follow me one evening. Up until this point, I had been telling her that I was working at night. But when she checked at my job, they told her I had not been there in weeks. When Kathy found out what I was doing, she blew up in anger. In order to patch things up, I had to come clean and promise her to never do it again. However, this was a promise I did not keep.

A Way of Escape

Unfortunately, I did not leave drug dealing, even though I knew it was wrong. I had lied to my wife and put our lives at risk, justifying my actions in my own mind. I lied to myself saying that I was dealing drugs to provide for my family. It's true that I did bring a lot of the money home and gave it to my wife for the household, but my methods of provision were dead wrong. It is a dangerous thing when a person can do evil and justify it because they say it is for a good cause.

How could I do such a thing? Because I was not in touch with God. I even went to church while I was in the lifestyle of drug dealing, and I didn't really feel guilty about it. I, like many other churchgoers today, was *religious*—I was honoring God with my lips, but my heart was far from Him (see Mark 7:6). Sadly, I had become trapped in a life of sin, putting on an act because I had gotten caught. There is a big difference between being *religious* and having a *personal relationship* with God. Without Him at the center of our life, there is truly no limit to the depth of sin that we will sink.

At this point, with all of the tension in our home and my desire to move forward and start my career, I decided to go ahead and enlist in the Navy. Unfortunately, I was still one class short of having my college degree. Ironically, I would have completed that class months earlier if I wouldn't have chosen to pursue a career of selling drugs. Another major disappointment I was dealing with was that I could not enter the Navy as a commissioned officer. Even though I had taken the exam for Officer Candidate School (OCS) and had scored in the eleven percentile (I scored better than 89% of the other candidates), I was told that it could possibly take a year or two before I could go to OCS. So I enlisted as an electronic technician (ET) with a Navy ranking of E-3.

As with everything else I did, I initially dove into my military career at full force, six months before I shoved off, Kathy and I got married. Interestingly, the military is very firm in getting your spouse's permission before you can enlist. Kathy understood that I would be gone for a long period of time, but she felt okay about it.

The Navy offered me a new start with many possibilities, and there were aspects about joining that really appealed to me. I knew that I needed more discipline in my life in order to be successful. I also liked how this career also focused on physical fitness, which I always felt was important. The thought of being able to try out for the All-Navy basketball team was very exciting. On top of that, I loved to travel and the Navy would provide that opportunity as well. All in all, I knew the military could definitely change my life for the better.

Although the military isn't for everybody, I do believe it would be beneficial for all young men to experience a boot camp environment at some point in their life. Some people look down on the military, but the things that the military can instill in a person are the very things many of our young people today are lacking (I was one of them). Being in the armed forces teaches responsibility, discipline, perseverance, and a spirit of unity that few other institutions can match. And when you look at the fate of many young black men, their chances of being killed or thrown in jail are far greater on the streets than they are in the military.

Prepared for Boot Camp

Thankfully, I had prepared myself very well for boot camp. The last few weeks before I left, I was working out three or four hours a day, four days a week. I had also prepared myself mentally for the challenges I would face.

I understood that drill sergeants used mind games in order to prepare you for the tasks that lay ahead. My background in psychology really helped prepare me for this aspect of my training.

The only time I really questioned whether or not I had made the right decision to enlist in the Navy was the first day of boot camp. At about 5 o'clock in the morning, I was abruptly awakened by the loud crashing sound of a large metal trash can banging against the tile floor. About three or four drill instructors came in yelling at the top of their lungs for us to get up and stand at attention. In that moment, I felt a strong sinking feeling in my gut and began to think, *This may have been a mistake!* However, I very quickly suppressed the feeling and braced myself to prepare for the tasks ahead.

Boot camp was not that difficult for me. I was twenty-four, I had been through college, and was a father helping to raise a daughter. I was also physically and mentally prepared for the training, so I moved through it with relative ease. On the other hand, many of the young men that went through boot camp with me were eighteen years old and had never been away from home.

The hardest part about boot camp to me was the anticipation of what was to come. There were a lot of "hurry up and wait" situations, which were used to increase everyone's stress level. This was all part of a psychological strategy to exert authority. The person who is in control of the meeting time assumes authority in a situation. This same tactic is used in sales and employment circles. When you are going to be interviewed by someone, it doesn't matter if you are early, late, or on time, they will usually make you wait. In the military it is vitally important that they reshape everyone's thinking. They have to get every soldier on the same page in order to be effective as a unit. A commanding officer has to try to re-teach everyone the Navy's way of doing things. This has to be done at the sake of all that person has learned up until that point. A unit must be in one accord in order to be effective, because there is *power in unity*.

God Himself recognizes the power in unity. In Genesis 11:6, "...the Lord said, 'Indeed the people are *one* and they all have one language, and this is what they begin to do; now nothing that they purpose to do will be withheld from them'" (NKJV). Unfortunately, when the unity of spirit and purpose is not used for the right reason, as it was in this case with the people building the tower of Babel, it is a very dangerous thing. But when people are unified for righteous reasons, it is a wonderful thing. Indeed, there is nothing quite as marvelous as seeing a well-disciplined group of people, like those in the military, performing marching maneuvers. I loved being a part of it!

Off to Naval School

After boot camp, I traveled to Orlando, Florida were I began Navy Electronics A School (ET-A). I loved Orlando and was excited about excelling in the new school. ET-A school is considered one of the toughest training programs in the country, including all college programs as well. It is an intense fifty-week course that is divided into two classes: "Basic Electronics and Electricity" and "Advanced Electronics." At the end of the training program, all participants will have the equivalent of an associate's degree in electronics.

In my estimation, the most difficult aspect of the schooling was being confined to classroom instruction for six straight hours, only pausing ten minutes each hour. A test was given at the end of each week, and every other week we started a new area of study. In addition, we still had to perform our military duties after our classroom instruction was complete. The only bright spot in the training was that the instructors provided plenty of support. Without a doubt, this period of training was intense and fast-paced.

The other major element of stress I was continually dealing with was the possibility of failing the program and all the consequences that came with it. It is said that the people who fail out of ET-A school are put into the category of *undesignated personnel*—a category of people who have entered the Navy but have not chosen a specific job. Undesignated personnel have very little to say about where they go or what job they are assigned. In fact, they are required to go wherever there is a need in the Navy. If there is a certain job that is undermanned, the undesignated personnel are used to fill it. I know of one person who failed out of ET-A school and he ended up receiving orders to go to Guam. I personally dreaded the thought of going to Guam.

Considering the intense schooling along with the rigorous schedule we had to keep, this certainly was one of the most difficult experiences I have ever been through. What intensified my stress level even more was the fact that Kathy chose to stay with her parents in Pennsylvania instead of coming to live with me while I was in training in Florida. To a great degree, the fault of this problem laid heavily upon me, as I would later learn. As Jesus clearly stated in Matthew 12:25, "…Any kingdom that is divided against itself is being brought to desolation and laid waste, and no city or house divided against itself will last or continue to stand" (AMP).

Out of Order

When an "out of order" sign is placed on a gas pump, it is because it is not working or functioning as it should. This image describes the condition of my marriage and home. Because I did not understand God's divine design for the relationship between husband and wife, my house was *out of order*. What does God have to say about marriage and the role of husbands and wives? Check out this passage from Ephesians 5:21-31:

> Submitting yourselves one to another in the fear of God. **Wives**, submit yourselves unto your own husbands, as unto the Lord. For the husband is the head of the wife, even as Christ is the head of the church: and he is the savior of the body. Therefore as the church is subject unto Christ, so let the wives be to their own husbands in everything.
>
> **Husbands**, love your wives, even as Christ also loved the church, and gave himself for it; That he might sanctify and cleanse it with the washing of water by the word, That he might present it to himself a glorious church, not having spot, or wrinkle, or any such thing; but that it should be holy and without blemish. So ought men to love their wives as their own bodies. He that loveth his wife loveth himself. For no man ever yet hated his own flesh; but nourisheth and cherisheth it, even as the Lord the church:
>
> For we are members of his body, of his flesh, and of his bones. For this cause shall a man leave his father and mother, and shall be joined unto his wife, and they two shall be one flesh (KJV).

God gave us the institution of marriage as a gift, and He has a perfect plan on how marriage and the family should work. As the husband, the man is to *sacrificially* love his wife and be the head of his home. As the wife, the woman is to submit to her husband's leadership. Regrettably, I did not love Kathy as God requires; I allowed my personal insecurities and fear of rejection to control me. Consequently, Kathy did not submit to me. As a result, our marriage was out of line with God's principles and we were suffering because of it.

Statistics show that today's church basically has about the same divorce rate as the rest of the world. I believe the main reason for this is because our marriage and homes are out of order and don't line up with God's plan. Many believers do not approach or view marriage as the sacred commitment it should be. We have women who are usurping authority over men and running the home, and we have men who are mistreating and neglecting their wives, failing to love them as Christ loved the church. Think about it: Christ *gave his life* for His church, and if husbands had this same type of unselfish, sacrificial love for their wives, they would act differently. Instead of disrespecting them by cheating on them, they would strive to treat them like a queen. How different would our homes be if we did this?

I don't want to give the impression that Kathy did everything right. On the contrary, she had her own set of issues. However, my desire is to share how God turned *my* life around by the power of the Holy Spirit. He enabled me to overcome many strongholds in my life, and He will enable you to do the same.

"ET" Part 2

As I began the second part of my ET-A School, I was transferred to Great Lakes, Illinois. This base was one of the oldest and largest Naval Training Centers in the country, and the schedule we kept was intense. From 6 a.m. to noon, we received training in electronic theory as well as practical theory on the equipment we would be using. From noon to 2 p.m., we ate lunch and then went back to school for a two-hour review of the day's lesson. This was followed by two hours of *company time* from 3 to 5 p.m., in which we had PT (physical training), military instruction, or cleaning time for our barracks inspection. When company time was over, most of us returned to the classroom from 5 to 7 p.m. to do our assignments for the next day. After all this, I went to the gym for two hours of training. I still had aspirations of going to flight school, and I knew my physical readiness was vital to seeing that happen.

After 9 p.m. was my time to relax. This meant running back to the barracks after gym, changing my clothes and hitting the streets. The misery of my home life attributed to my desire to always be on the go. I hated being in my barracks at night because the silence forced me to face the loneliness of being separated from my family. Looking back, I sometimes wonder what life would have been like had I been committed to my faith in Christ and living a godly life. More than likely, there would have been nothing I could not have accomplished. Unfortunately, I turned to alcohol and bar hopping instead as my way out.

One thing I'll never forget about Great Lakes is how bitterly cold it was. Located in the north part of Chicago, the training center sat geographically at the bottom of Lake Michigan. The day I left Florida, it was 90 degrees and sunny. When I got off the plane in Great Lakes, I stepped into 40-degree weather. It was quite an awakening!

Now, I was familiar with cold weather. Growing up in Pennsylvania, I had experienced many frigid mornings, waiting for the school bus and walking to school. Likewise, when I attended college, Pittsburgh was cold and windy too. Pitt's campus sits in the middle of a number of large buildings and concrete structures and is surrounded by three large rivers. I remember walking to class many mornings, thinking how much colder Pittsburgh was than Harrisburg. Great Lakes, however, was a whole new realm of coldness.

I arrived in Illinois in October, which gave me a full taste of autumn in Chicago. The wind was brutal. I remember being on duty one weekend when we had one of the biggest snowstorms of the season. It snowed twenty-two inches in less than twenty-four hours, and I had to wake up every three or four hours throughout the night to shovel snow. Our barracks were split into four *duty sections* at the time, which meant we were required to stay in the barracks one full weekend out of the month for security and maintenance purposes. I was in charge of our company's duty section that weekend, and it was my job to choose what each person's duty was. This gave me an opportunity to draw from the great leadership principles I learned while in school and playing sports. This was one aspect of military life I had grown to enjoy.

It is widely believed that Navy duty sections, which are also called watch sections, began back in 1941 when the Japanese attacked the U.S. base at Pearl Harbor in Hawaii. The sailors were caught off guard and the Japanese inflicted major damage to the U.S. forces. To help prevent such a tremendous loss from reoccurring, duty sections were established. Most of the Navy's basic procedures, such as duty sections, are practiced by sailors serving on a ship as well as on shore. This ensures that everyone is on the same page.

As time passed and the days turned colder, I became very lonely—even lonelier than I was in Florida. The growing coldness in the air symbolically reflected the growing coldness between Kathy and me. We saw each other less and less, and when we did get together, we really didn't have much of a relationship. To fill the void in my heart from not having my wife and daughter with me, I once again turned to my old buddy—the world. This only accelerated my downward spiral, causing me even greater struggles in school. The class work was becoming more and more intense as did our extracurricular military duties. Focusing on my training became very difficult, and I was close to failing school.

Once again, this would have been a perfect time for me to turn to God and cast my cares upon Him as the Bible tells us in 1 Peter 5:7. However, I turned to drinking and partying, trying to drown my sorrows in a bottle instead of dealing with them. I quickly gained a reputation for living life in the fast lane. I was still a good athlete, and most people felt I would soon become a naval officer. But the personal inadequacies I sensed within were overwhelming and really beginning to take their toll.

Anger Begins to Boil Over

With Kathy and Danielle several states away and my school struggles continuing to intensify, fresh anger began to build just beneath the surface and eventually started spilling over into my everyday life. Getting into fights became a common occurrence.

I remember one such instance when I was still in Florida that really scared me. At that time, we were on a training base and were not allowed to have alcohol in the barracks. There were also many young men in our company who were under the drinking age of twenty-one. So, before going out on the town, a group of us would get a hotel room and have a few drinks. On one such occasion, a couple of the guys in our company were out in the hallway, drinking and walking around the hotel. At one point, we heard a loud crashing noise just outside our door. Being one of the older guys in the room and usually one of the crew leaders, I felt I needed to check things out.

Right away, I came up on two guys fighting. One was a member of our company named Steve, and he was definitely getting the worst end of the deal. The other guy was not from our company but, based on his haircut, was serving in the Navy too. I immediately jumped into the fight to protect my shipmate (a name given to anyone assigned to the same command as you).

Now, I always prided myself on my physical ability. Growing up where I did, it was important to know how to fight. As a teenager, I had a heavy-duty punching bag in my basement on which I trained myself how to box. I had also wrestled in high school and spent years lifting weights, which gave me more than average strength. All these factors contributed to my confidence as a fighter. I never looked for fights and didn't really enjoy them. But if I got in one, I felt very capable of winning.

I moved in quickly towards the two men. The nameless man, who was extremely huge, was viciously pounding my friend Steve. I stepped into range and punched the guy directly on the chin. Most boxers understand that when you land a solid punch on your opponent's chin you have a good chance of knocking him out. By the velocity of the blow and the precision with which it struck, I believed that my hit would end the fight, but it didn't.

As I stood there in amazement, the enormous white "gentleman" slowly turned to face me. Although I had been drinking and some of the details are cloudy, I do clearly remember two things that happened. First, I ended up with a knot on my forehead and second, the other nameless man was carried out by the paramedics on a stretcher. Even though I probably didn't deserve it, I believe God had mercy on me and protected me that night.

Weeks later, as I was eating lunch in the mess hall, I saw a very large white sailor with a hideous looking bruise on the side of his face. It was my unnamed sparring partner. As I moved in to get a closer look, I saw that the white of his eye was almost unnoticeable. Instead of it being white, only a black and red glob was present. Suddenly, I felt a deep sorrow inside of me because I had inflicted such harm on this man. In my mind, fist fights were always to be a last resort—only to protect yourself or someone you love. This situation was a major awakening. I realized that my life was beginning to spin out of control. What also became clear around this time was that my marriage would soon be over.

Separate Ways

As my time in Great Lakes began to come to a close, I really started searching for answers. The problem was I didn't know where to find them. So I decided to use alcohol and wild living to sustain me until I figured things out. One weekend while I was at home visiting my family, Kathy and I had a long talk. She repeatedly told me how unhappy and lonely she felt because of our separation. I agreed and expressed the same feelings. I offered what I felt in my heart was the best solution: for her and Danielle to come and live with me. However, Kathy didn't want to. She was very dependent on her parents and didn't want to leave the safety of being close to them. At the emotional state I was in, this was an irreparable blow. I just couldn't get over the overwhelming sense of abandonment I felt because she chose to live with her parents instead of me, her husband.

Looking back, I now understand that if I had been a godly man who was striving to fulfill my God-given calling as the head of my home, I would have insisted that my family live with me in Great Lakes. But out of fear and insecurity, I didn't. Instead, I allowed Kathy's unwillingness to *leave* her parents and *cleave* to me rule our relationship. As a result of my negligence, I subconsciously began to withdraw from her— I began to think, feel, and act as though we were no longer married. More or less, this new mind-set became a self-fulfilling prophecy. In other words, I myself began to think, say, and do things to make it come to pass. I started to believe that there was no hope in having a peaceful marriage, so I began to protect myself by building walls and not totally giving of myself.

Several weeks went by, and during another conversation with Kathy, she again began to repeatedly tell me how unhappy and lonely she felt because we were apart. She said the stress of raising our daughter alone had become too much to bear, and she couldn't take it anymore. Of course, she was still not open to coming to live with me; instead, she wanted me to come live with her. At that point, I simply said, "Let's get a divorce." Immediately, my carnal mind felt such a surge of relief once I said that word. I began to think of all the "fun" I could have once the constraints of marriage were removed. I would no longer feel the burden of having to answer to anyone; I would be free to come and go as I pleased. My only concern was to continue to be a part of my daughter's life. So, I made a promise to myself to do so.

Just a few months before my training in Great Lakes would be completed; I went to Harrisburg to visit Kathy and Danielle. By this time I had already made up my mind that Kathy and I were through and divorce was imminent. So when she presented me with the separation papers, I wasn't sad at all. In essence, I felt it would be best for both of us because we would no longer have the stress of maintaining a long- distance relationship. I could concentrate on my career as well as being a father to my daughter.

I will say, however, that I never, ever wanted to be divorced. On the contrary, I wanted to take my marriage vows very seriously and make them work. But because the Lord was not first in my life, I was not emotionally strong enough to deal with the type of marriage I was in. I felt that if I stayed married any longer, I would self-destruct in one way or another. In my mind, divorce became my only option.

Choosing My Ultimate Destination

Now when a person completes a naval training program, such as ET-A school, he usually chooses the orders for his *ultimate duty station* just before finishing training. By the time I had reached this point, my marriage was basically over. Consequently, I wanted to get as far away from Kathy and Harrisburg as I possibly could. I first sought orders in San Diego, California. I had lived on the east coast all of my life and I thought it would be great to get a fresh start on the west coast. Visiting San Diego was also something I had always wanted to do, and being on the west coast meant traveling to Japan and other places in the Pacific Ocean.

When I mentioned this idea to Kathy, she seemed saddened by it, which in a strange way, made me feel good. Oh, it didn't change my mind about the divorce, but the fact that she was saddened meant she still had some feelings for me, which brought me a certain sense of satisfaction. Still, my biggest concern was making sure I stayed connected to Danielle and that I had enough time with her. I didn't want to be too far away and unable to see here as often as I wanted.

As it turned out, the ultimate duty station I chose was Jacksonville, Florida. Jacksonville wasn't as far from Kathy as I wanted to be, but it was far enough to put a distance between me and my pain—or so I thought. I would soon realize that most of my troubles were still very close and very real—they were inside me, to be exact. And if we don't deal with them, we just take them with us wherever we go.

Chapter 7

Virginia Beach Living

Before going to my ultimate duty station in Florida, I had to attend what is called C-School. C-School is the place where a person receives specific training on the electronic equipment on which he will be working. My C-School was in Norfolk, Virginia. By this time in my naval career, I really didn't want to do any more learning, but since I really didn't have any choice, I was off to Virginia.

Paradise of Pleasure

Virginia Beach was a true Navy town, and it was my first experience with the real Navy. Up until that point, I had only been stationed on training commands, which were generally strict and demanded greater accountability. On training commands, men are constantly mustering, which means coming together for roll call, inspection, and instruction. The musters in Great Lakes took place at 6 o'clock in the morning. Due to the wild partying I was doing, I usually made it to muster right at six, still half-drunk from the night before.

My schedule in Great Lakes was so intense and I partied so much at night that I usually only got about three or four hours of sleep a night. My day began around 4:30 a.m., and many mornings I returned to the barracks just in time to shower, shave, and put on my uniform to be ready for muster. I practically lived on NoDoz and Vivarin, which are over-the-counter stimulants equivalent to two or three cups of caffeinated coffee. Countless times, I stood at attention with my eyes glazed over and the taste of liquor still in my mouth. I had all my uniforms professionally cleaned and pressed with extra starch so that I didn't have to iron them, because when you stand at muster, if your uniform is messed up, you were written up.

Weekends were really my only time to sleep. Oh, I still partied and made sure I spent time in the gym, but other than that, I rested. When I look back at the life I was leading, I am amazed I survived. If I had not been in my mid-twenties and in great physical shape, my lifestyle would have more than likely landed me in the hospital with a heart attack.

So Virginia Beach was a big switch from Great Lakes. I spent the first four or five months on temporary duty at a base in Little Creek. It was much more relaxed than the training commands I had been stationed at previously. At Little Creek I had a regular desk job from 8 a.m. to 4 p.m. that was primarily made up of busy work. Once work was done, I had the rest of the day to myself. This gave me the ability to really explore the night life. And because Kathy and I were officially separated, I felt no guilt about cheating on her.

Indeed, Virginia Beach seemed like the perfect place for me to forget about my failed marriage and all the grief in my life. It was filled with clubs and lots of women—about seven or eight women for every man. When you add in the "Navy widows," who were women whose boyfriend or husband was on a ship at sea, you had a virtual paradise of pleasure for any man willing and able to indulge himself in this lifestyle. I usually maintained relationships with four or five women. I had a certain night that I spent with each one. It was the perfect setup because they didn't require me to make any promises and, for the most part, I didn't lie to them or give them any false pretenses. We just spent time together and enjoyed each other.

Aside from my job in the military, my life was about women and partying. I certainly held my own with the best of them. Satan had once again succeeded in helping me to justify my sin. However, my sin was still sin. No matter how nice it looked or how much fun I seemed to be having, the fornication I was involved in was sin in God's sight. Any person having sex outside of marriage is sinning, and the wages of sin is death (see Romans 6:23). Amazingly, God did not bring judgment on me when I deserved it. Instead, He had mercy on me, and I believe He did this because of the great emotional pain in my heart. Through my experience, God proved to me that the Bible is 100 percent true all the time. Without question, I can personally testify that a life of sin and sex is truly *lonely* and *empty*, and because of all the sin I had in my life, I began to die spiritually. What I thought was fun was actually an empty attempt at fulfillment that was killing me inside.

The Best & Worst of Times

While I was in Virginia Beach, I reconnected with my father who lived about four hours from the naval base. I had actually run in to him while living in Maryland, but we quickly lost contact again after I got married.

My impression of him was rather unique. When I was with him, he was the best dad in the world. But he gave me the feeling that when I was out of sight, I was out of mind. He rarely initiated a phone call and never came to visit. The only time I saw him was when I called or went to visit him. I really resented him for his lack of interest in my life. I was looking for a chance to tell him how I felt about all the years he was not around.

The initial reason I wanted to pursue my dad was to get back what I felt he owed me. This happened while I was still in college. I knew he was a Vietnam-veteran and I believed I was entitled to get any financial help that was rightfully mine. When he and my mother got divorced, the judge ordered him to pay $50 a month for child support, but according to my Mom, he only paid one month. Years later when I was going to school and living in Maryland, I could have really used his help financially. While Kathy's parents fully funded and supported her academic pursuits, I worked several jobs and struggled to make ends meet every semester. Ironically, by the time I reconnected with my dad, I was in my last year of college and had made it pretty far *without* his help.

The last time I had seen my father I was about four or five years old. He took me to a toy store and bought me a couple of toys, and we had a great time. Now, eighteen years later, I had only a vague remembrance of him. We met for breakfast in Danville, VA, outside of a Piggly Wiggly grocery store. Amazingly, when I saw him, all the negative feelings I had towards him immediately melted away. I believe the Spirit of God gave me the ability to forgive him.

As we sat and talked for the first time in a long time, a few things came to mind. First, I realized that regardless of what someone else does to us, the Bible says we must forgive them as God has forgiven us—there are no exceptions. In Matthew 6:15, Jesus says, "But if you do not forgive others their trespasses [their reckless and willful sins, leaving them, letting them go, and giving up resentment], neither will your Father forgive you your trespasses" (AMP).

The best example of this kind of forgiveness in Scripture is found in the lives of Jesus and Stephen. Jesus Christ was without sin and had never harmed anyone, yet he was beaten until he was hardly recognizable and then nailed to a cross. Even when He was mocked and spit upon, he would not speak against his accusers. Instead, he begged God to forgive them. Similarly, when Stephen was being stoned to death by an angry mob, he prayed for God to forgive his murderers (see Acts 7:59,60).

So God requires us to forgive everyone, even those toward whom we have had negative feelings. When I reunited with my father, his big, loving heart made it very hard for me to harbor hatred towards him. Even though I carried the pain of his absence with me for years even after we got back together, I did not hold a grudge against him. This enabled us to move forward and become good friends.

An *Un-Godly* Common Interest

Unfortunately, the thing that brought my father and me close together was the worst thing possible—the common interest of sin. I was truly amazed at how many of his characteristics I had inherited. The DNA connection between us was incredible. Even though I had spent most of my life apart from him, we were so much alike. When we were together, it was like we had never been apart. My appetite for women, alcohol, and partying were just like his, and sadly this was what I admired most about him. While I didn't respect his lack of responsibility, I was drawn to his personality, which was the basis for many of the poor choices I had made in my life.

As I said, my father lived about four hours from the Navy base in a small country town in Virginia, where most of the jobs consisted of either farming or factory work. It was pretty much a blue-collar town that was made up of second- and third-generation workers. Many of the people worked seasonally in the tobacco fields or warehouses, and during the off season they worked odd jobs. I was from the north, and because of my father's popularity it was almost like I was royalty. He even taught me some things about the country that I never knew.

One person my father was friends with was a woman named Marabel. She was very popular in town and came from a big family that was notorious for bootleg liquor, drugs, and gambling. Marabel had a very charismatic personality, and we hit it off right away. At first it was just about having a good time, but before long our relationship took on a whole new twist of intensity. She became instrumental in luring me back into drug dealing—a business I knew I should have stayed away from.

I spent a lot of time driving back and forth from Virginia Beach to my dad's town to hang out with him and Marabel. Although they were friends, my dad was more "old school," so cocaine was not a part of his world like it was for Marabel. He preferred liquor, and consequently was managing a local bar with a good friend of his. Before that, he had spent many years working in one of the larger industrial plants in the area. Although the bar was relatively small, it was the only game in town. By the time I was stationed in Virginia, the bar had moved to another location and had grown much larger. It was now considered a full-fledged night club with a bar and a restaurant.

The time I spent with my father was strictly to fulfill my carnal appetite. As we drank and hung out together, the women came to me with great ease, which amazed me. Other than going to school and working out at the gym, my time was spent with my dad at his club or the clubs in Virginia Beach. Basically, my life revolved around two things: sex and alcohol. I had started down a path of destruction and thought I was having a good time. Indeed, this was a pivotal point of my life, and Marabel would be instrumental in turning me totally to the dark side.

Taking Another Stab at It

During this time, Kathy and I were still somewhat connected. We often talked, but just about every conversation we had ended in an argument. Most of the people at my temporary duty station at Little Creek overheard our heated phone conversations, but they learned to ignore them. I found myself constantly getting into shouting matches with her. The anger and hatred that I allowed to build up in me toward her was overwhelming. As a result, I stayed away from her as much as possible. If it weren't for Danielle, our daughter, I am sure that I would never have spoken to her. Trying to forget the pain of my failed relationship with Kathy was an ongoing thing. I believed that as long as I continued to numb myself with booze and wild living, I would not have to face the pain.

Ironically, by the end of the summer in Virginia Beach, Kathy and I were actually thinking about reconciling. We were still legally married, and the thought of someone else raising my daughter was not a pleasant one. In an effort to patch things up, I began traveling back and forth from the base to Harrisburg every other weekend. Even though it seemed at times like I was the only one working on our relationship, I still felt like the five and a half hour drive was worth the try. Yet there was still a lot of pain that we never really dealt with. And the fact that we were both seeing other people didn't help either. For the most part, we were just going through the motions.

But something happened one weekend in October that signified a true finality to our relationship. At the time I was still trying to get into Officer Candidate School (OCS), so I was going to the gym at 5:00 a.m. and then going to work afterward. Normally, when I went to visit Kathy, I would leave work on Friday and go home to take a nap before getting on the road. Kathy, however, was not pleased with me getting to her place late on Friday evenings. In an effort to appease her, I decided one Friday to drive straight to her house from work *without* taking a nap.

Now, if you have ever been very tired and tried to drive, you know how difficult and unwise it can be. I have always had a hard time driving while tired, and I can't tell you how many close calls I've had. I have literally driven down the highway for moments at a time with my eyes closed from exhaustion. On this particular trip, I had my trusty box of Vivarin beside me, but it really wasn't helping. My body was past the point of being propped up by pills. There was only one thing that was going to help it, and that was sleep. I know that the hand of God has protected me and kept me from death numerous times. But God was about to show me in a very tangible way just how much he was protecting me.

As I was coming up the highway, I knew instinctively that I was in trouble. With my Acura's cruise control set at about 65 miles an hour, I crossed into Maryland and suddenly dozed off. I am not sure how long I was asleep, but I believe it was God who woke me up just in time to avoid running into a flat bed tow truck that was parked on the side of the road. My car skimmed the side of the truck, flipped over, and skidded upside down for several yards on route I-83 North. After blacking out for a moment, I regained consciousness and found myself suspended upside down in the car. Still in shock, I unhooked myself and crawled out on my hands and knees. All I can say is **thank God** for seat belts! To this day, the only thing that I have to show for this near fatal accident is a small, barely noticeable scar on the middle finger of my right hand, which is nothing short of a miracle.

Unfortunately, when Kathy came to pick me up, we got into a heated argument over what happened. All she could think about was how much our car insurance was going to go up because of *my* accident. At that moment, I began to totally shut down emotionally and shut her out. By January of 1994, we decided to finalize the divorce and move on with our lives. But the thought of knowing my marriage had failed brought deep despair into my life. From then on, I spent very little time with my daughter. To make matters worse, my Navy life also became very unpleasant because of all the negative feedback I was receiving regarding OCS. Again, this would have been a perfect time for me to get on my knees and cry out to the Lord for help, but I chose to turn to the world instead.

Receiving Mixed Signals

The end of my relationship with Kathy started a chain reaction of events that almost ended my Navy career. Even though I still had a desire to go to OCS, my outside activities were eating away at my commitment to my career. At this time, I also began seeing a lot of inconsistencies in regards to what the Navy authorities *said* and actually *did*. Before joining the military, I had heard that there was a lot of prejudice in the armed forces, and with what I was experiencing; I began to wonder if it was true. I knew that historically there had been segregation in the military, just as there was segregation in the U.S. itself. For example, during World War II there were a number of companies that were all black because they were not allowed to serve alongside their white comrades. I cannot say if this was truly racism, but I did personally run into a lot of double talk concerning the opportunities that the Navy had to offer.

When I first enlisted in the Navy, I was told that going directly in as an officer was *not* the way to go. This information had been given to me by an enlisted recruiter. In contrast, I was advised by a high ranking officer in Washington, DC I spoke with not to go in enlisted. I was also repeatedly warned by people in the officer programs not to enter as just an enlisted man. Unfortunately, because of the strife between Kathy and me over my involvement in drug dealing, I didn't feel I had the time to wait and sort out who had the best advice. I felt I had to enlist and leave as soon as possible, so that's what I did.

As time passed, I became more and more frustrated with the responses I was getting from non-commissioned officers. These were the officials who were supposed to help people like me put together the packet of information for OCS. At every training command I was stationed, one of the first things I did was to seek out the command career counselor (CCC) and ask him questions about applying for OCS. The CCC was usually an E-7 or E-8 officer who had the job of helping enlisted men further their Navy career. Unfortunately, I very rarely got a worthwhile response. I even had one CCC tell me, "If you are not smart enough to fill out your own packet, then maybe you don't need to be an officer." I attributed the overall lack of help to several things, including jealously, laziness, and on a few occasions, incompetence. Needless to say, my mountain of frustrations was continuing to grow, and I was running out of places to turn for help.

The Last Straw

Of all the disappointing and frustrating situations I was dealing with, the thing that I ultimately sealed my decision to turn away from God completely was the declining health of my Pop Pop. Throughout my life, he was the one person I felt I could always turn to when times were bad—he was the one stable force that I always knew I could count on. Now his health was failing and there was nothing I could do.

A wise man once said, "Time waits for no man," and this certainly rang true in Pop Pop's life. He was always a very active man who had a sharp mind and ample strength to work many part-time jobs even into his

70s. But by the time I had left for the Navy, he had reached his 80s and his health began to deteriorate rapidly. Physically, his body was feeling the effects of taking insulin and battling diabetes for many years. He also began experiencing problems with his right hip which significantly slowed his ability to get around. However, the thing that took the greatest toll on his body was the onset of Alzheimer's.

There are few diseases that steal a person's dignity like Alzheimer's. It disables a person from functioning normally and puts a lot of stress on their family. Someone with Alzheimer's disease becomes a prisoner in their own mind. This once vibrant and dignified man was now confined to sitting in a wheelchair or lying on the hospital bed we had purchased. I watched him sit in a room staring blankly into space, not knowing where he was or how he got there. Although his mind would come and go, near the end it was mostly gone. I remember going home to visit Pop Pop and seeing him in the process of dying. To sit and watch this man I had known and admired my entire life look at me as if he never knew me saddened me deeply. The feelings of despair were overwhelming.

As Pop Pop neared death, I began to lose all the faith and hope I had. Although he was a good man and a tremendous example of honesty and integrity in my life, he was still just a man. Unfortunately, I had put my trust in a man and the world instead of God. As a result, I came to the place where I just didn't care about anything any more—a very dangerous place for any person to be. Not only was my loss of hope a danger to me, it was also a danger to others.

Chapter 8

Deep, Troubled Waters

The pain of my past and Pop Pop's imminent death were really beginning to weigh heavily on me. Fortunately for me, I was about to make another big change in my life. I was finishing C-School in Virginia Beach and was finally headed to my permanent duty station in Jacksonville, Florida. My check-in date was May 22, 1994, in Staten Island, NY. But before I left, I and the other soon-to-be sailors were given a thirty-day leave.

I wish that I would have gone back to Harrisburg to spend time with Pop Pop and my daughter, but I didn't. Instead, I decided to go to my dad's place and hang out with Marabel. As you may have expected, I took up my old hobby of selling drugs again. With her tight connections with the area drug hustlers and my ability to get cocaine cheap in New York, our relationship was truly a match made in hell. Regrettably, my thirty days of leave were spent in Virginia, selling drugs and getting high. Instead of preparing myself for the high road of becoming a naval officer, I became more and more attracted to the streets.

A New Station in Life

As I said earlier, my permanent duty station was a ship with a home port that was going to be in Florida. However, it was presently docked in Staten Island, NY, and that was where I was to report. I wasn't sure when we were going to change ports, so I had planned on doing as much in New York as I possibly could before we left. I had envisioned being able to make some extra money by hustling coke from New York to Virginia. Marabel and I had developed what seemed to be a solid partnership. I felt I could trust her because of the physical relationship we had. Sadly, this made it much easier for me to do my unlawful deeds.

The ship I would be serving on was named the Oliver Hazard Perry FFG-7 (OHG). It was a relatively small vessel that normally had a crew of about 150 sailors. I was very much looking forward to being on board.

After almost a year and a half in the Navy, I was finally going to be at sea. This was a very exciting time in my life. I had also been told by all of the CCCs that once I was assigned to a permanent duty station, it would be much easier to complete my OCS packet and hopefully start my career as a naval officer.

Now, when a person reports to their duty station, their orders normally state that they are to register no later than midnight of their check-in date. I, of course, waited until the last possible moment to report. As I drove onto the naval base on Staten Island, I was greeted by a large billboard that read "Farewell Oliver Hazard Perry, May 22. We will miss you!" I didn't think much of the sign until I got to the ship. The watchman on duty met me with all the necessary paperwork for me to officially sign in. Even though I still had mischief on my mind, I was very excited about this new chapter in my life. As I started to bring my belongings on board, I asked the officer in charge where we were going. When he responded, "Russia," I felt like someone punched me in the stomach. Yes, we were changing home ports from New York to Florida, but first we were heading to Russia.

Although I didn't realize it at the time, God had a purpose in this shocking change of course. He is all-knowing and knew what I needed most at that time in my life. Because of my plans to resume drug dealing, He sent me to Russia on the Navy ship I was now assigned to. No matter what our plans are, God's will prevails when He has a plan for our lives.

Life at Sea

Overall, I loved being in the Navy, but I especially loved it when I was at sea. While many sailors are usually stationed on ships, others are stationed on land. But even those who serve at land-based duty stations have at least two tours at sea. This would be my first, and I was excited. During my travels, I went to some very interesting places, such as Russia, Latvia, Denmark, Estonia, and many other European countries. I also traveled to Cuba, Haiti, and virtually every state on the East Coast of the U.S. I thank God for allowing these experiences in my life, even though I did not acknowledge Him during that time. There is just nothing quite like being on the open sea and witnessing the awesomeness of God's creation around the world. It is a marvelous, exhilarating experience!

I've seen waves that were as tall as a building, and I have been on the bridge of the ship when all that could be seen for miles and miles was nothing but ocean. Once I was on board the OHG and saw how beautiful the ocean was, I understood how men have fallen in love with sailing for centuries. I fondly recall sailing in the north Baltic Sea during the season when the sun doesn't set until around 1:00 or 2:00 a.m. I sat on the rear flight deck of the ship and just marveled at God's creation. I can only imagine what it will be like in heaven. Indeed, "...eye hath not seen, nor ear heard, neither have entered into the heart of man, the things which God hath prepared for them that love him" (1 Corinthians 2:9).

Now, life at sea was very simple. Each person had his duty section and assignments to perform, along with drills that had to be done and watches on which he had to stand guard. Other than that, there were not a lot of things to distract you. Most of the younger guys on the ship spent time playing video games or watching movies in the berthing. I spent most of my time working out and reading. Clearly, it is much easier to be a good person while out to sea because you don't have as many temptations.

In many ways, I equate being at sea with being in prison—but in a positive way. Many people who are sent to prison experience a spiritual transformation. They often get saved or accept a new belief system, such as Islam or one of the many other religions. Some decide that they want to change from a life of crime to something more respectable, while others simply choose to recommit themselves to their family. In many cases, however, they do not experience a true transformation. Just because a person makes a proclamation that they've changed while in confinement, does not mean it's valid. I believe many people who make decrees like these are sincere when they make them, but until they have the opportunity to do wrong, it is not necessarily true and lasting. I, for one, have experienced this phenomenon firsthand.

While at sea, I was finally able to complete my OCS packet. Many of the officers on board, including my executive officer who was second in command, really helped me to get all my information together. It finally seemed as though I was going to fulfill my dream of becoming a naval officer.

Leading a Double Life

Meanwhile, I was enjoying a lot of popularity on the ship. I received perfect evaluations from my commanding officers and was well-liked by my crew members. While at sea, I was the perfect sailor. On land I was a different person altogether. While the ship was in port, I was able to explore and live out my wild side. I remember the first port we stopped at on our way to Russia; it was in Nova Scotia, Canada. I was really surprised to find out how many black people lived in Canada. Historically many slaves journeyed to Canada to escape slavery and racial discrimination. I was delighted to find out that although they lived in a different country, they still knew how to party like people back home. After a wild night of partying, I ended up spending the night with a young lady I had met at a party. This would be one of many one-night flings.

At this time I was an E-4, and all E-4s had a 1:00 a.m. curfew while in Canada. However, because of my heavy drinking and the long hours I had put in on the ship, I overslept by about an hour. Fortunately for me, one of my fellow sailors had also overslept at the same party, so I had a partner in crime. Failing to return to the ship by your assigned curfew was a punishable offense. As usual, I managed to avoid punishment by jumping from the pier to another part of the ship and avoiding the officer on watch. This stunt was actually very dangerous. If I had underestimated the distance, I would have fallen into the harbor, which was very dark and bitterly cold at night. (The things we do for "fun!")

The Navy has a reputation of swashbuckling, womanizing, beer-guzzling men who work hard and play hard. This described me to the tee. I quickly gained a reputation as a diehard partier. I could drink with the best of them, and I was very smooth at picking up women—even those who barely spoke English. Of course, I was able to justify my actions in my mind, and the admiration of my peers made it even easier for me to convince myself that everything I was doing was okay. But nothing could have been further from the truth. By the time our port stops were complete, I was usually glad to be back at sea. It enabled me to escape the demons that were steering my life in a direction that was very far from the life God intended me to live. Being at sea was the only time I really got any rest.

Our arrival back in the states did not slow me down one bit. Once we home ported in Jacksonville, Florida, I quickly picked up where I had left off in Europe. I was a regular at the local clubs, and my womanizing reputation quickly spread all over the base. I wore this title as a badge of honor, even though I was dying inside more and more every day. As Romans 6:23 says, I was earning the wages, or payment, for my sins. I was experiencing spiritual death, which unfortunately only made it easier to sin. Please hear my heart: no matter what anyone ever tells you, the more you sin the easier it gets. You can never get sin "out of your system" in your own strength. You must humble yourself before God and ask for His mercy and grace.

Turning Point

Then it happened—the turning point of my life. I received the news that I was not accepted to OCS, and I was devastated. I had all the necessary qualifications: I had perfect evaluations, I was ranked number 11 out of 89 in test scores, and I was a minority. I had been told over and over by naval OCS recruiters that the Navy had a lack of minority officer candidates for the program, so recruits like me were in high demand. Yet, I was denied. It just made no sense. When I inquired as to why I was not accepted, I was not given a straight answer. Instead, I was told to keep trying.

I had many theories as to why I was not accepted. One was that my ship was relatively small, and since I was in a highly technical field, my command would not allow me to go until it had someone with my same credentials to fill my place. I was also told that because OCS was extended schooling, the Navy was reluctant to send me and thus lose my expertise. But in reality, none of this mattered. I had put all my efforts into something that I wanted very badly, yet I was unable to achieve it. Again, I could have turned to the Lord for help in my time of trouble, but instead I allowed myself to sink deeper and deeper into despair.

From this turning point, I came to another major crossroads. It was around Thanksgiving 1994, and I received the news that a cousin of mine had died. She was only thirty-five years old and had passed away from Parkinson's disease. At the time, I had lost so many things that I was kind of numb to her death. Nevertheless, I wanted to take this time to get away and sort things out. So I requested to go on leave in order to be with my family. We were in Florida at the time and were running some special operations near Cuba. After we arrived back in port, I pushed hard to get a five-day pass to go home to Pennsylvania. Once I got it, I foolishly called Marabel and let her know what was going on. She ended up meeting me on the way and, consequently, I never made it to the funeral.

On my leave slip, I had requested five days off and was scheduled to return on the fifth day, which would have been a Saturday. However, I was so glad to get away that I filled out the slip incorrectly and actually wrote down that I would be back on Friday. I was now late, and this was not good because coming back a day late from leave is a serious offense in the Navy.

To make matters worse, I had done something similar just a few weeks earlier. While we were in Norfolk, VA, getting the ship serviced in dry dock, I overslept and returned to the ship two hours late. Because of this, I had almost gone to Non-Judicial Punishment (NJP) a few weeks earlier. NJP is when a person is sent to a formal hearing in front of his commanding officer, and he receives punishment for the violations he has committed. These punishments can be very severe and range from a reduction in pay *or* pay grade, to confinement on the ship. Some punishments entail all of the above. My tardiness was a serious offense and could have warranted severe punishment. But because of my good record and rapport with my commanding officers, I was only given a verbal reprimand. Having another serious offense so close to the first would have almost guaranteed a much stiffer penalty. So instead of going back to the ship and facing the consequences of my actions, I simply didn't return. Instead, I went to Atlanta with Marabel and hung out with some friends.

There are many different terms for not reporting back to duty: AWOL (Absent Without Leave), desertion (which usually happens during war time), and the most popular was UA (which stands for Unauthorized Absence). There are many crossroads that we all must face in life, and the decisions we make at these times can affect us for the rest of our days. In this situation, I made the worst possible choice I could have made. I believe the sin that I had allowed to take over my life had actually corrupted my conscience. I permitted my disappointments and my blatant sinful lifestyle to cloud my judgment. As a result, I became an ungodly, lawless person who felt like whatever I could do and get away with was okay. Indeed, I was a very miserable person.

Actually, I almost went back to the base and reported to the ship, but the devil convinced me that staying away was a chance to get some much-needed rest and relaxation away from the hustle and bustle of Navy life. Emotionally and mentally I felt like I was on the brink of a nervous breakdown. Everything I had put my trust and energy in had failed me miserably. The truth is, however, I was the one who had failed, but I couldn't see it. When a person is in denial, he tends to blame everything and everyone else for his misfortunes. Again, the Lord was there gently speaking to me saying, "Come unto me, all ye that labour and are heavy laden, and I will give you rest" (Matthew 11:28 KJV). But I rejected His invitation and turned to the streets to escape.

Section 2
MY LIFE ON THE DARK SIDE

Chapter 9

Life on the Run

I could have very easily gone back to the ship to face the authorities and receive my punishment for being late. It really was a simple mistake on my part. My leave slip said five days; I had just put the wrong departure date on it. Any commissioned officer (CO) worth his weight in gold would not have "stuck it to" one of his best sailors over a little typo. Now that I look back on it, I am pretty sure I probably would have gotten off with just a light slap on the wrist. However, my corrupt mind was operating at a carnal level, and I was only able to see the situation as a golden opportunity to get away from the ship.

When a person's mind turns to evil, common sense usually goes out the window, which is exactly what happened to me. I began thinking of ways in which I could beat the system. My carnal, worldly view of thinking was, *Whatever you can do and get away with, go for it*. Romans 8:6,7 says that

> ...the mind of the flesh [which is sense and reason without the Holy Spirit] is death [death that comprises all the miseries arising from sin, both here and hereafter]. But the mind of the [Holy] Spirit is life and [soul] peace [both now and forever]. [That is] because the mind of the flesh [with its carnal thoughts and purposes] is hostile to God, for it does not submit itself to God's Law; indeed it cannot (AMP).

Indeed, having the mind of the flesh is a sad and miserable existence; I can attest to that personally. Yet, through it all, God allowed me to see just how low a person can sink when the fear of the Lord is not the driving force of his life.

I quickly began trying to devise a story I could give the Navy officials for not going back to the ship on time. I knew that technically the moment I did not return as scheduled, I was considered a fugitive. So coming up with a good story was vital. But first, I had more important things to do, like stopping in Atlanta to "holla" at my boys!

Marabel and I had some friends who lived in Atlanta who were also in "the business," or "the game" as it was called. Of course these were just nice terms to say we sold drugs. We spent the entire weekend partying and getting high. When it was all over, I still didn't know exactly what I was going to do, but I knew I needed to do something quick.

SIDELINED IN BETHESDA

After much thought, I came up with a plan. Instead of going back to the ship in Jacksonville, I went home to Harrisburg and decided to act as though I was having a nervous breakdown, which was truer than I realized. Once I contacted the naval authorities, they sent me to the naval hospital in Bethesda, MD, which is right outside Washington, DC, about two hours from Harrisburg. Shortly after arriving, I was diagnosed with depression and began taking medication. I then spent several weeks in a ward for people suffering from psychiatric problems. Although I didn't think I needed to be away in a hospital, I believe God knew I needed it and that I would benefit best from being away from the ship. I didn't know it then, but I would never again set foot on the Oliver Hazard Perry FFG-7.

What I also did not realize was that I had almost reached my emotional breaking point. The effects of my failed marriage and the inability to see my daughter like I wanted to were really weighing heavily upon me. To compensate for this, I had tried pouring all my energy into my career, which also turned out to be a major disappointment. To make matters worse, Pop Pop was dying and they didn't give him much time to live. His mind was all but gone due to the scourge of Alzheimer's, and his body had deteriorated from both malnutrition and many years of diabetes. As a result of these things and the emptiness produced from my wild living, I had lost all confidence and felt as though I had nothing to live for. Had I not been placed in the hospital when I was, there is no telling what I may have done.

The only two people in my life that I felt I could confide in were Marabel and my mother. Unfortunately, my relationship with my mom was still strained. I didn't like the living conditions at her house with her husband and the step-children. In addition to regularly cheating on my mother, my stepfather never really contributed anything to the household income. Consequently, I never had much respect for him. So in essence, the only person I felt I could depend on was Marabel. In my mind, she was a very close friend that I felt comfortable talking with—even about things that I wanted to keep hidden from the rest of my friends and family. We were literally and figuratively partners in crime.

After a few weeks in Bethesda, I began to show signs of improvement. The rest and relaxation had done me wonders. The heavy burdens I had been carrying around seemed to have been lifted off me. As a result, the Navy deemed I was well enough to return to active duty. They moved me from the psychiatric ward to the medical barracks across the street to finish my recovery. Most of the people there were recovering from some form of physical ailment and were assigned light duty work. Initially, I was assigned similar work, but I quickly managed to get out of it. My only remaining responsibilities were to wake up and gather for muster each morning. Then I could leave and go about my own business and report back to the base at the end of the work day. I couldn't have had it any easier.

Playing a Very Dangerous Game

Well, as you may have expected, it wasn't long before I very rarely showed up for muster. I did faithfully keep a weekly doctor's appointment with a psychiatrist, but other than that, I was very rarely on the base. I reconnected with Marabel and some of her associates and I began running drugs between New York, Harrisburg, and Virginia. I was playing a very dangerous game. I was still a member of the Navy, traveling with a military ID, but I was now carrying large amounts of cocaine and money with me.

I used my networking skills to become a middleman in the illegal trade. I connected with people who needed large amounts of drugs, and I knew how to get them better and cheaper than most people in the area. I minimized my risk and my exposure by only dealing with drug dealers and not users. I also limited the amount of time that I had drugs in my possession by selling only in "weight." I would buy one or two kilos of coke for $18,000 or $19,000 and then sell it for $23,000 to $24,000. This was 'easy money' for me at the time, but I would later discover that the price to pay for making 'easy money' is never worth it.

Needless to say, an abundance of cash was coming into my hands. At the peak of my drug business, I was earning between $1,500 and $3,000 a day. Although dealing drugs was my main source of income, I had a few other side hustles. One of them was selling "burners"—illegal cell phones that could be used as much as a person wanted without paying a bill. My associates in Atlanta were connected with a guy who would get cell phones and put a chip in them that allowed a person to make unlimited calls at no charge. This was back in 1995 when cell phone plans were very expensive and not everyone had one. I would buy these illegal phones and then resell them, making a profit of $100 on each. At the time, I didn't really care how I made money—as long as I made it.

In my mind, I was "living the life." I stayed very busy for several months, transporting drugs up and down the highway. I felt no guilt nor was I concerned with the consequences of my actions. On the contrary, I felt justified. I had always been taught that if you worked hard and did the right thing, things would turn out good for you. This was the American Dream, but to me the American Dream was a lie. I no longer believed that it was true because I had tried to do things the right way in the past, but they seldom seemed to turn out to my advantage.

The Car Story

My crimes were not limited to drug dealing or hustling burners. There were other things I was in to, one of which involved the purchase of a car. To understand the situation, you need to know a few things about the used car business in Virginia Beach. For starters, most of the dealerships there at the time were owned by foreigners, which always made us very suspicious of their dealings. Many of them preyed on service members who had a guaranteed income but not a lot of wisdom when it came to buying a vehicle. In fact, some of the lots had interest rates as high as 33 percent. However, because we liked the flashiness of their cars, we reluctantly became their clients. These dealerships featured many early model BMWs, Mercedes, etc. Although the cars looked very expensive, they usually weren't.

In any event, while I was stationed in Virginia, I purchased a used Audi. I wasn't overly concerned about the financing or anything like that. I liked the car, so I bought it. That was a big mistake. I should have never rushed into it so quickly without having the car thoroughly inspected. Just three weeks after I bought it, it left me stranded on the expressway while going to work early one morning. Of course, I was furious and as soon as I got to the base, I called the dealership and gave them an earful.

Several days later, the dealership had the car picked up, and at the time, I believed they intended to fix it and return it to me. They informed me that the engine had overheated and locked up, and it would need to be rebuilt. Naturally, I realized that a repair of this kind for an Audi would be quite costly. Most European cars are very expensive to have serviced, and not all mechanics are equipped to fix them. Nevertheless, because I had the car for less than thirty days, I assumed that the dealership would get it done and pay for the repairs.

About three weeks passed, and I decided to catch a ride to the dealership to check on the progress of the repairs. When I arrived at the dealership, I noticed a car sitting on the lot with a price tag on it that looked strikingly similar to my Audi. As I got closer to the car, I noticed a couple of tell-tale scratches that made it very clear that it was indeed my car. Immediately, my blood pressure skyrocketed and my anger began to boil.

When I approached the owner of the car lot and asked him if the car on the lot was mine, he very calmly told me that it was. Like a volcano, my fury erupted, and I came very close to punching the guy out. Thankfully, I was able to control my rage to an extent. Instead of physically abusing him, I verbally assaulted him for about ten minutes. I stood very close to the man's face and shouted some very nasty things at him, which in no way reflected my Christian upbringing. After feeling as though I had made my point, I turned away and left the lot.

Sometime later, I went back and made a deal with one of the assistant managers. (The owner would always seem to make himself scarce whenever I came around.) The deal I agreed to was to pay for half the cost of the repairs for the Audi, which was about $1,500, and in return they took the money as a down payment on another car. I exchanged the Audi for a shiny red BMW 318i. Although the episode had passed without any bloodshed, the matter was far from over.

Not So Sweet Revenge

So there I was driving my new, *used* BMW, but I really couldn't enjoy it. I was still harboring hatred in my heart, and I felt I needed to get revenge on the dealership for trying to take advantage of me. The Bible clearly states, "…do not avenge yourselves, but rather give place to wrath: for it is written, 'Vengeance is Mine, I will repay,' says the Lord," and, "If you do not forgive men their trespasses, neither will your Father forgive your trespasses" (Romans 12:19; Matthew 6:15 NKJV). The funny thing about revenge and unforgiveness is, although the Bible indicates they are both sin, we can often justify them in our minds—just like I did in this situation.

Unfortunately, because of my lack of consideration and respect for God's laws and myself, there were few things I would not do at the time. One night I employed the services of one of my buddies, and we went to the car lot and simply drove the Audi off the lot. In essence, I stole the car, but in my mind I had convinced myself that the lot owner had it coming to him and he owed me.

Sadly, once I gave in to the dark side of life, I began to think like a criminal. After stealing the Audi, I realized that driving a car around with no license plate on it would really draw attention. So once I spotted a car of similar make and model, I unscrewed the license plate and put it on the one I had stolen. Only the devil could have given me the idea to do something like that. What's worse is that I felt no remorse or conviction for doing it.

For about two weeks, I drove the Audi around, looking for a chop shop to sell it to. I traveled from Virginia Beach to Pennsylvania and back to Virginia where my dad lived, but much to my dismay, I couldn't find anyone who would take the car off my hands. Eventually, I took the tags off it and left it parked somewhere in Virginia. The car was taken away by someone some time after I left it.

In spite of my attitude and my actions, God once again mercifully protected me and kept me from going too far. Time and time again, I could have and should have met disaster, but the Lord always seemed to keep me from completely going over the edge. I believe the reason He did this was because I had sincerely dedicated my life to Him at a very early age. He honored my vow, even while I was living an ungodly life.

Facing Unforeseen Obstacles

Meanwhile, my drug-dealing days continued. My goal was to sell enough drugs to be independent and do what I always wanted to do—have my own business. I didn't know the exact details about what type of business I wanted to own, but I had come to the conclusion that I no longer wanted to spend twenty years in the Navy. One underlying problem at this point, however, was that I was burning so many bridges with others that I probably would be unable to get a good job when the time came. Nevertheless, I figured if I were able to accumulate a couple of hundred thousand dollars, I could be my own boss.

In time, some unforeseen factors began to put a damper on my plans. The first one was, as they say on the streets, I "came up quick." In other words, I made it big in the drug industry very fast. This gave way to an increased amount of jealousy in the places where I hustled. What made the jealousy toward me even worse was that I always gave the impression that I was just cruising along without any difficulties—even though I was working myself silly behind the scenes.

What people did not see were all the days I went without sleep, driving up and down the road hauling drugs and making sure I had the right amount of money for my next load. They did not know how many times I was drunk out of my mind trying to get over the nervousness of what my fate might be if I were caught or a deal went sour. Every time I made a big drug purchase, I became a sitting duck. I never knew who tipped off whom or who was watching me. And because I was living by the rules of the streets, I didn't have the law to back me up. Just think about how many people would try to take you out if they knew you were carrying $20,000 to $30,000 in cash. If they got the jump on you, what could you do? I did always carry a gun with me, but in the streets it is often a matter of who gets the jump on whom.

The other major complication to achieving my goal was my purchase of a Lexus. Marabel and I were making so much money that we decided to splurge a little. So on one of my trips to Virginia Beach, I spotted a Lexus two-door coupe. The car was maroon with a spoiler and the gold trim package. This was the hottest vehicle on the streets, and I had to have it. Well once I bought it, it set off shock waves on the streets. When a drug hustler buys his first high-dollar car, it is a sign to the people on the streets that he has graduated from "small time" to "big time." This immediately gets the boys to talking.

Once I purchased the Lexus, things went downhill quickly. One contributing factor to this was that I paid the car off in less than a month. Like many of the auto dealers in Virginia Beach, the man I bought the car from agreed to help me hide the fact that I paid for it in cash. This is called money laundering, and it happens a lot with used car lots. It puts not only the drug dealers at high risk but also the car dealers for helping them. In return, the dealer gets to do business with a person who walks in and lays a large amount of cash on the table. To them it is a fast and simple way to make money.

Well, when I went to the Department of Motor Vehicles in Virginia, I discovered a major problem. The lady behind the counter informed me that there was a lien on my car. Immediately, I got very angry and started having flashbacks from the Audi incident that happened earlier. I called the owner of the car lot where I purchased the Lexus, and he told me to come see him right away. When I arrived at the lot, he notified me that the Drug Enforcement Agency (DEA) had been there to see him, asking him questions about the car I had bought. He also said they had requested to see the payment record for the car and that they had taken its vehicle identification number (VIN).

Meanwhile, my mother and some of my friends were getting some very strange telephone calls from people claiming to have been stationed with me in the Navy. When this began happening, I thought it might be a good time to return to the base to check things out. When I arrived, I was informed that the Navy Investigative Service (NIS) had been inquiring of my whereabouts. At that point, I knew things were getting serious! Consequently, I took a couple of days off to get away and sort things out in my head.

Until then, I had never really feared law enforcement. I always believed I was smart enough and careful enough to stay one step ahead of the local and state police. However, this was a different situation. It involved two federal agencies—the DEA and the NIS. They had the massive amount of resources needed to conduct a thorough investigation. I couldn't just leave a city or a state to avoid them. Therefore, I knew I had to change my direction.

Cautiously Counting the Cost

I had seen firsthand the type of punishment given to people who deal drugs, and I certainly wanted no part of it. As a criminal, I made it my goal to operate as smoothly as possible. I always watched my back and I took every necessary precaution I knew to take. For instance, I never said anything careless on the phone. Instead, I used code words for the product and the quantity I was selling to my customers. I'd use words like "onion" when referring to the number of ounces of cocaine, and "brick" or "cake" for a kilo. If someone only wanted a half or a quarter of a kilo, it would be a half or a quarter of a cake. I am sure the cops had an idea of what we were talking about, but this terminology gave us a certain level of discretion when discussing deals over the phone.

I was also constantly changing routines and routes. I never went the same way twice, and I never returned on the same route that I came. I was always on my guard. Ironically, even the most cautious of people tend to get caught. If it is not because of their own carelessness, then it's because of those they are around. Most drug dealers are very flashy, sporting a lot of jewelry and talking a lot of bull. The only flashy thing I remember doing was buying the Lexus, and as I said it was a main reason for my downfall.

As the old saying goes, "There is no honor among thieves," and this is very true, especially when it comes to "snitches." A snitch is someone that tells the police about the illegal activities of someone else. Snitches can be undercover or they can testify in court against someone who is on trial for a crime. Because of the current drug laws in the U.S. and the large amount of jail time connected with drug crimes, snitching has become more and more prominent. It might sound strange, but the lack of integrity in our society has also contributed to this trend. Even when I was dealing drugs, I could not understand why a person would tell on someone else instead of taking responsibility for what he or she had done, but it happened all the time.

Unfortunately, the punishment usually does not fit the crime. The stiffer penalties are usually given to the street-level crack dealers as opposed to the higher up main suppliers who bring the drugs into the area to be processed into crack. It never ceases to amaze me how the small and medium drug dealers who directly supply drug addicts often get *three* to *four* times the sentence that a main supplier receives when he gets caught. For example, I know a man who got caught transporting *two kilos* of powder cocaine, and he did six years in prison. I know another man who got caught buying *less than a half of a kilo* (12 ounces) of cocaine, and he got twenty-years out of a possible twenty-eight year sentence. Needless to say, the system is not always fair.

Indeed, I learned a lot from living a life of crime. When a person is living as a drug dealer, you have to constantly be aware of the people around you. Yes, you have to worry about the police, but the police are somewhat limited in what they can do. If a person is discreet about their business dealings, it is sometimes very difficult for them to get caught by law enforcement. One way or another, however, everyone does get caught. The truth is, most people know when they are doing wrong, and I believe it is their subconscious that ultimately gets them caught. It stands to reason that the best way not to get caught is to not participate in illegal activity to begin with. Unfortunately for me, I was already beyond this point.

A Deal Gone Sour

In spite of all the danger signals around me, I chose to further abandon my sense of decency in order to get to the next level in the drug game. I had reached the point, like most people in this lifestyle do, in which I decided to get in the game *all the way*. While I was in the drug world, I had gotten into several fist fights over relatively small amounts of money. When it came to larger amounts, fist fighting usually wasn't enough. I had been faced with this dilemma several times, and although I had every intention of shooting a person over the money they owed me, I always chose to back away.

One time, in particular, I know that God stepped in to help me avoid bloodshed. I had an order to deliver two kilos of cocaine to someone in Virginia. At the time, a kilo was going for about $19,000 or $20,000. Selling two kilos meant I was going to clear $8,000 in cash. However, the deal went sour, and I ended up *losing* $3,000 instead. My connection, who we will call "Bill," was expecting me to come up with a total of $48,000 to pay for the cocaine. But I only had about $39,000 in cash. I had to quickly come up with a way to get the additional money.

My first thought was to go to the guys that shorted me and threaten them at gunpoint to give me what they owed me. But something inside of me would not let me do it because I knew that I would probably have to actually shoot them. I just could not bring myself to that point. I had done many things, but taking a life for money was where I drew the line. Even though I went to them and intended on going through with the shooting, I believe that the Holy Spirit prevented me from doing it.

In His mercy, I believe God kept me from taking a life because He had plans for me to help build His kingdom, and He didn't want me to miss out on it. This reminds me of how King David was not allowed to build the Temple of God because there was blood on his hands. In 1 Chronicles 22:8 David says, "But the word of the LORD came to me, saying, Thou hast shed blood abundantly, and hast made great wars: thou shalt not build a house unto my name, because thou hast shed much blood upon the earth in my sight" (KJV). David missed out on this special blessing, but for some reason God mercifully kept me from crossing this line, and I'm grateful He did.

Of course, this left me with the dilemma of being $9,000 short. Somehow, I didn't think that Bill was going to have the same amount of compassion that I did. So I stalled him for a couple of days, telling him that I was stuck in Virginia and I was being watched too closely to move. In the meantime, I was trying to quickly flip a couple of kilos in order to make up the money I needed. Due to my time limitations, I chose not to drive all the way to New York; instead, I tried to make a quick flip on the streets of Harrisburg.

Unfortunately, the word got out that I was shopping around for some "major weight," and it got back to Bill. He, of course, thought that I was trying to pull a fast one on him, so instead of being willing to work with me through the situation, he sought to take my life. I called him and requested a conference with him. Although he agreed to talk with me, he had an alternate plan up his sleeve.

The night that we were supposed to meet, I waited and waited for him. Although I was carrying a weapon just in case I needed it, I did not intend to use it. Suddenly, Bill and one of his partners showed up and held me at gunpoint and searched my house for the money I owed him. Finding nothing, they threw me in the back of their car and proceeded to drive me around town still at gunpoint.

Ironically, I never felt as though I was going to die that night. As I've said before, I believe God was with me even during this time. As Psalm 139:8 confirms, "If I ascend up into heaven, thou art there: if I make my bed in hell, behold, thou art there" (KJV). Indeed, God was with me and protected me—even when I didn't deserve it.

Eventually, I was able to escape from Bill and his associate by jumping out his vehicle in the middle of morning rush-hour traffic. I knew, from experience, that no smart hustler would bring attention to himself by shooting someone with a lot of witnesses around. So by the grace of God, I got away without any blood being shed.

Bill had taken my Lexus in return for the money that I owed him, and he had also taken my keys, which meant I couldn't go back to my house right away. Furious over what happened, I thought long and hard about getting revenge for what he did. I had even planned how I was going to ambush him and shoot him when he was coming out of his house. I felt as though I had to get him before he got to me. Many nights, I drove by his house looking for the opportunity to exact revenge. After awhile, though, I decided to leave him alone and return to the naval base and face my awaiting punishment.

Return to the Navy

When I finally went in to talk to the NIS, I discovered that they really didn't have much on me except some telephone calls from people who told them about my whereabouts and my activities. Up until then, it was all just rumors and innuendos. They did know, however, that I had not been reporting on the base every morning like I was supposed to, and that was enough to write me up. I was immediately put on confinement until a further investigation could be done. While on confinement, I had to muster about five times a day with the last muster being at 10:00 p.m. This made it very difficult to run my drug business, so I put it on hold. This was a good thing for me because the DEA was actively checking me out. I knew it was only a matter of time before I got caught and faced some really serious charges.

My confinement was supposed to last thirty days, but after two weeks, they presented me with a way out of the Navy. Up till then, Navy officials were preparing to certify me "fit for duty" again and send me to another ship. But with all the new allegations that were against me and the fact that I was UA again, I guess they felt it was in their best interests to just part ways. Needless to say, I was thrilled and gladly signed the paperwork to receive an administrative discharge under the category of "other than honorable" (OTH) circumstances. Although this was much better than a dishonorable discharge, it wasn't really a good thing. However, the only thing I could think of at the time was getting out of the Navy and getting back to my "business."

Once I signed the release forms, I felt a great burden lift off of me. I couldn't wait to be free once and for all from my ties to the Navy. I felt as though they had let me down just like so many other things in my life. It seemed like I had been used and tossed aside by everything and everyone I had put my trust in or cared about. I desperately wanted to begin taking control of my life.

Well, like most governmental processes, there was still some "red tape" holding things up. Not wanting to wait another day, I again left the base *without* permission. I took everything from my locker along with about $3,000 in cash and I left. In my mind, I justified that leaving was okay since I had already signed the release papers and accepted the "other than honorable" discharge. Of course, the Navy felt otherwise.

Pride Goes Before a Fall

Leaving the naval base before I was officially released was just another tell-tale sign of the *pride* growing in my heart. Pride is the first and worst sin of the devil. The Bible clearly shows us that pride was the root reason Lucifer was thrown out of heaven. Isaiah 14:12-15 reveals:

> "How art thou fallen from heaven, O Lucifer, son of the morning! How art thou cut down to the ground, which didst weaken the nations! For thou hast said in thine heart, I will ascend into heaven, I will exalt my throne above the stars of God: I will sit also upon the mount of the congregation, in the sides of the north: I will ascend above the heights of the clouds; I will be like the most High. Yet thou shalt be brought down to hell, to the sides of the pit" (KJV).

Because Lucifer was filled with pride and wanted to be above God, he was thrown out of heaven. In the same way, Adam and Eve also gave into the pride of wanting to be like God. In the Garden of Eden, Satan tricked them into disobeying God by telling them that when they ate of the fruit they would know as much as Him. Genesis 3:4,5 says:

> And the serpent said unto the woman, Ye shall not surely die: For God doth know that in the day ye eat thereof, then your eyes shall be opened, and ye shall be as gods, knowing good and evil.

We know the rest of the story. They gave into the temptation, separating us from fellowship with the Father and opening the door to sin and death. Indeed, "Pride goeth before destruction, and a haughty spirit before a fall" (Proverbs 16:18 KJV).

Once I had given in to the temptation to sell drugs, I felt as though I was untouchable. I stared disaster in the face many times and walked away unscathed. By God's mercy I continually got out of one jam after another.

Back then, however, I thought it was *my charm* that saved me. In pride, I began to feel like I was super human and there was nothing that I could not accomplish. But I was headed for a very rude awakening.

Chapter 10

Full-Time Dealer

At this point, I was deep into it—I was a full-fledged, full-time drug dealer. I began traveling back and forth between Virginia and Pennsylvania, selling drugs, but I really couldn't travel as freely as I wanted. I had left the base without being officially released, and as a result, I became a fugitive from the law. My name was now placed on the National Crime Information Center (NCIC). This alerted authorities of criminal activity nationwide; therefore, I knew that I had to be very careful.

The pressure of this situation, coupled with the fact that I had lost a lot of money in a bad drug deal, really began to affect me. To make matters worse, my drug business had lapsed because I had been in confinement for a couple of weeks. The thing about the drug business is if your customers can't find you, they will go somewhere else for the product. The drug game goes on regardless of who is around. With stress beginning to mount from many different directions, I really didn't know what I was going to do.

A Self-Satisfying Lifestyle

In spite of it all, my lifestyle became very flamboyant. So much so that $3,000 became pocket change for me. I was living a life of shopping, traveling, and eating out every day. There were even times when I traveled that I didn't take an overnight bag. When I needed clothes, I just went shopping and bought more. I remember flying to Miami Beach once to look for a new connection. I stayed there for about three days, and while I was there I ate out every night and went to some of the clubs on South Beach. I even had the opportunity to see part of the filming of the movie "Bad Boys," starring Will Smith and Martin Lawrence. I didn't know which movie was being filmed at the time, but seeing scenes from it later made me realize that I had been right in the middle of the movie shoots.

Sometimes when I think about how much money I wasted living the way I lived, it really blows my mind. It was bad enough that I spent tons of money, but what made it worse was I spent it all on myself, having total disregard for everyone else. That is what the drug-dealer lifestyle is all about—satisfying **self**. The devil had convinced me that I deserved to treat myself to basically anything I wanted. I even believed the twisted idea that God was paying me back for all I had missed out on while trying to be a good person. Indeed, I can see how the lifestyle of a drug dealer can be very addictive.

As we learned in Romans 8:6-7 earlier, the carnal, worldly mind is against God and His ways and leads to death. But following the mind of the Spirit produces life and peace. I have found that without the wisdom of God, we as humans automatically revert back to self-centered, carnal ways. Indeed, everything I did at this time in my life was all about me and what *I wanted*.

Selfishness is the fruit of a carnal, worldly mind, and it is in direct opposition to God. Usually the ways of the world and the ways of God are opposite. For instance, Jesus demonstrated *selflessness* instead of *selfishness*, and as a child of God we, too, must develop this quality through the power of the Holy Spirit. Jesus said in Matthew 16:24, "…If any man will come after me, let him *deny himself*, and take up his cross and follow me" (KJV). Interestingly, God knows what we have need of and has promised to supply it when we make Him our top priority (see Matthew 6:33). He has set up a scenario that would create a perfect society, if we would only put Him first in everything we do and how we deal with each other.

An Eyewitness to the Depths of Sin

Along with living selfishly, I also lived incognito. For about eleven months, I was like a shadow. No one called me by my real name; I was known as "Buck." When I talked to family members and friends, I was always vague concerning my whereabouts. I was always looking over my shoulder to make sure I wasn't being followed, and I always took the back route whenever I drove somewhere. Eventually, my income was reduced to a little bit of hustling. I couldn't really move any significant "weight" for fear of drawing too much attention to myself. I had all but completely given in to the dark side. The light of God was all but extinguished in my life.

During this time, I witnessed with my own eyes some of the worst aspects of human existence. Because I was only hustling small amounts of drugs, I began to sell crack cocaine as well. Crack, also known as "rocks" on the streets, is a drug that brings out the worst in anyone who takes it. I saw people using it and sinking to such great depths of depravity that I began calling crack "the devil." A true crack addict will do *anything* to acquire more crack cocaine. I've seen this addiction turn women into prostitutes and men into homosexuals who performed sex acts for money.

I have been in houses that were converted to a "rock house"—a place where crack is regularly bought, sold, and used. These are either vacant houses that no one lives in any longer, or they are homes in which the residents have become so entrenched in using crack that they are incapable of functioning. Unable to pay their bills, the electricity and water get turned off, and the house is left in shambles.

The women who hang out in these houses will give sexual favors to anyone with money or rocks. For as little as $2.00, a man can receive oral sex from someone looking to acquire some crack. I have seen a pregnant woman smoke crack until she vomited and wondered what would happen to her child. I just can't imagine what the future holds for a baby born with such a severe addiction. I still remember feeling repulsed to see the men who paid for sexual favors from a six-month, pregnant woman who desperately needed crack cocaine to feed her addiction. Seeing women constantly pulling tricks to get money or drugs to keep their high going was one of the most unspeakable things I have ever seen in my life. Without question, rock houses are the image of depravity to which man can sink.

The worst rock house I have been in was one located in Virginia. It was surrounded by many "boot houses" or "juke joints." These are houses in which people sell beer and liquor without a license. They usually sell store-bought alcohol, but many times they also sell bootleg, or illegally-made, liquor. At any rate, this one rock house I frequented had no lights or running water, and the few full-time residents were in a constant cycle of getting high, eating, and sleeping—but mostly getting high. Because there was no running water, people used the bath tub to relieve themselves whenever necessary. There were also plastic containers throughout the house in which people urinated. You can just imagine the smell during the summer months.

Crack is a very dangerous drug because once a person takes a "hit," the "blast" usually only lasts about ten to twenty minutes, and then the person has to go about trying to find more rocks to smoke to regain their high. I have seen many people shoot heroin, but it usually incapacitates them for a certain period of time. Crack, on the other hand, charges the user up, giving them great surges of sustained energy and an increased appetite to use more drugs. Amazingly, a person on a crack binge can stay awake for days without feeling a need for sleep.

The temporary euphoric feelings resulting from using crack also give people an increased sex drive. When women first begin to use crack, it arouses them and gives them a heightened sense of desire for sex. After repeatedly using the drug, however, the desire may still be there, but their bodies become so dried up that the only form of sex they are capable of providing is oral sex. Crack seems to have a similar effect on men.

Without question, I have personally seen people sink to unbelievable lows as a result of their crack addiction. I thank God that I never had the desire to become a crack user. I snorted cocaine on a regular basis, but I never truly became addicted. I did get a temporary rush from it, but I never had any crazy thoughts or desires. The reason I used it so frequently was because I usually had an abundance of it and it was convenient. Ironically, I never really craved cocaine, and when I didn't have it, it didn't really matter. Indeed, I was very fortunate that I escaped getting totally strung out on cocaine.

Personally Sinking to New Lows

During my time of hiding from the feds, I sank to new moral lows myself. Throughout all the things I had done in the past, I still usually had some limits as to what I would do. However, during this period, my standards dropped dramatically. I remember one time in particular when I set up another drug dealer and robbed him. His name was "Frank," and I had done business with him some time earlier. He came to me and asked me if I was holding any "weight" because he was looking to buy half a kilo (18 ounces) of cocaine.

Knowing he had the money to buy the drugs, I contacted another close acquaintance of mine, who I'll call "Rick," to arrange the scam. I knew from experience Rick would do just about whatever was necessary in order to make money. I told him the details of the deal that was going to go down, including where Frank and I were meeting. Once he knew his cue and what he was to do, we proceeded with our plan.

Frank and I drove to pick up the drugs from a contact at a specific store. I pulled up in front, parked the car, and pretended to go inside and get the stuff. When I came back to the car, Rick stepped out from around the building and forced his way into the car, pretending to hold us up at gunpoint. He took Frank's bag, which contained about $12,000, and my bag, which of course was empty. After Rick abruptly left, I was able to convince Frank that I was just as upset about getting robbed as he was. I even went into my house and came back with a loaded .38 revolver, vowing to get revenge on the guy who had done it. Rick and I met up later and divided up the spoils.

Occasionally, I got a scare from the law enforcement agents that would come by the place where I was staying with pictures looking for me. Most people living in a criminal environment don't want to tell the police anything. In fact, true criminals usually don't even offer their name unless they are forced to. Most of the core group I hung out with would lie to the police and tell them they either didn't know me or that they hadn't seen me in years.

On more than one occasion, I was actually hiding inside the house while the police were at the door, questioning people about my whereabouts.

Another scary moment happened when I attempted to rob another drug dealer named "Tom." Tom was an ex-boyfriend of Marabel. She had mentioned some things to me in passing about him, including where he hid his drugs and money in his apartment. Knowing she still occasionally did deals with him, I knew the information was accurate. Once I was able to get the overall layout of his apartment from Marabel, I again employed the help of Rick to go in and get his goods.

The first night we planned to break into his apartment, we couldn't locate Tom. Fearing he might come home while we were still in his apartment, we decided to wait. The next afternoon, I stationed another female friend of mine with a cell phone to just sit outside of Tom's business where I knew he would be for most of the day. At about 3 p.m., Rick and I took a crowbar, pried open Tom's apartment door, and walked right in. After about 30 minutes of rummaging through his house, we were only able to find some jewelry. At that point, I decided it was time to go.

Even though I was really far gone in my thinking, I still exercised caution by wearing gloves while searching through Tom's stuff. Rick, on the other hand, didn't have any gloves on, so I made him leave first to be sure he got away. By the time I came out of the apartment, it was late afternoon and I saw the kids coming home from school. Suddenly, I was met with a police car sitting right outside of Tom's apartment complex. Not knowing if they had been called by the neighbors or not, I immediately ran around the back of the building and removed the white sweatshirt I was wearing. When I returned to the front to get picked up by my ride, the cops were gone; the alert was for nothing. To this day, I believe someone tipped Tom off, because we were unable to find the drugs or the money that I knew he normally had hidden in his place.

Sometime later, I found out Tom had gotten busted for drugs and had spent three years in prison. Similarly, Rick had pulled a big bank robbery and had been put in jail for about twenty years. Frank, unfortunately, had been tragically killed in a motorcycle accident. As the timeless truth says, **crime doesn't pay**. I know that even though I was living a horrible, criminal lifestyle, God mercifully spared me. He kept me from self-destructing and prevented me from getting locked up for many, many years.

Picked Up by Police

I stayed on the run for nearly a year and began to wonder if and when life as I knew it would come to an end. Things continued to spiral downward with no signs of turning around. I was drinking about a pint or two of gin and snorting coke every single day.

In June of 1995, my best friend Randy was getting married, and I was asked to stand in his wedding. It was in Philadelphia, which is quite a distance from Virginia. Even though I was living a life of crime, I went through the wedding ceremony as if everything was going well. My ex-wife, Kathy, was at the wedding, and she was eagerly trying to hold a conversation with me. But she was a part of my past that I had no interest in returning to.

As we moved from the wedding to the reception, I received a page from my mother. Instinctively, I knew why she was calling me; Pop Pop had died. When I called her, I firmly told her to wait until I came to Harrisburg to tell me what she needed to tell me. Somehow I felt if I didn't actually hear the news spoken, I could hold myself together and help my friend Randy enjoy his special day. The last thing I wanted to do was put a damper on his celebration. Amazingly, I put up a very good front, and no one at the wedding had any idea of all the turmoil that I was experiencing in my life.

Time passed, and I was back in Harrisburg visiting my mom. Pop Pop had indeed passed away, and since his house was available, I stayed there in order to avoid being around my stepfather. I was planning on traveling to New York to pick up some coke. But because I was still on the run, I purposely chose to deal in small quantities. I understood the consequences of getting stopped with a large amount of cocaine and wanted to avoid it at all costs.

One evening as I left my mom's house, I was just about to stop at a neighborhood bar to get some drinks before going to Pop Pop's house for the night. On the way, I was pulled over by the Harrisburg Police, and they immediately asked me if they could search my car. I told them "yes," and it quickly became evident that they were looking for something specific (drugs, I'm sure). Obviously, someone who knew I would be in Harrisburg had tipped them off as to my whereabouts.

Much to my surprise, they let me go without a ticket or even a warning. At the time, I attributed it to a "good luck" charm I had in my pocket. During our time together, Marabel had taken me to several "root doctors" that are very prevalent in the south. These root doctors would read your palms and tarot cards and mix up potions for good luck. For the right price, they would even put curses on people for you. Ironically, I was so far into darkness that this seemed insignificant. However, it was probably one of the worst things I did!

Deuteronomy 18:9-12 declares, "When thou art come into the land which the Lord thy God giveth thee, thou shall not learn to do after the abominations of those nations. There shall not be found among you anyone that maketh his son or his daughter to pass through the fire, or that useth divination, or an observer of times, or an enchanter or a witch, or a charmer, or a consulter with familiar spirits, or a wizard, or a necromancer. For all that do these things are an abomination unto the Lord: and because of these abominations the Lord thy God doth drive them out from before thee" (KJV). Ultimately, I know now that there is no such thing as luck, and it was by the grace of God that my circumstances were not far worse than they were. I would come to this understanding later and repent for participating in this demonic activity.

After the police let me go, I went into Les & Tiny's bar, which was right down the street from Pop Pop's place. A few minutes later, I looked up and about ten police officers were coming into the bar to get me. As they arrested me, they told me that they had run my name through the NCIC computer, and it revealed that I was a military deserter. I knew it was only a matter of time before this happened. Nevertheless, I protested and continued to tell them it was a mistake. They transported me to Dauphin County Prison (DCP) in Harrisburg, PA, where I waited for the Navy to come and get me. It was a Friday, so I knew I would be there at least for the weekend. Finally, my eleven months on the run had come to an end.

Booked and Discharged from the Navy

Strangely, while I was in DCP, I saw many people I knew from both childhood and the streets. In a way, I felt relieved that I didn't have to look over my shoulder any more. Being arrested was probably best because I really don't know that I would have ever turned myself in.

The following Tuesday, two federal marshals, a man and a woman, came to pick me up. I still remember walking through the Harrisburg airport escorted by these federal agents with my hands and feet shackled together. It was a very different experience. Sadly, my thinking was so off base that I actually felt important—like one of those gangsters in the movies. They took me in handcuffs back to Norfolk, VA, to be processed and put into prison. I was not looking forward to this because of the stories I had heard concerning military prison. I wasn't really afraid, but I was anxious because I didn't know what to expect.

From the time I had been picked up by the local police in Harrisburg until the time I arrived at the military prison in Norfolk, five days had elapsed. While being processed, I was given a complete physical and tested for a number of diseases, such as AIDS, syphilis, etc. I was also given a drug test. Usually cocaine leaves your system after three days. I still had a high level of coke in my bloodstream, and I had not used any drugs for over five days. Once the processing was complete, I was placed behind bars.

Military prison, also known as *the brig*, is a lot different from a normal jail. There are many strict rules a person must follow, such as always keeping your hands at your side and walking on the right side of the hall. The military does not have to follow the same rules as the public prison system. If a person in the brig violates the rules of the brig, committing an additional serious offense, he can be sentenced to bread and water. In other words, that's all you get to eat and drink. Needless to say, it was not a very pleasant experience, but I made it through the process. I appeared in a military court hearing and was ultimately released from the U.S. Navy with an administrative discharge under *other than honorable* circumstances.

One of the biggest problems people have is a lack of genuine repentance. Such was the case with me even after I was caught. Most of us would rather change our perception of what is right and wrong instead of actually changing our behavior and our mind-set. But right and wrong do not change; our actions are what must change and come into agreement with what is right. The Bible says that David was "a man after God's heart." In other words, he was a model of what we are to be. He wasn't perfect from the standpoint of his *actions*; he was considered perfect because of the condition of his heart. Whenever he realized he had sinned, his desire was to repent and get back into right fellowship with God. That's true repentance— changing your mind about what you are doing that is wrong and doing what is right by God's strength. Although I did not immediately repent and change my mind after being placed in a military prison, that change would soon come.

AGAIN AND AGAIN, GOD SHOWS MERCY

After I had officially been released from the Navy, I went out and got a job, but I still continued to hustle cocaine. In 1997 I bought a Mercedes Benz from a gentleman that was the manager of a local steak house in Virginia. I purchased it on a Friday, and because it was a Friday, I couldn't get new tags for it until the following Monday. Nevertheless, I wanted to show the car off, so I drove it that Friday to my dad's nightclub. After I had been in the club drinking for awhile, a friend of mine named "Don" came and asked me for a ride home. Now, my house was around the corner from the club, and I didn't have any problems getting to it—even with a couple of drinks in my system. On the other hand, Don's house was all the way across town. Although I had initially told him I wouldn't take him, I eventually gave in and agreed to give him a ride home.

About half way to Don's house, a policeman got behind me and began to follow me. I believe he did this for several reasons: First, I was a young black man driving a large, expensive-looking car. Second, the officer may have recognized the license plate and thought I had stolen the car. The third and most obvious reason, however, was I been drinking alcohol and my driving probably showed it.

In any event, the officer followed me for about two miles, and during that time I tried my best to do everything correctly. I made sure I used my turn signals, came to a complete stop at each stop sign, and so forth. In spite of all my efforts, the officer pulled me over and asked if I had been drinking. I believe he saw me leave the night club, so he assumed that I was drinking alcohol.

This may not seem like a big deal, but as I told you, I had returned to my drug-dealing ways. On that particular night, I was riding very "dirty," which is a term that means a person has illegal materials on them. When that officer pulled me over, I had half a kilo of crack cocaine (18 ounces), approximately $14,000 in cash, and a stolen gun that I had bought hot off the street. If the police officer would have arrested me, he would have searched my car and found everything. Consequently, I would have been looking at probably about thirty or forty years in jail.

To put this in perspective, a close associate of mine had been arrested with just 14 ounces of crack, and he was facing twenty to twenty-eight years in jail. He cooperated with the authorities and only received twenty years. Amazingly, even though my blood-alcohol level was at the legal limit, the officer let me go with only a warning not to drive the car anymore that night.

In another instance, I was at the house of one of my girlfriends, talking and having some drinks when suddenly Marabel showed up. At the time, she and I were not seeing each other, but for some reason she always felt like she could dictate to me what to do. She was a very street-smart woman who had a bad temper and reputation, as did her entire family, as being a "hell-raiser." Once I realized that she had come to make a scene, I attempted to leave the house in order to avoid a bad situation. When I did, Marabel tried to run me over with her car. Enraged, I began to scream obscenities at her, and when she got too close to me with her car, I shattered the driver side car window with my bare hands.

Needless to say, the neighbors called the police who quickly showed up and began asking questions. They immediately asked Marabel if I had hit her, which I had not done nor would I ever do. I always believed in defending myself, but I never believed in hitting women. Fortunately for me Marabel confirmed this. It was pretty obvious what had happened; I was standing beside Marabel's car with shattered glass all over me. The officer later told me that because of the rash of domestic violence cases, they were instructed to automatically take the woman's side whenever there was an altercation between a man and a woman. Again, I could have been arrested and charged with domestic violence, which would not have been good on my record for the future.

After talking to Marabel, the police then turned their attention to me. They asked me if I was armed, which of course I was. At that time in my life, I very rarely left the house without having at least one gun on me. I told the officer that I did have a gun in my pocket, and once I did, I was arrested. What I did *not* tell him was that I had about four grams of powdered cocaine in my pocket as well. I had it tightly wrapped in paper to sell to my customers. To get caught with a gun *and* drugs usually results in a longer sentence. Therefore, when he found it, I made up a story as to what it was. Amazingly, the cop bought it and promptly placed the drugs back into my pocket. I was arrested that night and only charged with having a concealed weapon. I walked away with only having to pay a $75.00 fine and a year of probation. Only God's mercy allowed me to escape these situations without being arrested and charged with some very serious jail time.

These are not very pleasant memories for me. There is much more I could write about, but I do not want to give the impression that I am glorifying crime or myself in any way. I share these transgressions because I believe it is necessary in order to truly communicate my testimony and tell how the power of God delivered me from all unrighteousness. We must be transparent enough to tell how far we have fallen in order for others to see how far God has brought us.

I have since repented for all of my wrongdoings, and God has renewed my mind and continues to do so each day. Philippians 2:5 says to "Let this mind be in you, which was also in Christ Jesus" (KJV). The more I study the Word of God, the more my thinking is transformed to think the way God thinks about what is right and what is wrong.

I said it before and I'll say it again: Even when I didn't deserve it, God showed me mercy and kept me from disaster. He did allow me to go through many trials and tribulations because of my disobedience, but He always kept me from going totally over the edge. I do believe that if it had not been for His mercy and grace, I would have spent many years in jail or I would probably be dead by now. God kept me in order to fulfill the mission and purpose He has called me to.

Section 3
RETURNING TO THE LIGHT

Chapter 11

The Path to Repentance

So far, I have given you a pretty clear picture of just how far my life had drifted off the path of God. From the time I finally received my discharge from the Navy in 1996 until the end of 1999, I continued down a path of destruction and death—maintaining my drug dealing and wild partying. I had worked a couple of very good jobs, but my lifestyle made it hard for me to keep them for more than a year or so. With each passing day, I was dying more and more because of the amount of unrepentant sin that I was carrying around. But sometime around 1998, God really began to work on me, and by the end of that year, I went through one of the lowest points of my life. Again, God was trying to get my attention, but I was still not hearing Him.

This reminds me of the stories of Jonah and Saul, who later became the apostle Paul. God had chosen them for specific purposes, but they were both heading in the wrong direction. Saul, as he was originally known, was on his way to Damascus to persecute Christians, and he was struck blind by Jesus Christ Himself. Knowing it was Saul's desire to serve God with all his heart, Jesus revealed the truth of who He was to him; He redirected his passion, gave him a new name, and put him on the right path to fulfill his destiny. Indeed, Paul was instrumental in spreading the gospel of Jesus Christ to the Gentiles through his preaching and his writing. At least thirteen books of the New Testament are attributed to him.

Similarly, Jonah was given a word from God to deliver to the people of Nineveh. But because of the bitterness he had in his heart toward them for their harsh treatment of Israel, he didn't want to go. Instead, he decided to board a ship that was headed in the opposite direction. To get Jonah's attention, God sent a very big storm his way and a fish to swallow him up once he had been thrown into the water. In the end, God's will prevailed in and through Jonah's life—he preached the message of repentance to the people of Nineveh, and they repented.

These examples from scripture clearly declare that when God really wants to get your attention, He will! Although my conversion was not as dramatic as Jonah's or Paul's, God did get my attention. He brought circumstances into my life to break my will and put me on the path He had purposed for me to follow.

Very Troubled in Heart

In 1998, I began to get a very troubled feeling in my spirit. Over and over again, I had this gnawing sense in my gut that I was not doing what God wanted me to do, but I didn't know what it was. This got me to thinking of the days when I was in grade school and how I used to calculate how old I would be in the year 2000. I did the math and realized I would be 33 years old. This didn't seem like a big deal when I was in sixth grade, but since the century was coming to an end, it became very relevant.

Jesus Christ died on the cross at the age of 33. At the time of His death, He had completed the job God the Father had given Him to do. His mere 33 years here on earth changed the course of human history and reopened the door of relationship between God and man. Matthew 27:51 reveals that when Jesus died, "…the veil of the temple was rent in twain from the top to the bottom; and the earth did quake, and the rocks rent" (KJV).

Indeed, the life of Jesus Christ has had an enormous impact on the world. Even today, some 2,000 years later, His life still affects us. Our entire calendar system is based upon His life and death. The time before Christ is classified as B.C., and the time after His death and resurrection is classified as A.D., which is a Latin abbreviation meaning, "In the Year of Our Lord."

As I crept toward my 33rd birthday, I started to examine the impact of my life on the earth. I began to question whether or not my death would affect anyone in the world around me other than those in my immediate vicinity. Then one day, the Lord clearly questioned me within my spirit, asking me, *My son, Jesus changed the course of history in 33 years; what will you have done in 33 years?* That question began gnawing at me day and night, but I did not know how to answer it. Looking back, I now believe this was the beginning of God placing His call on my life. He knows exactly what buttons to push and when to push them.

Clearly, from 1997 until 2000 was probably the worst period in my life. Financially, I had hit an all-time low. Interestingly, at one point in my life I owned a Lexus two-door coupe, a Mercedes 300SD, and an Infinity Q45. I also owned two houses that were completely paid for. As the century drew to a close, however, I was struggling to maintain a job and hustling small amounts of drugs just to make ends meet. Eventually, I ended up homeless and lost almost all of my worldly possessions. I had gone from having an abundance of money and driving fancy cars to having nothing.

It was now the year 2000, and God certainly had my attention. When He finally convinced me that it was time to change my life, I moved back to Harrisburg driving a seventeen-year-old car with mix-matched seats and everything I owned in the trunk. Without question, I knew I needed to turn away from a life of crime and drugs. However, I was still not completely convinced that God had to be in charge. So I did not completely surrender my life to Him…yet.

A Season of Restoration

Moving back to Harrisburg marked the beginning of a new season in my life—a season of restoration. During that time, God began to work a miracle in my relationship with my mother. Even before I had totally surrendered myself to Him, He began putting the pieces of my life back together in a way that I could never have imagined.

For many years, my relationship with my mother had been strained and distant. I had been upset with her because she had allowed my stepfather to treat her so disrespectfully. As I said before, he did not provide for the family, and he cheated on her constantly. I didn't want our relationship to remain damaged, so I began to pray that God would help me mend it, and He answered my prayer, coordinating restoration in a way that no man ever could.

What had happened was my stepfather had been sent to jail in 1998 for two years on a burglary charge. He had broken into his girlfriend's house and hit her with a chain. At the time, he was on a crack binge and was basically out of his mind. His two-year sentence was just coming to an end in 2000. My mother had made up her mind that this situation was the last straw—she would not take him back. However, she also knew from past experience that she was too weak to tell him "no" when he tried to return. When she learned of my homeless situation and invited me to move back to Harrisburg to live with her, God had made it so that I needed to move back as much as, if not more than, she needed me back. This gave us time to bond and repair our relationship, which I believe is vitally important for parents and children to have.

Incredibly, God gave me the desire of my heart even *before* I knew what to pray for. This is what Romans 8:26,27 means when it says, "Likewise the Spirit also helpeth our infirmities: for we know not what we should pray for as we ought: but the Spirit itself maketh intercession for us with groanings which cannot be uttered. And he that searcheth the hearts knoweth what is the mind of the Spirit, because he maketh intercession for the saints according to the will of God" (KJV).

We must always realize that God wants the best for His children. In Jeremiah 29:11 He declares, "For I know the thoughts and plans I have for you, says the Lord, thoughts and plans for *welfare* and *peace* and not for evil, to give you hope in your final outcome" (AMP). He only chastens, or disciplines, us and allows pain and suffering in our lives to make us better and mold us into the image of Jesus Christ. Actually, His discipline is an expression of His love: "For the Lord corrects and disciplines everyone whom He loves, and He punishes, even scourges, every son whom He accepts and welcomes to His heart and cherishes" (Hebrews 12:6 AMP).

Not only did God restore our relationship, He also used my mother to help me get a new job. Through her recommendation, I was soon hired as an adult parole/probation officer for Dauphin County, PA. Indeed, this was probably one of the last places on earth I would have ever thought of working, but it turned out to be just the place I needed to be.

A Surprising and Strange Job Opportunity

God's will for my life was playing out right before my eyes. Like most people, I did not see the big picture of what was going on; God had only given me enough information to take the next step, as He usually does. But with Him orchestrating our life's journey, that's the only thing we need to know.

As Romans 8:28-30 says, "We know that all things work together for good to them that love God, to them who are the called according to his purpose. For whom he did foreknow, he also did predestinate to be conformed to the image of his Son, that he might be the firstborn among many brethren. Moreover whom he did predestinate, them he also called: and whom he called, them he also justified: and whom he justified, them he also glorified" (KJV). As we learn to trust and follow Him daily, He will lead and carry us to where we need to be.

Miraculously, through all I had experienced God had kept me, and the only criminal record I had was the concealed weapon misdemeanor in Virginia. My military record only showed that I had an administrative discharge, but it did not show up as a civilian offense. Even the time I spent in the military prison did not reflect on my criminal record. Amazingly, with all the crimes I had committed, I still had a clean slate. This was totally the result of God's mercy.

Being a former criminal, it was very ironic that I would get a job as a probation officer. Yet, after living a life of crime for so many years and doing so much evil, I felt as though I was better equipped to supervise criminals because I understood how they thought. I really believed I could make a big difference in their lives because of my life's experiences. I had tried that lifestyle, and I knew beyond a shadow of a doubt that it was fruitless.

During my time as a parole officer, God really began to change my thinking. He was preparing me for the future path He would be taking me on, even though I had still not put Him first in my life. I was now on the side of law enforcement, and I began to look at things from a totally different perspective. I gained new insights into the mind of criminals, and I had the chance to see just how sad and pitiful it was to live a lost life of lawlessness.

God also gave me the opportunity to counsel men and women who were living their lives outside the order of the law. It didn't take long for all the wisdom that Pop Pop and other mentors had instilled in me to come back. I knew I had it in me, but I had suppressed it for so long with drugs, sex, and alcohol, I had forgotten it was there. I felt a surge of peace as I was able to instill things into people and set them on the right track. It felt good to be on the right side of the law, doing things to help to build up society instead of tear it down.

In the process, I met a lot of very nice guys who had lost their way. I was able to sow positive seeds of hope into their lives by letting them know that there was a better way to live—a life behind bars was *not* the way to go. I also let them know that when they went to jail, their sentence not only affected them but also their family members and friends who cared about them. If I were there today, I would confidently say without fear of contradiction that no matter what your circumstances are, you can overcome them. You may have more obstacles to overcome than the next person, but with the right amount of perseverance, patience, and commitment, you can accomplish great things.

Recognizing the Real Problem

After spending almost three years as a parole officer, one of the things that really became clear to me was the mentality of drug dealers. Unquestionably, they are selfish and always seek the fastest way to make easy money. A dealer will usually distribute his poison to whoever has the money to buy it. Actually, drug dealers are not the only ones who are selfish. This is also the mentality of a majority of people who are repeat offenders in the criminal justice system. They tend to blame everything and everyone else for their problems. They make claims like, "The system is set up to make me fail," or "I had a bad childhood," or some other type of conspiracy is keeping them down. As a result, they go in and out of prison like a revolving door, and they never change.

The vast majority of the people who did this didn't seem to have any desire to do the right thing. They lied about the least little thing. I often said they would spend ten minutes trying to get out of five minutes of work. They refused any type of treatment offered and only did the minimum of what was required of them. Eventually, I became disgusted with dealing with people like this; they just would not do anything to better their lives, and it really frustrated me. More and more my eyes were opened, and I saw just how ugly a life devoid of God can make a person.

I often hear people talk about how the criminal justice system is set up to make people fail, and I disagree with that. Looking at the system from the inside out, the real problem I see at work is what psychology calls a "self-fulfilling prophecy." What this means is people very often bring to pass in their lives what they *think* and *speak*. For instance, if a person continually makes the statement, "I am going to lose my job," he usually begins to withdraw, showing up late for work and not giving his best effort. In essence, because he believes he is going to lose his job, his actions bring it to pass. I watched this happen repeatedly among offenders. Many believe they are doomed for disaster, so they take on an attitude of not caring. They decide to not even try to do the right thing because they feel they're going to fail anyway. As a result, they usually do, but what they fail to see is that they made it happen.

There are actually a couple of key scriptures in the Bible that confirm this. After Job loses everything of value in his life, he says, "For the thing which I greatly feared is come upon me, and that which I was afraid of is come unto me" (Job 3:25 KJV). In other words, Job's fear allowed him to fall victim to the very thing which he feared. In a similar way, Proverbs 23:7 shows the connection between the way a person thinks and what becomes reality in their life: "For as he thinketh in his heart, so is he..." (KJV). Without question, what we think and believe is the mold in which our lives are poured.

Understanding & Dealing with Repeat Offenders

I have always found that in life we either win or lose, and we usually lose because we either didn't try or we simply didn't do the right things— we made wrong choices. To put this into perspective, here is a list of stipulations that most parolees have to adhere to in order to avoid being placed back in jail: (1) Maintain steady employment. (2) If you change residences or jobs, inform your probation officer (P.O.) about it. (3) Pay your fines and costs. (4) Do not use any illegal drugs. (5) If you have any police interaction, inform your P.O. about it. (6) You may be told not to drink alcohol or hang out in bars. (7) No weapons (guns, knives, etc.). These are the basic stipulations that most people on parole/probation have to follow. They are really not too hard. The deciding factor determining whether or not a person succeeds is the person's attitude.

As I said, people who lead a continual life of crime are very selfish. These are repeat offenders—they only think about themselves and act on impulse, doing what feels good at that moment. They usually don't consider the long-term consequences, or if they do, they don't take them seriously. I have seen many people do the same wrong thing over and over again, and they always seem to feel remorse when they get caught. Sometimes the remorse is for what they have done, but often it is just because they got caught.

The reason I keep using the words *repeat offenders* is because they are what really drain the system. I can personally attest to the fact that many people lose their way and do things wrong; my life is a prime example of that. Everyone is human, and as a result, everyone makes mistakes. Making mistakes is not the problem. The problem is making the *same* mistakes over and over again, expecting to get different results. This is what repeat offenders do, and it is just plain foolishness.

It's been said that the definition of insanity is doing the same thing over and over again and expecting to get different results. Based on my experience as a parole officer, there are a large number of insane people in the world. The criminal justice system was never set up to accommodate people who go in and out of jail. On the contrary, it is supposed to be a deterrent from crime and a place for rehabilitation. They purposely try to make prison as unpleasant as possible for inmates so that they don't want to come back!

Dealing with repeat offenders really did begin to burn me out and cause me to lose faith in humanity. I came to the place where I felt like I was dying on the inside. In the midst of it all, I caught a glimpse of the despair that God must sometimes feel when he looks down on man, His prized creation. Thankfully, He moved me from being a parole officer when He did. Nevertheless, He used the entire experience to turn my life away from crime.

RECEIVING DIRECTION IN AN UNEXPECTED WAY

While being a parole officer, I made some very good friends—with co-workers and even with some of the people I was supervising. One person I met was David Ray, and clearly, God had put him in my life to change my direction and place me on the right path. Even though he was assigned to the work release center where I supervised, I became his friend.

Now David was a very good talker—so good that he probably could have sold ice to the Eskimos. Oddly, I liked being around him, but I was also disappointed with him. He had a great gift of communication, but he never used it to reach his full potential. Unfortunately, many people fall into this category—they use their gifts to gain minor victories, but they fail to use them to excel in the field they are called to.

Nevertheless, David was originally from Brooklyn, NY, and he had the classic New York, fast-talk approach for everything. I had spent a lot of time in New York City hustling drugs, so I was used to the way he talked and could understand him, even though many others could not. I have learned not to listen to what a person says as much as look at the fruit that his or her life bears. In other words, results are more important than talk.

Interestingly, David began taking music classes at the local community college, and he had a young friend who was an aspiring rapper that he was managing. What was even more fascinating, though, was learning about some of the people of influence in the entertainment field that he knew. In fact, it just so happened that these bigwigs were looking to have a concert in the Hershey Giant Center—a 12,000-seat auditorium right next to the famous Hershey Park and Hershey Chocolate Factory. At first I did not believe it was true. However, David produced documents, confirming that he had actually talked his way into a pretty big deal, and he wanted me to be a part of it!

The thought of being a part of a big rap concert really sparked my attention. I had always been a big rap fan, and at the time my entire playlist of music was about 99 percent rap. When David's connection in New York offered me the chance to be in charge of security for the event, I really got excited! As a parole officer, I had a license to carry a gun, which made me a logical choice to guard the entertainers. Knowing I couldn't do it alone, I employed the services of some of the other parole officers as well as some of the local police with which I had been working. This opportunity would give me the chance to make some extra income and be in the middle of something I really loved.

Surprisingly, the investor sponsoring the concert backed out at the last minute, which left David and his associates without the cash to pull it off. Consequently, I was offered the opportunity to promote the concert—if I could find someone to put up the money. The total cost for the performers and the promotions would be approximately $100,000, which initially seemed like a lot of money. But when I took into account that the auditorium had 12,000 seats, each bringing in $30 to $50, I realized I was looking at a net return of about $200,000 after all the bills were paid. I could definitely work with that kind of money.

Immediately, I began to learn all that I could and tried to secure the needed support so that the concert could go on. Although I got close to my goal, I was never able to secure the investors necessary to make the concert a reality. Nevertheless, this event birthed my desire to be a concert promoter—it gave me a new passion in life and pointed me in the direction that God was taking me.

A Promotions Company Is Born

More and more, I began to strategize on how to put together big concerts. Like everything else I was interested in, I totally engulfed myself in learning the business. I made contacts with people from all aspects of the industry—from insurance agents who insured events to booking agents for stars to people in charge of the stadiums and auditoriums. Each person I spoke with gave me a piece of the puzzle as to how the promotions business worked. When I started to crunch the numbers, I began to realize just how much money a concert promoter could make with just one tour. A person could literally retire with a good ten- to twenty-city tour under his belt. Of course, I was looking at this as a career move, not just a one-time deal.

Up till then, all of my efforts had been merely projections and speculation. I had a lot of potential, but I had not done anything that would give someone enough confidence to pour $50,000 to $100,000 into a project that I was putting together. Then it happened—I received some of the best advice possible. I spoke with a woman who worked with one of the larger radio stations in Philadelphia and I asked her for advice on putting together a big, successful concert. She said the most practical thing for me to do would be to begin putting together some small, local events in order to get experience and get my name out in the community. Then I could go after the big bucks!

Upon receiving this advice, I knew I had to form my own company and come up with a name for it. Since David and I were working together, I combined my last name with part of his last name and came up with Greener Management Group (GMG). As GMG, I started trying to plan and put together small events to get the name out. I began calling local nightclubs to see where I could hold an event. I recognized that just as in real estate, location was a major key to holding an event like this.

The next most important thing I needed to do was to put together a budget. At that time, I was still a parole officer in Harrisburg, and I wasn't making a lot of money. Therefore, my budget was basically zero. I did, however, have a friend from high school who was a comedian. His name was Kenny Rob, and he had been on BET's Comic View a couple of times. In my mind, this designated him as a celebrity. My connection with Kenny motivated me to begin putting together comedy shows at local bars and restaurants. I also had some very good comics who came from all over the east coast. Through persistence, I was able to put together one show a month for most of the year 2002. I believe we did nine or ten shows altogether that year, which is a good number for a small promoter. Occasionally the turnout was extremely small, but we usually had nice-sized crowds.

When I look back over my life, I actually began putting together events in 1996 when I was in Virginia. Soon after I got out of the Navy, Marabel threw a birthday party for one of her brothers and me. My birthday is July 9, and her brother's was July 5. Our party was probably the event of the year. Marabel hired a limousine to drive us to my dad's club. Once we arrived, her brother and I made a grand entrance! The cabaret was such a big success that we began doing more of them every couple of months. We formed the "Player's Club and the Foxy Ladies." It consisted of two men and me along with our three girlfriends. Most of us were drug dealers, so the elaborate cabarets attracted many people. This was my introduction to the promotion business. Again, God was directing my life, even when I had no clue.

Persistence Is the Key

Up until that point, most of the money to do the shows was coming out of my pocket. David really didn't have any, which opened my eyes as to why he hadn't gotten any further in life. I once read a book titled *Think and Grow Rich* that gave testimonies of several people who had made it big in the business world. One of the common themes in all of their stories was *persistence*. Just about all of them talked about having to push forward even when things didn't seem to be going their way. Ironically, some of the richest people had bounced back from the brink of suicide, homelessness, and a deep desire to quit. Indeed, I learned an important lesson about persistence from their examples.

The Bible talks about persistence as well. The apostle Paul declares the importance of *pressing toward the goal of the high calling in Christ Jesus* and *fighting the good fight of faith* (see Philippians 3:12-14; 1 Timothy 6:12). Galatians 6:9 also reveals that there is a reward for those who do not faint but remain faithful in doing what's right, even when they are weary. Of course, the Bible is talking about those who are doing God's work, but the theme of persistence is still the key principle to obtaining the reward the person is pursuing.

By the end of 2002, I began to move in a new direction. I was still putting together comedy shows, but I was also trying to plan and organize other kinds of events. I wanted to see how much money I could earn by catering events and planning out all of the details. I was also exploring other avenues of obtaining wealth. For the first time, I began to see just how much money a person could make *legally* without worrying about getting arrested, going to jail, getting robbed, or being killed like in the drug business.

Little by little, I began to gain a good name in the community and met some very influential people. At one of the first comedy shows I promoted, a good friend of mine who was a lobbyist invited several state senators and representatives to my show. This sparked ideas of trying to get into political event planning as well. Indeed, a whole new world was opening up to me. Nevertheless, God had plans for my life, and when God has plans for you, all the planning in the world cannot change that. Oh, we can try to do something else, but true joy and fulfillment are only found in fulfilling His specific call on our life.

CHAPTER 12

A NEW LIFE BRINGS CHANGE

Time passed and it was spring 2003. Although I had reduced my womanizing ways, I was still sexually active and not living in accordance with God's will for my life. During this time, something happened which would drastically affect my plans for the future. In April, one of the young ladies I was seeing told me that she was pregnant. God used this news of the impending birth of another child to draw me back to Him. It was a wake-up call showing me that I needed to get serious about my spiritual life more than ever. Thankfully, He had worked on my heart enough for me to know that abortion was not an option. My son Jayden would be born in January 2004, but before the miracle of his birth took place, another miraculous new life was on the horizon.

NOT YET...BUT GETTING CLOSER

The summer of 2003 was very unique—it was the time in which *God's* plan and purpose for my life intersected with *my* plan and purpose. Once again, I began to ponder the accomplishments of my life and the direction in which I was headed. Although I had turned my back on many of my former ways, I still had not recommitted my life to God—but I was getting closer.

Interestingly, I had a female friend at the time who was a devout Christian. We were casually seeing each other, but because I wasn't living committed to God, we never had anything more than just a friendship. At one point, she prophesied a word from God over me, proclaiming that He was going to use me in a big way. Soon after she spoke this message into my life, I woke up in the middle of the night with a very heavy feeling on my chest. The sensation I was experiencing was similar to a heart attack but without any real pain.

At the time, I was working out about three or four days a week and in excellent physical condition. Nevertheless, I felt like I was going to die. The sensation intensified and I began to feel as if I were drowning, even though I was not in water. At first I thought I was dreaming, but my eyes were wide open and I knew I was completely conscious. I then called on the only name that I knew could save me—the name of Jesus. Within moments He came and rescued me, and the feelings were gone. Looking back, I believe Satan was trying to kill me because of the prophetic word that had been spoken over my life.

Unfortunately, I didn't change my ways immediately. After the distress of that night was over, I didn't think much of calling out to Jesus and being rescued. Up until then, I had always used God like a *fire extinguisher*. The only time I wanted to "bother" Him was when something arose that I could not handle on my own. Think about it: We walk past fire extinguishers in buildings all the time, and we only reach for them when there is an emergency. But God doesn't want us to treat Him like a fire extinguisher— He wants us to call on Him at all times and welcome Him into every part of our lives.

Looking and Longing for Success

Sadly, I was unaware of God's desire to be in relationship with me, so life went on as usual. I was still dating regularly, working as a parole officer, and running my promotions business. I really wanted to go to the next level in 2003. I had a strong sense that it would be a breakout year for my business. Consequently, I began planning a large show at the Whitaker Center, which was a 700-seat auditorium located in downtown Harrisburg. To me, the Whitaker Center represented the next level. In my mind, this would take me from putting together small shows in bars and nightclubs to arranging big shows that would bring in bigger names, bigger crowds, and consequently, bigger money.

I started talking with some big name comics that I believed would help me bring in a large, sell-out crowd. Unfortunately, the comics that would guarantee a sellout were too expensive for an auditorium the size of the Whitaker Center. As I mentioned before, location is vitally important when putting together a show. The cost of the performer can only be justified by the size of the venue. Simply put, the larger the name, the larger the cost to bring them in, and the larger the venue needed in which to house the event.

As I was working on one of my shows, I met and fell deeply in love with a woman named Sherry. We hit it off from the beginning, frequently going to lunch and dinner together and communicating often through e-mails and instant messaging. The only problem was she was married. She had told me she was happily married when we first met, but the attraction between us was so intense I couldn't seem to get her out of my mind. Up until that point in my life, I had always tried to steer clear of married women. Although I now understand that premarital sex is wrong, back then I could always justify sex between two unmarried people. However, "Thou shalt not commit adultery" was one of the Ten Commandments, and I had reverential fear of breaking it.

Once Sherry told me she was considering leaving her husband so that we could be together, I was faced with a major dilemma. Although I had deep feelings for her, the guilt of breaking up her marriage was too much for me to bear, not to mention the fact that I had a child on the way that she knew nothing about.

Through much crying and pain, we eventually made the right decision and ended the relationship. During this highly emotional time in my life, God was giving me an ultimatum: Serve Him and live, or serve myself and suffer heartache and destruction. My spirit had become deeply troubled beyond comprehension. So much so that I actually felt like I was going to lose my mind. Ironically, it is often at times like these, when we are at our point of greatest despair, that God can come in and bring us great hope and deliverance if we will surrender to His will. I am so grateful that I chose to side with Him and discontinue the relationship. Had I not, there is no telling what may have become of me.

Hitting Rock Bottom

Meanwhile, the crowds for my shows began growing smaller and smaller, and as a result, my business began to tank. Even though I was making almost $40,000 a year as a parole officer, I ended up getting evicted from my apartment and having my car repossessed. Clearly, things were not looking good.

Putting on a big show at the Whitaker Center became my primary focus. Since I couldn't afford a big-name comic, I scrapped the idea of doing a comedy show and decided to put on a Gospel Showcase. I had seen how many "church folks" came out to see a show, and I believed that a show highlighting some of the local church choirs and singers would draw a large crowd. A Gospel Showcase allowed me to have many talented people perform without having to pay them. This idea would help me save about $20,000 that I would have paid a professional performer. My goal was to sell enough tickets to not only pay for the venue, but also pay back whoever had invested in the project and make a profit at the same time.

The other major event that took place during this time was I parted ways with Dauphin County Probation and Parole. I was still fighting some of the demons that had plagued me in the past, including an all-consuming drive to make money. I was spending more and more time promoting the show at the Whitaker Center and, consequently, I wasn't taking care of my other responsibilities. I had recently received a promotion, which meant I had gained more responsibilities and more people under my supervision. I was very well-respected by my supervisors, but some errors in judgment on my part caused me to very quickly fall from their grace.

That being said, I didn't leave my job totally by choice. My boss, Terry Davis, and I disagreed on some very key points, and because of that I left under his suggestion. To this day I have great respect for him and harbor no hard feelings. I believe he had a real heart to help criminal offenders get back on the right track. Nevertheless, I ended up resigning.

So along with all the other things going on in my life, I was also without a job. Inevitably, I was coming to another crossroads in my life. I had a child on the way, I had lost my job, and I had broken up with a married woman for whom I had developed deep feelings. My pursuit of financial wealth had caused me to lose my apartment and my car. I had truly hit rock bottom...for the second time.

The Show Must Go On!

It was now the week leading up to the showcase, and it was one of great stress. More and more, the pressure began to build as the program got bigger and bigger. But my spirit was lifted every time I listened to the gospel singers practice. Amazingly, the more that stress and tension surrounded me, the more my spirit was lifted by the sweet sounds of the gospel being sung. It had been about twenty years since I had listened to spiritual music, and hearing it brought me great comfort.

Even though the cost of the showcase was nowhere near the $20,000 that I had intended to spend on a major comic, the total amount to produce it was still around $6,000. Thankfully, I was able to get a couple of investors to finance the part that I didn't have. The truth is, however, that most of the show was based on totally on faith—not faith in God, but faith in the people giving me advice and faith in my ability as a promoter to get the word out. I had begun working with a few radio stations to put together advertisements for the show. This was an avenue God was reintroducing me to that I had not thought about since my college days in Maryland.

Finally, the time of the big Gospel Showcase had arrived. It was Labor Day weekend 2003, and the night of the show was a very hectic one. As usual, my leadership instincts kicked in, and I felt an inner-confidence mingled with an energizing flow of adrenaline. All the performers were at the top of their game, and everyone associated with the show had high expectations. Along with my natural ability to sell things, I was also very good at motivating people. This worked in my favor as far as the performers were concerned, but it did not produce the large turnout I had hoped for. Quite frankly, the show was a bust! Of the 700 seats in the auditorium, only about 100 to 150 were filled; the Whitaker Center was all but empty.

Total Surrender

I received many compliments concerning the show that night, but in the promotions business, attendance is what determines success or failure. In view of the low attendance, I considered the show a huge failure. I was devastated and I did not know where to turn. I felt more lost than ever. I had poured everything I had into my pursuit of having a successful promotions business. I had lost my home, my car and my job, and with the failure of the showcase, I also felt as though I had lost the confidence of those close to me. *The up and coming businessman in the community has fallen flat on his face*, I thought. Indeed, I felt as if the whole world had crashed down around me, and on top of it all, I had a baby on the way.

I felt so strongly that the Gospel Showcase was the thing that was going to put me on the map and really change my fortunes, but it didn't. However, instead of it bringing the financial breakthrough I yearned for, it brought the spiritual breakthrough I desperately needed. Through all the trials and disappointments, I finally came to the realization of how much I needed God. For the first time I clearly understood that I could not run my life by myself; my own intellect and abilities were nothing without the Lord's help. I was now a broken vessel.

In Acts 9:5, we find Saul, soon to be Paul, running into the blinding light of Jesus Christ. "And He said, who art thou, Lord? And the Lord said I am Jesus whom thou persecutest: It is hard for thee to kick against the pricks" (KJV). This scripture was so relevant to me at that point in my life. Like Saul, I was "kicking against the pricks"—I was fighting the Lord's calling and going against the good thing He had intended for my life. When I finally got tired of kicking against the pricks, I cried out to the Lord and *totally* surrendered myself to Him, embracing His plan and purpose for my life.

A New Life Begins

It was now October 2003, just a few weeks after I had surrendered my life to the Lord. By God's grace, I was hired as an account executive with Clear Channel Communications (CCC). CCC was the largest radio station owner in the world, owning approximately 1,500 radio stations and 500 TV stations in the U.S. As an account executive, I was basically a sales representative for the station. In addition to going out and getting business, I was also responsible for servicing the clients and making sure their needs were met. In other words, I acted as a liaison between the advertisers and the radio station. Indeed, account executives are the heart of a radio station because they bring in the revenue necessary for the station to operate.

As usual, I poured myself into my new position and hit the ground running. After just a couple of months of training, I was on fire and making things happen. In the first six months of 2004, I was number one in new direct business and new direct accounts. Again, God's gift of selling was tangibly at work in my life. For many years, I had used it to manipulate people for my own personal gain, but I couldn't do that any longer. Instead, I would sell to clients with the intent of helping them see an improvement in their business. I knew firsthand how it felt to struggle trying to see your business succeed, and as a result, I never tried to take advantage of people. Indeed, the Spirit of God began to shape the way I did business.

In the meantime, I had also started attending church on a regular basis. While I was putting together the Gospel Showcase, I had actually visited a number of churches, trying to spark an interest in the show. By patronizing them, I increased my chances of them participating. Little did I know, the entire time I was calling on churches, my spirit was being fed what it had lacked for many years—the Word of God. My visiting helped me select a church with which I could connect and call home.

Growing By Leaps & Bounds

One Sunday, Mrs. Audrey Jackson, one of the spiritual mothers of our church, told me something that put me on a path of powerful spiritual growth. She mentioned to me the benefits of fasting and how it greatly affects a person's spiritual maturity. It is a way to put our flesh under subjection and allow our spirit to grow.

As humans, we are made up of three parts: spirit, soul and body. Before we accept Jesus Christ into our lives, our spirit is dead (see Ephesians 2:1-6). However, once we receive Him as our Lord and Savior, the Spirit of God comes and makes His home inside us and quickens, or awakens, our spirit. Our "flesh" is our sinful, carnal nature, which is a combination of our unrenewed soul and body. Unless we *starve* our flesh, it will dominate and control our lives. Fasting is a way of strengthening our spirit to take control of our lives. Once I began to understand the power of fasting and put it into practice, my life began to irreversibly change.

More and more, I became hungry for God. I began reading the Word every day and spending time in prayer before work and throughout the day. I even fasted at least one day a week, which really caused me problems when trying to sell advertising to people. Fasting had humbled me so much that at times, I really didn't have the "fire" to close the deal. But I didn't care. My passion for God was growing within me, and my relationship with Him was the only thing that mattered.

With God's help, I still maintained a level of success, but working at CCC became increasingly miserable. As strange as it may seem, talking about money and business became boring to me. I only wanted to talk about the Lord. I also began to hate being around the profanity and coarse jokes that are prevalent in many secular companies. Every curse word began to feel like a needle sticking me in the side. More and more it became evident that the Spirit of God had taken over, and the old Joe Green was fading away. I knew that if I continued to work on my spiritual maturity at my current pace, working at CCC would soon be unbearable. Yet, I felt like slowing down or stopping was not an option.

The Point of No Return

I owe a lot of my spiritual growth to my pastor, Earl L. Harris. He always encouraged me to *live* the Bible and not just read it. Consequently, I began looking at Scripture in a whole new way. Instead of seeing it as just good reading material, I began to see it as a blueprint on how to get closer to God. I began to read about David, Moses, Elijah, Paul, etc., not just as people to admire or idolize, but as examples of how God can use anyone He chooses to do miraculous things here on earth. Indeed, Jesus said, "Verily, verily I say unto you, He that believeth on me, the works that I do shall he do also; and *greater works* than these shall he do; because I go unto my Father" (John 14:12 KJV).

Holding tightly to this verse, I began to seek God for all I believed He would give me, and I prayed that He would use me in whatever way He chose. I specifically remember lying on my face one day in my prayer room, telling God that wherever He wanted me to go and whatever He wanted me to do, I would do it. I completely pledged myself to *His* purpose for Joe Green, no matter what it was. To me, this is part of what Paul means when he says, "I beseech you therefore, brethren, by the mercies of God, that ye present your bodies a living sacrifice, holy, acceptable unto God, which is your reasonable service" (Romans 12:1 KJV).

During the spring of 2004 is when, I believe, I reached a point of no return. It was during that time my pastor entered a forty-day fast, and invited others to join him. As a result of joining him, I came into greater harmony with him and began to fast for longer periods of time on my own. Instead of just one day a week, I began fasting three days some weeks. I even went on a seven-day fast where I only drank water and fruit juice. While this was going on, I was in constant study of God's Word. I also took time out to pray in the middle of the day and in the evening. I had jumped into the deep waters of God, and I was receiving healing from many years of living a life outside of His will for my life.

After the fast, everything at my job went downhill. I had become so spiritually minded that I couldn't sell anything—not even a bucket of water to a man on fire. I knew in my heart God was moving me from my career at Clear Channel Communications, but I didn't know where. What I did know was that wherever He was taking me, I would willingly follow.

A Divine Connection

At that time, God put an important person in my life. His name was Dean Lebo, and the way we met had God's fingerprints all over it! Initially, I didn't know much about him, but what I had heard were all good things. He was truly a man of God who became very instrumental in helping me *grow* to the next level in my relationship with the Lord.

While I was still working at CCC, I came across a church that had opened a school and wanted to advertise it. Of course, me being the "great salesperson" that I was, I sold them commercial time on one of our top forty stations—one that played rap music. My rationale was that most parents with day-care aged children went out to night clubs, and because this particular station played music catering to that demographic, the church should advertise on it. After about a week, the church pulled their ads because of the content on the station, and I really didn't blame them. The obscene lyrics in the songs being aired were very offensive to me as well. Unfortunately, this is the case on a number of popular radio stations.

Realizing I didn't have a station that met the church's needs, I told them about Dean Lebo who owned a Christian radio station called 720 AM "THE ROCK." Even though I couldn't get a commission from the sale, I believed it was important for the church to have success in advertising their school. Now this was definitely not the typical thinking of most salespeople. Usually, an account executive doesn't look to help a client unless they can get compensated for it, so my sincere desire to see them succeed was another tangible sign that God was changing my thinking from evil to good.

Sure enough, the church ended up buying advertising on 720 AM and consequently, a bond between Dean and me was formed. I got a call from him one afternoon, and he told me he wanted to take me to lunch to thank me for what I did. I really didn't think it was a big deal, but I accepted his invitation nonetheless.

From the moment Dean and I sat down to have lunch, we began to build a close friendship. I had no idea how much God was going to use him to influence my life and order my steps. I was truly amazed at how his life was a living demonstration of someone dedicated to building the kingdom of God. It seemed like everything he did was centered on doing God's work. From owning and managing a Christian radio station, to ministering in prisons two days a week, his primary focus was winning souls for Christ. The only other man that I was close to who had so clearly demonstrated the transforming power of God was my Pop Pop.

Dean and I built a very godly bond and met regularly just to have lunch and talk about the Lord. I shared with him about my time as a parole officer, and he shared with me his experiences ministering to prison inmates. Interestingly, we knew many of the same people that were incarcerated and were very like-minded as to who had really changed and who had not.

I also marveled at how God spoke into my life through Dean. There were many times when I was praying about something and Dean would unknowingly provide me with a confirmation of what I was praying about. Before long, it became apparent that God uses people and situations to verify a word from Him as well as the direction in which we are to go. I have seen this happen so many times in my life, I cannot number them. For instance, one afternoon during lunch, Dean made a very interesting proposition: He asked me to do a program on his radio station. Interestingly, when he asked me this, I was already seriously considering becoming a radio personality at the station where I worked. Knowing that we played a lot of rap music, I thought there may be a place for an "old school" hip hop show. I had pitched the idea to my program director, and he told me he would consider it; but he wasn't sure it was something he wanted to do. Needless to say, when Dean offered me an opportunity to be on the radio, it was a clear confirmation that I was supposed to pursue being an on-air personality.

TRAINING FOR MINISTRY

At this point, I was really on fire for God. I was fasting, praying, and really trying to live the Word. God was moving powerfully in my life, and

A NEW LIFE BRINGS CHANGE

I was very conscious of His call on me. He even showed me the plan He had for my ministry. More and more, I began to feel like the apostle Paul. After Jesus met him on the road to Damascus, he was sent into the desert of Arabia for three years where he was given the gospel he was to preach:

> "But I certify you, brethren, that the gospel which was preached of me is **not after man.** For I neither received it of man, neither was I taught it, but by the revelation of Jesus Christ. For ye have heard of my conversation in time past in the Jews' religion, how that beyond measure I persecuted the church of God, and wasted it. And profited in the Jews' religion above many my equals in mine own nation, being more exceedingly zealous of the traditions of my fathers. But when it pleased God, who separated me from my mother's womb, and called me by his grace, to reveal his Son in me, that I might preach him among the heathen; immediately I conferred not with flesh and blood. Neither went me up to Jerusalem to them which were apostles before me; but I went into Arabia, and returned again unto Damascus. Then after three years I went up to Jerusalem to see Peter, and abode with him fifteen days" (Galatians 1:11-18 KJV).

God often ministers to us and directs us through His Word, and I really believe He was showing me something through Paul's story in Galatians. When Paul said that the gospel he learned was "not after man," he was telling us that Jesus Himself taught him and gave him his assignment. I took this to mean that God Himself was going to be preparing me for ministry over the next three years. I began to feel as though I was being called into a higher relationship with Him. I had earnestly prayed to be used by Him, and my prayers were being answered.

As strange as it may seem, from the time I was a young man I had envisioned being a minister of the gospel. I had never really pursued it, but I believed that was where God would ultimately use me. Even though I temporarily departed from my calling and had lived a wild and selfish life for a number of years, I knew in my heart that what He said would come to pass.

When God ordains you to do something, He will equip you to do it. Romans 8:29-31 confirms this, declaring that those "...he did foreknow, he also did predestinate to be conformed to the image of his Son, that he might be the firstborn among many brethren. Moreover whom he did predestinate, them he also called: and whom he called, them he also justified: and whom he justified, them he also glorified. What shall we then say to these things? If God be for us, who can be against us?" (KJV.)

Through Dean Lebo, God was directing me on the path He had for my life. I don't believe that either of us knew how everything would play out, but because we both had strong faith in God, we understood that we were to just take the next step and wait for God to work out the details. Clearly, I was living out Proverbs 3:5,6: "Trust in the LORD with all thine heart; and lean not unto thine own understanding. In all thy ways acknowledge him, and he shall direct thy paths" (KJV).

ON THE AIR

After Dean invited me to do a program on his radio station, I asked him what he thought I should do. He replied, "Do whatever God leads you to do." He even hinted to me that if I felt led to preach, I should preach. Indeed, this was a really interesting offer. Of course, since 720 AM "THE ROCK" was an all-Christian radio station, I was not going to be doing an old school hip hop show like I had originally considered. But I really didn't know what I was going to do.

Then I began to think about several organizations in the community with which I had been working. A couple of them were dedicated to building up the African-American community by increasing the amount of opportunities offered to minority business people. In August 2004, about a month earlier, I had organized a "Day of Empowerment," which was a huge block party thrown at a park in Harrisburg, encouraging community involvement and voter participation.

In light of all this, I decided to do a show about people that were making a positive impact and bringing change in the community. Thus, "Community Builders" was born, and I began doing the show in September 2004, just about one year after I had totally surrendered my life to God.

Before long, I really began to feel comfortable talking on the radio, and God began to show me favor with the program. He brought me great joy and fulfillment by allowing me to be on the air and gain a strong following. He also connected me with some very famous people, giving me the opportunity to interview Elizabeth Edwards, wife of then vice-presidential candidate John Edwards, and many others. I also had the chance to interview some community activists who were making a positive change in the community. Clearly, Community Builders gained popularity and became a hit with listeners—a level of success I was truly grateful for.

The Impact of Music

Even though I was growing spiritually, I still loved listening to rap music. When I was alone in my car, I would rap along with some of my favorite rappers such as Jay-Z, 50 Cent, Nas, and others. Although I would say the lyrics, I would *not* repeat the profanity when it came up. God had taken away my desire to *use* profanity, but I still listened to it. Without question, this music had a **stronghold** in my mind.

For a large part of my life I had been wrapped up in the hip-hop mentality of being a "thug" or a "gangsta," as it is commonly known. I believed that this was an acceptable way to carry myself, and that the lifestyle would be good for me. This, however, was a powerful deception from the devil that he used to fool me in an attempt to destroy my life. He continues to use it on young men and women today. I thank God that He rescued me from that mentality before it was too late. Almost every person I have ever known that stayed in the thug lifestyle is either a drug addict, a former prisoner, a current prisoner, or dead. Their lives are so messed up that without the merciful intervention of God, they will probably not recover.

The images we watch on TV and the music we listen to have a major impact on our thought processes. When we constantly meditate on lyrics that talk about sex, drugs, violence, and misogyny (hatred of women), it begins to influence the way we think about these subjects, as well as life in general. Music also has a powerful effect on our emotions. While a quiet, gentle lullaby can soothe a fussy baby, a majestic chorus can make us swell with excitement. Indeed, music is powerful!

Diane Bales, Ph.D., talks about how music affects the brains of very young babies. She writes that "musical training actually creates new pathways in the brain." In recent years, we've learned a lot about how the brain develops. Babies are born with billions of brain cells, and during the first few years of life, those cells form connections with other brain cells. Over time, the connections we use regularly become stronger. Children who grow up listening to music develop strong music-related connections, and some of these pathways affect the way we think. For instance, listening to classical music can improve our spatial reasoning, at least for a short time. And learning to play an instrument may have an even longer effect on certain thinking skills.

Without question, what we put into our minds has a definite degree of effect on us consciously and subconsciously. Not everyone who listens to thug-style music will go out and begin selling drugs and living like a thug. However, those who listen to it will begin to look at life in a different way. Violent, crude behavior will no longer be shocking or appalling to whoever is constantly exposed to it. Now, I am not blaming the music I listened to for the sin in my life, but I know for sure that it did have a huge effect on how I looked at life. I began to think that the music I heard and videos I watched were an example of reality.

So there I was—thirty-something, on the road to spiritual recovery and in desperate need of a new playlist. Other than the conventional hymns and church songs I had sung from the time I was a small child in the church, I had not listened to any spiritual music for many years. But after discovering scriptures like Philippians 4:8, I knew I needed to make some changes: "Finally, brethren, whatsoever things are *true*, whatsoever things are *honest*, whatsoever things are *just*, whatsoever things are *pure*, whatsoever things are *lovely*, whatsoever things are of *good report*; if there be any *virtue*, and if there be any praise, think on these things" (KJV).

THE STRUGGLE CONTINUES

The reason I talked about what I was listening to and what I was watching during this time of my life is because I believe it was a major hindrance to my spiritual growth. Although I was really growing in my walk with God, I was also being tripped up from time to time by what I was putting before my eyes and ears, not to mention the friends I was still hanging out with that partied hard.

Consequently, I was still struggling with lust in my life, as well as a number of other things from which I had not been fully delivered. Even though I was attending church every Sunday, I still had my little "hiccups" of sin. Even after I had recommitted myself to the Lord, I occasionally used cocaine, fornicated, and did other things that I did before my recommitment. I can recall sitting in church some Sunday mornings with the taste of alcohol in my mouth and cocaine in the back of my throat.

Why am I sharing so many of the details from my past failures? I am trying to demonstrate that lasting change doesn't usually happen overnight—it is a *process*. I had spent many years practicing a lifestyle of corrupt living, and it took time for me to get my thinking and my living right—even after I asked the Lord to change me. But I am grateful that over the years I allowed Him to take me through the process until I became totally cleansed and transformed from my corrupt thinking and living.

If we're willing to change, He will change us. In our weaknesses He is glorified, as we trust in Him. Psalm 51:16,17 says, "For thou desirest not sacrifice; else would I give it: thou delightest not in burnt offering. The sacrifices of God are a broken spirit: a broken and a contrite heart, O God, thou wilt not despise." That is what God is looking for—a humble spirit that is broken down with sorrow for sin and humbly and thoroughly repentant. A person in this condition will fully receive God's goodness and be used to bring Him glory.

Section 4
THE CALLING

CHAPTER 13

RECOGNIZING & ACCEPTING THE CALL OF GOD

More and more, it became evident that God was preparing me for something new. And as He had typically done throughout my life before taking me to a new level, He once again began to shake things up. This drove me to press into Him in order to be purged from unrighteousness. The more I did, the more He answered my prayers.

Philippians 2:12-14 says, "Wherefore, my beloved, as ye have always obeyed, not as in my presence only, but now much more in my absence, work out your own salvation with fear and trembling. For it is God which worketh in you both to will and to do of his good pleasure. Do all things without murmurings and disputings."

To me, *working out my salvation* means becoming more and more like God, which means becoming holy. Holiness is very important in the Kingdom of God. To be holy means to be separate and set apart—noticeably different than those in the world. As long as we live like the world lives, we will never gain victory in our personal lives. If we cannot gain victory over our personal lives, then we will never be the conquerors we are called to be.

Now, holiness is not just about our actions—it is also about our thinking. When we listen to secular songs that promote sex, violence, idolatry, and all other forms of ungodliness, we are shaping our minds to think the way the world thinks. Likewise, when we watch soap operas that glorify lying, cheating, and the ruthless pursuits of the fleshly desires, it shapes our thinking to believe that this behavior is acceptable.

When we meditate on godly things and the truth of God's Word, however, the Scripture becomes our picture of reality. Consequently, we are able to be His *true children*—"...a chosen generation, a royal priesthood, a holy nation, a peculiar people; that ye should show forth the praises of him who hath called you out of darkness into his marvelous light" (1 Peter 2:9 KJV).

THE 2004 ELECTIONS

During the presidential campaign of 2004, I was spending a lot of time helping to campaign for the Democratic Party. I helped to organize an event in which prominent party leaders spoke. I also wrote and voiced several ads for the Democratic Party. At this time, my perspective on some very key issues really began to change. Through fasting and prayer, God began to reveal to me His heart. On several occasions, I remember waking up and weeping for the state of humanity. I drove around the city with my heart broken for all the lost souls who didn't know Christ and were living in darkness.

I also received a revelation concerning two issues that I believe are very important to God. As you may remember, two of the hot topics in the 2004 elections were abortion and same-sex marriage. Up until that point in my life, like many other people, I simply felt that we should "live and let live" in regards to these issues. I had personally encouraged four women I had dated to have abortions, so who was I to judge? As for homosexuality, I knew it was unnatural, but I always felt that as long as a person didn't make a pass at me or kiss in front of me, it was okay. They weren't bothering me, so I didn't bother with them.

However, God made it clear to me that He wants us to speak out against unrighteousness, with the objective of restoring each other in love. Jesus died as a sacrifice for the atonement of our sins—not so that we could sin and it no longer matter. Abortion is murder and homosexuality is unnatural in God's eyes. We must realize this in order for us to encourage repentance; we must give people the truth of God's Word with love. Shouting derogatory comments at gay people is not going to bring them to Christ. Likewise, bombing abortion clinics only hurts the mission Jesus has called us to; it does not encourage people to turn away from abortion, and it does nothing to strengthen the body of Christ.

I realize that these topics are extremely controversial. Nevertheless, we must keep in mind that they are just sins. Homosexuality and abortion are sins just like fornication, adultery, lying, stealing, gossiping, etc. I say this because many of us have knowingly or unknowingly categorized sin in our mind, and as a result, we have been hypocritical in how we have treated people who are trapped in certain sins. For instance, many of the same people who gossip or hold grudges against their neighbors have the audacity to turn their nose up at gay people. The reality is sin is sin. God hates it, but He loves the person caught in it.

Just before the elections of 2004, I remember praying and asking God for guidance on these key issues. The Lord made it very clear to me what was important to Him: stop the shedding of innocent blood (abortion) and stop justifying what He says is unnatural and wrong (homosexuality). Again, sin is sin, and we do not have the right to say something is right when God says it is wrong.

A Major Shift in Desires & Priorities

Meanwhile, as I was heavily involved in campaigning, my work at Clear Channel Communications began to suffer. My growing relationship with God made me fit less and less in the CCC environment. Additionally, my desire to bring positive change in the lives of others had now superseded my desire to make money. These two factors combined caused me to become increasingly miserable. Indeed, "No man can serve two masters; for either he will hate the one and love the other, or he will stand by and be devoted to the one and despise and be against the other. You cannot serve God and mammon (deceitful riches, money, possession, or whatever is trusted in)" (Matthew 6:24 AMP).

More and more, it became apparent that extremely large companies like CCC that do not have God at the center of what they do are only concerned about one thing—the almighty dollar. On many occasions, I came across opportunities to better the community through promoting events and at the same time provide some good publicity for the company. But before agreeing to it, the sales managers always needed to know how CCC could generate revenue from it.

Don't get me wrong, I understand business and the importance of making a profit. However, my heart had begun to change. I had come to the realization that making money should not be the driving force in everything we do. Increasingly, my only concern became bettering others and advancing the kingdom of God. It was clear to all those around me that something was different. Even my speech was changing, and all I wanted to talk about were spiritual things. So much so that when I had lunch with a good friend I had known for many years, he expressed to me how uncomfortable it made him feel that "all I wanted to talk about was Jesus." This, of course, I took as a compliment.

As Election Day drew near, I had not only become disillusioned with the entire political system, but also disliked talking about worldly things that didn't have any eternal value. After the elections, I found myself very discouraged. I was disappointed with corporate America because I had seen firsthand how much the love of money drives our culture. I was also disappointed with many community and church organizations that were supposed to be helping the community but were more concerned for their own well-being—a problem the majority of the world suffers from. I was frustrated with the political system on both the Democratic and Republican side because I felt that both parties had too many politicians with a lack of concern for the benefit of those less fortunate.

Generally speaking, our society is a "me" society. This included many churches—everything centers on *my* church, *my* denomination, and *my* ministry. As a result, we are cheating God out of His glory by looking and acting just like the rest of the world. I believe this is one of the biggest reasons why the country is going further and further down the road to destruction. The church is the moral compass of America, and it is failing to do its job. Instead of being what God has called us to be, which is the salt of the earth and the light of the world, we have allowed the world to dictate the standard of what is right and wrong.

Again, I was at a crossroads. I believe God allowed me to see all these things so that I would not be as wrapped up in and swayed by worldly affairs. As He says in Romans 12:2, "And be not conformed to this world: but be ye transformed by the renewing of your mind, that ye may prove what is that good, and acceptable, and perfect, will of God" (KJV). God was about to put some finishing touches on my transformation, and in order to do so, He needed to separate me from the environment I was in. As long as I was surrounded by the worries and cares of the carnal world, I was limited in just how far I could go with God. I had come to the place where the only thing that brought me pleasure was focusing on godly things. So, as God had done many times before in my life, He prepared me to move.

My Next Move

After the 2004 elections, I began to seriously ponder the future. I had made more money in October and November working for the Democratic Party than I did at CCC. Interestingly, I had invested more time and effort working on political commercials than doing business for my employer. This was just one more confirmation that it was time for me to move on to another job, and my boss at CCC agreed. So in November 2004, I was once again unemployed.

I really didn't know exactly where I would go or what I would do. I did, however, have a certain level of anticipation that God had something big planned for me. I went into a season of self-examination, prayer, and reading the Word. I wasn't exactly sure how to get direction from God, but I knew in my heart He had the answer I needed. I began to pray more and more, asking Him to order my steps and use me in whatever way He chose.

One of the things I contemplated was opening up an independent advertising agency. Ad agencies can be very profitable, and they only need a couple of large clients to generate enough funds to make a living. There are a number of very big national companies that spend hundreds of thousands of dollars, or even millions, every month in advertising. When you take into account that an ad agency is typically compensated fifteen percent of its client's advertising budget, they can pull in a considerable amount of revenue.

With this in mind, I approached Dean Lebo that same month with the intention of asking him to allow me to act as the sole advertising agency for his station. I figured that once I had at least one guaranteed client, I would only need to pick up one or two more in order to have a solid start. God, on the other hand, had already planned the path I was to take. Before I could propose my idea to Dean, he was already offering me a full-time position with the station as an on-air personality, salesperson, and pretty much whatever else I wanted to do.

Amazingly, God had already made arrangements for my next move *before* I knew I needed it. Evidently, He had already told Dean that I was to be a part of the station. When he offered me a job, I immediately knew it was God's divine will for the next step of my life. Consequently, I said yes even before Dean had finished making me an offer.

The Start of Something Big

In January 2005, I started full time with radio station 720 AM. Although I was extremely excited, I really didn't know what I was doing. In desperation, I turned to the only person who could help me—Jesus. Every day before I got to the station, I prayed and asked Him to take over. I only wanted to say what He wanted me to say and do what He wanted me to do. I also made it a point to fast everyday while I was at work so that God would be totally in charge and my flesh would not have the upper hand. On most days, I fasted the entire day until 6:00 p.m. Sometimes I fasted until 9:00 p.m., and other times I wouldn't eat until 6:00 p.m. or 9:00 p.m. the next day.

It was amazing to watch God's plan for my life unfold before my eyes. My spiritual life began to grow in a miraculous way. This was the beginning of the second year of my three-year training period that I felt God had put me on. As a result of being submerged in nothing but spiritual music and programs, my understanding of God's Word began to deepen and accelerate at an unbelievable pace. Consequently, my faith in Him also began to grow stronger and stronger.

When I first went on the air, I was a little slow and hesitant to talk about the Word of God. Up until that time, my relationship with God had been very personal. In addition to my participation in Bible studies and church services, I made it a point to spend many hours *alone* praying and reading the Word outside the walls of my church. I have always valued God's approval above man's, so I never wanted to be a person who was merely putting on a *religious act* in front of others.

Jesus didn't like it when people put on religious acts, and He told them that up front. Mark 7:6-9 says, "He answered and said unto them. Well hath Esaias prophesied of you hypocrites, as it is written, this people honoureth me with their lips, but their heart is far from me. In vain do they worship me, teaching for doctrines the commandments of men. For laying aside the commandment of God, ye hold the tradition of men, as the washing of pots and cups; and many other such like things ye do. And he said unto them, Full well ye reject the commandment of God, that ye may keep your own tradition" (KJV). Needless to say, this is something I definitely didn't want to do.

Over time I became more and more comfortable with speaking on the radio about the Lord. The more I delved into the Word, the more confident I became when I spoke. Indeed, God was really beginning to work through me, and my spirit felt peace like never before. I also learned a lot from Dean. He was always on the lookout for *divine appointments*—meetings set up by God in which a believer's path intersects with a non-believer. Dean seized these orchestrated opportunities to share the gospel with others and introduce them to Jesus Christ. He believed they were never a coincidence. In his unique way, He would often say, "God wants us to catch 'em and He will clean 'em."

Dean was always open to doing whatever the Lord wanted him to do. It didn't matter if he planted the seed or watered it—just as long as he could share in the process. This is what the apostle Paul was talking about in 1 Corinthians 3:5-10: "Who then is Paul and who is Apollos, but ministers by whom ye believed, even as the Lord gave to every man? I have planted, Apollos watered; but *God gave the increase*. So then neither is he that planteth anything, neither he that watereth; but God that giveth the increase. Now he that planteth and he that watereth are one: and every man shall receive his own reward according to his own labor. For we are laborers together with God: ye are God's husbandry, ye are God's building. According to the grace of God which is given unto me, as a wise master builder, I have laid the foundation, and another buildeth thereon. But let every man take heed how he buildeth thereupon" (KJV).

I remember one divine appointment Dean shared with me that took place when he was watching one of his grandchildren. Now, he loved his

RECOGNIZING & ACCEPTING THE CALL OF GOD

grandkids; so much so that when he was buried, he was wearing a sweatshirt that read "World's Greatest Granddad"—a title in which he took great pride. Anyway, Dean had dropped off his grandson and was headed for his house when he came across a lady walking with a very small child in her arms. Since he still had his grandson's car seat, he asked her if he could give her a ride. She accepted and Dean took the opportunity to witness to her about the goodness of Jesus. If he would not have had the car seat, he would not have been able to offer the woman help and, consequently, witness to her. Divine appointments like these were recurring in Dean's life and something he always marveled at.

About six months after being at the radio station, I encountered a divine appointment of my own. Dean approached me with a surprising proposal: He offered to sell me the station if I could secure the needed investors. This to me was a major confirmation from God. Although I didn't know how I was going to do it, I jumped at the chance. Somehow, someway I believed that if God was in it, He would make a way for it to happen.

Putting All the Pieces Together

To fully appreciate the miraculous hand of God in the way I acquired the station, you have to really look at the series of events that made it possible in such a very brief period of time. As I previously stated, I started full-time at the station in January 2005. Six months later, Dean offered to sell me the station if I could secure the needed financing. Although I didn't know it then, God had strategically placed me at 720 AM in order to fulfill His purpose for my life.

For the first few months after Dean made me the offer, I began to fast and pray even more fervently. I gave up trying to sell advertising and I focused all my attention on studying the Word and praying for direction. I had absolutely no money saved up, and purchasing the station was going to cost close to one million dollars.

Then in December 2005, less than a year later, my beloved friend Dean Lebo went home to be with the Lord. He had left the station that morning to go to do his prison ministry, as he had done so many times before. A few hours later, I received a call from one of the prison guards, asking me who his next of kin was. Just after leading an inmate through the prayer of salvation, Dean had a massive heart attack and died. Amazingly, he started his prayer talking to Jesus from earth and woke up looking at Him face-to-face.

Once Dean passed away, I was in a very strange position. I had already begun the process of putting together my business plan to secure the necessary financing to purchase the station, but I had no guarantee. The price for it and the land it was on was about $900,000, but I didn't have anywhere near that amount. The truth is, I didn't have any money at all. However, I had something better than money—I had faith! "Now faith is the substance of things hoped for, the evidence of things not seen" (Hebrews 11:1 KJV). I knew that if God was opening the door and had given me the station, He would provide all that I needed to make the purchase.

Another concern I had after Dean's death was that his family would not want to sell the station, or they might want sell it to someone else. There was a co-owner, or partner, named Carl Kuehn who lived in Florida, and although he had been more than cooperative when I initially attempted to purchase the station, I had nothing in writing stating that they would sell it to me. Thankfully, by this time in my walk with the Lord I had learned to trust Him and take all my cares to Him. Immediately, I began to pray, and like always, God didn't let me down.

As it turned out, Dean's family was very supportive throughout the entire eighteen-month process. They could have put the station on the market and sold it to the highest bidder, but they didn't. They knew Dean specifically wanted me to purchase the station before he passed away. Consequently, they honored his request, which was definitely the favor of God! In fact, the Lebo family gave me the vital help I needed to purchase the station.

As time passed, I put my faith in action and secured the remaining financing I needed. Shortly after that, I signed the sales agreement and eagerly awaited the anticipated closing date. It was only by God's grace and mercy and my yielding to His leading that I arrived at that point. For many a mile, I walked the journey alone with nothing but faith and Jesus as my guide. Very few people actually believed I could do it. Even some of my closest friends tried to get me to look at my pursuit of buying a radio station as unrealistic. Nevertheless, I stood on the promises of God, and He didn't let me down.

In June 2007, I was blessed to finalize the purchase of radio station WWII 720 AM "THE ROCK" in Shiremanstown, Pennsylvania. Just imagine… I started the journey with no knowledge or understanding of finances and no money. At the close of the journey, I ended up with $875,000 worth of financing and a sales agreement to purchase the station. On top of that, I was able to make history by becoming the first African-American to ever own an FCC licensed radio station in central Pennsylvania. Indeed, this was definitely the work of God!

The Lord knew when Dean Lebo would leave the earth, so He allowed him to put things in motion before his death. Once I was in place and correctly trained, Dean was relieved of his duties at the station and given rest in the bosom of Jesus. I felt honored that God had chosen me to carry on the legacy of such a great, godly man. To God be the glory!

I am so grateful the Lord has used me to spread His message of hope and redemption on radio station 720 AM "THE ROCK." It never ceases to amaze me that God chose to use me as an on-air radio personality to shine His bright light to the masses. My life was totally confused and unstable in every way. I was a misguided young man who was a menacing influence to society, but God has radically changed my thinking! I am now a stable family man, a legitimate business owner, and a positive influence in the community. I was once on sinking sand, but now I'm standing on the solid rock of Jesus Christ!

Indeed, my life truly proves that through God **all things are possible** regardless of failures, setbacks, wrong choices, or disadvantages an individual has faced in life.

Successes & Setbacks

Since purchasing my first radio station in 2007, followed by the purchase of my second station in 2008, I have experienced victories as well as challenges. But overall I have had some very worthwhile experiences which have helped me to learn from my successes and setbacks.

As previously stated, I bought the stock of Hensley Broadcasting and its WWII-AM radio station back in 2007 after securing $875,000 worth of financing to get the station from Carl Kuehn II and the estate of Dean Lebo. The station, a Class D daytimer on 720 kHz with 2 kW and a non-directional antenna, serves the Harrisburg-Lebanon-Troy market. In 2010, I handed the station over to a lender in return for forgiveness of debt, which ultimately led to the station being in the hands of noncommercial Holy Family Radio Inc., a new owner with a new valuation. Although it was not easy for me to part with 720 AM "THE ROCK," I am glad that the station that is now Holy Family Radio, WHYF 720 AM, still has a mission to spread the good news. Betty Girven, a retired elementary school teacher serving as Holy Family Radio board president, stated "We hope to help motivate listeners to seek a deeper relationship with Jesus Christ and his church."

In 2008, before parting with 720 AM, I partnered with Bruce Collier, using licensee name Trustworthy Radio, to acquire WHYL-960 AM, at that time my second AM station in Pennsylvania's centrally-located capital market, Harrisburg-Lebanon-Carlisle. While acting as co-owner of WHYL-960 AM in Carlisle, Pennsylvania, I am also currently fulfilling my mission as the pastor and founder of the Antioch Assembly Church in

Harrisburg, Pennsylvania, and as founder of Josiah Generation Ministries, an international ministry providing public speaking, training, and Bible teaching.

The Gift of Forgiveness

The wonderful thing about God's Word is that He always confirms it. Whenever you stand on a biblical principle through faith, you will absolutely see God move in your life to honor the Word. Although I have seen this happen so many times in my life, I don't think there was a better example than what God did in regards to my relationship with my stepfather.

As I have previously stated, I developed a strong dislike and even a hatred for my stepfather, Raymond Scott. But I want to emphasize that this was past tense. When I spoke of "hating" him, it was the feelings I had during my years of growing up and seeing how he treated my mother and how he operated as a man. Some of my stepfather's children—my "step-siblings"—expressed their displeasure because they felt I was out of line for writing about my issues with my stepfather in my first book. They wanted me to forgive and to forget what was done in years past. What they did not understand at the time is that I had already forgiven my stepfather; I was simply using the testimony to demonstrate how God miraculously changed me in spite of the circumstances from my tumultuous past.

An amazing thing happened after my first book, *From Kilos to the Kingdom*, was released. My stepfather got a copy and read it. At the time it had been a couple of years since I had really spoken with him. He called my mother and told her how much the book had affected him, explaining how he regretted what he had done and how he felt responsible for some of the bad choices I made. He expressed that if he had been a better father, then maybe I would have had a better life. God had started working on his heart after he read the book.

I want to say for the record that I do not blame anyone for any of the mistakes that I made in life. There were times that I may have been reacting to what someone else had done to me, but ultimately I made choices that I cannot blame anyone else for.

As with all things of faith, at some point in time we have to put it into practice. The Bible says that faith without works is dead. If we do not act on the things that we profess, then it is questionable as to whether or not we truly believe them.

My test of faith with Raymond was an interesting one. On a regular basis, I began to pray for him and to profess that I had forgiven him. I

RECOGNIZING & ACCEPTING THE CALL OF GOD

continued this for months even when I had no contact with Raymond. One Wednesday afternoon I was heading to my office when the Holy Spirit began reminding me of a promise I had made to a personal friend who was a pastor. This friend ran a weekly food ministry at a local church for the homeless and needy. I had told him that I was going to come by and visit with him on that particular Wednesday to check out the ministry.

I had several errands to run and was just making up in my mind an excuse to tell the pastor why I would not come by to visit him. I felt a strong urging from the Holy Spirit, however, to go there that day; I received a reminder of how I always talk about keeping your word and not ignoring verbal commitments that we make. When I reluctantly drove over to the pastor's food ministry in an effort to keep my word, I walked into the back of the crowded sanctuary in time to catch a portion of the pastor's message for the day. I was only in the room for less than two minutes when I heard the pastor say, "We don't show each other enough love; turn to your neighbor and show some love!" I turned to my right and of course, as only God could have set it up, I unexpectedly found myself face-to-face with my stepfather, Raymond Scott! As I looked him in the eyes and said the words "I love you," I had a feeling of pure love emanate from my entire being. I reached over and hugged Raymond and felt nothing but pure love for him, knowing that my heart had been totally cleansed by the power of God. With tears in his eyes, Raymond looked back at me and said "I love you too."

The next day I got a frantic call from my mother.

"What did you say to Raymond?" she asked.

"What do you mean?" I replied.

She said, "He told me he saw you and you told him you loved him… and he believed you!"

I explained to my mom that this was true and that I felt nothing but pure love in my heart for Raymond. All our years of alienation from one another had ended due to one brief moment that was divinely orchestrated by God.

A few weeks later, I got a call from my stepsister Tamika informing me that Raymond was in the hospital and the doctors did not expect him to pull through. Over the years the drug abuse and hard living had taken their toll on Raymond's body, and he had developed life-threatening illnesses. Tamika then went on to tell me that Raymond had shared the story from the food ministry with her and explained how much it had touched his heart. Tamika shared that he had also accepted Jesus Christ as his Lord and savior because of that feeling of love he felt from me on that day in the church.

By the grace of God, in spite of his critical sickness, Raymond defied the odds and made a pretty remarkable recovery. After he got out of the hospital, I would see him from time to time and would always go out of my way to hug him and tell him how much I loved him.

In January 2010 my wife and I started a church called Antioch Assembly. I was out at another pastor's church preaching when I looked in the congregation and saw Raymond. He was in a motorized wheelchair and had lost much of his strength, but his spirit was still strong. After church I went over to greet him, and he told me "I am coming to your church."

Once Raymond found out where our church was, he would usually beat us all to the church on Sunday mornings without the use of a car, only riding in his motorized wheelchair. Approximately six months after Raymond joined the church I pastored, he passed away. One of the last times I spoke with him he prayed with me, squeezed my hand, and told me "It's OK if I die, I know that I am going to be with the Lord."

I preached Raymond's eulogy, and all my siblings hugged afterwards as we all spoke about how Raymond Scott died as a child of God. I salute my stepfather and I believe that he is in Heaven with Jesus! Just imagine what would have happened if I would have continued to hold a grudge or if I had not been able to forgive Raymond for the things that happened many years ago. God is truly faithful to His Word and I thank Him for giving us the ability to be obedient to it. My life is much better off because I forgave.

CHAPTER 14

GROWING IN THE WISDOM & FREEDOM OF GOD

Whether you are the president of the United States or a homeless person living in the gutter, you are special in God's eyes. Jesus died for the "bum" just as much as He died for the richest man in the world. Through Christ, each of us has been given a mission and purpose in life, and our unique backgrounds, talents, desires, and experiences make us perfectly prepared for our God-ordained job. Nothing thrills Him more than to use the "nobodies" of the world to do His work. According to 1 Corinthians 1:27, "God hath chosen the foolish things of the world to confound the wise; and God hath chosen the weak things of the world to confound the things which are mighty" (KJV). He does this to show man that He is in control.

Once you realize God is sovereign and in control, you can begin to learn from all the experiences He allows in your life. If God allows something negative to happen to you, He can also use it for your good. The Scriptures show us again and again that the devil cannot do anything to us unless God allows it. God has the hairs on our heads numbered (see Matthew 10:30), and He declares the end from the beginning (see Isaiah 46:9-10). He is truly in control and wants the best for us. Although He doesn't cause us to make bad choices, He can use them to make us more effective in reaching others. Indeed, He "…is able to do exceeding abundantly above all that we ask or think, according to the power that worketh in us" (Ephesians 3:20 KJV). And my life is a perfect example.

HE WAS THERE ALL THE TIME

Although this book is about my life, it is *not* meant to be about me. It is meant to demonstrate how God has miraculously moved in my life, bringing me through one difficult situation after another. Amazingly, He has used the most difficult and sinful situations I went through to mold me into the person He needed me to be for the mission He had planned for my life.

As I said in the beginning, I was saved at the age of nine, and I grew up in the church. I knew *about* God, but I really didn't *know* Him. Through His deep love and desire to be in close relationship with me, He allowed me to make many choices that were contrary to His ways. Consequently, I saw for myself that His Word is true: The wages of sin and the way that seems right to a man really do produce death (see Romans 6:23; Proverbs 14:12; 16:25). He also let me see that when I trust in Him with all my heart and lean not on my own understanding, He will direct my path (see Proverbs 3:5-6). Once I turned my life over to God and began to consistently obey His Word, my path became prosperous and productive.

Looking back, I can clearly see how God used all of my choices to prepare me for His call on my life—to help build His kingdom through mass media. When I decided to switch my major in college to communications because of my girlfriend, God used my choice to fulfill His plan. When I chose to transfer to Towson University, I received valuable training in the radio field, including the opportunity to work in the radio lab. Years later, I went into the Navy with the goal of becoming a pilot. Ironically, I ended up becoming an electronic technician who worked on radio and radar equipment. The specialized training I received now allows me to understand the technical language for the operation of the station. Again, when I started doing promotions for the big rap concert and the numerous other shows I produced, I did it with the aim of making money. God, on the other hand, used the experiences to teach me how to book talent, advertise on the radio, and put on large-scale events. Today, all this knowledge helps me as a broadcaster.

During the three years that God helped me mature and draw closer to Him, I didn't know what direction He was taking me. I knew in my spirit that He was calling me to be a minister of the gospel, but I didn't know when or how it would happen. He had given me the revelation about Paul being directed by Him into the desert for three years to be trained to preach. Consequently, I believed I was to spend three years being equipped myself. Landing the job at the radio station was a major part of that training and a defining decision that propelled me into my destiny.

Ultimately, God was preparing me to be a preacher of the gospel— *one* of many preachers. He had been ordering my steps my entire life. In each situation I faced, He applied the precise amount of pressure I needed and gave me just enough direction to get me moving in the way He wanted me to go. Although I had many different plans for my life, God used **everything** I went through to work together for my good and His purpose—just like His Word says in Romans 8:28. He has shaped me into what He needed me to be and trained me for the mission I am ordained to do. He gave me a desire to help introduce more and more people to His kingdom and the vehicle to carry it out. What a mighty God we serve!

Finding True Love & Freedom from Lust

After I recommitted myself to the Lord, I realized that in order for me to fulfill the calling God had on my life, I needed to find a godly woman to be my wife. The Word of God tells us in Genesis 2:18 that man was not meant to be alone; God created woman to be his "help meet"—to stand beside him as he walks through life. The word *meet* comes from the Hebrew word *neged* (pronounced neh'-ghed), which means "a counterpart or a companion." In September 2006, several years after my painful divorce, the God of a second chance blessed me with just such a companion.

Now, I had struggled with lust for many years, so I knew that just getting married would not solve the problem. I would never be able to be the husband God intended me to be until I had overcome it. As stubborn as this stain of sin was on my soul, I was able to overcome it. And Mark 9:29 held the key: "…This kind can come forth by nothing, but by *prayer* and *fasting*" (KJV). This was Jesus' response to His disciples when they asked Him why they could not cast out certain demons from a little boy.

This is actually a very important clue to spiritual warfare. The only way to truly overcome major strongholds in our lives is by crucifying our flesh daily and strengthening our spirits. As followers of Christ, we sometimes kid ourselves into believing that once we have surrendered ourselves to Him, strongholds can no longer be built in our lives, but that is not true. Although each of us is a new creature in Christ and has received the Holy Spirit, we must work to build up our spirit so that we can effectively bind and cast off any evil spirit that comes against us.

Once an evil spirit is removed and we are clean within, it is vital that we fill the empty place in our soul with godly things. In Luke 11:24-26, Jesus reveals that "When the unclean spirit is gone out of a man, he walketh through dry places, seeking rest; and finding none, he saith, I will return unto my house whence I came out. And when he cometh, he findeth it swept and garnished. Then goeth he, and taketh to him seven other spirits more wicked than himself; and they enter in, and dwell there: and the last state of that man is worse than the first" (KJV).

In my life, I knew lust was a familiar spirit, and I had allowed it to live and gain strength in me over many years as a result of my lifestyle. A person fighting with an addiction to lust usually doesn't grow weary of sinning—the urge usually gets stronger. Indeed, lust is not a spirit that goes away on its own, which I can personally attest to. As believers, we must take proactive measures to keep it, as well as every other evil spirit, from rising up and taking control of our lives.

I personally believe that many priests fall victim to a spirit of lust because they are not called to a celibate lifestyle. The Bible tells us that celibacy is a gift from God, and not every man has it. The idea of forbidding marriage is actually a sign of the end times mentioned in 1 Timothy 4:1-3. As I said before, God intended for a man and woman to dwell together in marital unity, enjoying the pleasures of sexual intimacy and the power of procreation. It is not typical for a man to abstain from sex with a woman. Consequently, Paul says, "If they have not self-control (restraint of their passions), they should marry. For it is better to marry than to be aflame [with passion and tortured continually with ungratified desire]" (1 Corinthians 7:9 AMP).

If I had not dealt with my problem of lust *before* I got married, I would surely have fallen into adultery again. Thankfully, I dedicated myself to prayer and fasting, and the stronghold of lust in my life was destroyed as a result. I then committed myself to a life of celibacy until I found the wife God had for me. Through a heart of repentance, He helped me overcome lust and a wandering eye; I am now happily married to Gwendolyn. Still, I realize I am human, and if I were to become filled with pride, I could easily fall back into my old sinful lifestyle. Consequently, I make it a point to continually renew my mind with the Word of God and repent of any sin in my life (see Romans 12:2; 1 John 1:9).

Recognizing the Spiritual Battle

One of the biggest problems plaguing the church today is ignorance concerning spiritual warfare. Paul tells us in 2 Corinthians 2:11 that we are not to be ignorant of Satan's devices. "For we wrestle not against flesh and blood, but against principalities, against powers, against the rulers of the darkness of this world, against spiritual wickedness in high places" (Ephesians 6:12 KJV). To a great degree, the strongholds of wrong thinking that we, as believers, face on a regular basis come from the spiritual baggage we are carrying around. This baggage is from previous generations as well as the "luggage of lies" we have picked up on our own. Sadly, many of us are clueless about this.

The Bible identifies some demonic spirits as "familiar spirits." This is because they are *familiar* with your family line and have been capitalizing on their weaknesses for centuries. Some of these spirits have gained legal access to your ancestors through their willful sin and have been traveling through generation after generation, producing the same sinful behavior in your family members. Sexual sin is one of these familiar spirits that continues to grow and eventually manifests itself in ways in which we do not want. A familiar spirit not dealt with will get stronger and stronger with each successive generation.

How do these familiar spirits of lust gain entrance into our lives as believers? One of the biggest ways is through what we *watch* and what we *listen* to. Listening to songs and watching movies, TV shows, and music videos that are filled with sexual content opens a spiritual door for spirits of lust and perversion to come into a person's soul and take root. Likewise, viewing and reading pornographic materials opens us up to impurity and feeds and strengthens these evil spirits. If we are consuming a steady diet of this kind of "entertainment," it's no wonder we are losing the battle for sexual purity, monogamy, and long-term marriages—it's no wonder that spouses are cheating on each other at an alarming rate and children are becoming sexually active earlier and earlier.

What's the answer? Paul tells us in Philippians 4:8: "Finally, brethren, whatsoever things are true, whatsoever things are honest, whatsoever things are just, whatsoever things are pure, whatsoever things are lovely, whatsoever things are of good report; if there be any virtue, and if there be any praise, think on these things" (KJV). Psalm 101:3,4 also provides powerful instruction, stating, "I will set no base or wicked thing before my eyes. I hate the work of them who turn aside [from the right path]; it shall not grasp hold of me. A perverse heart shall depart from me; I will know no evil person or thing" (AMP).

Mankind, apart from God, continually tries to figure things out on his own. However, God's ways have always been right—whether man acknowledges it or not. When God gave His name to Moses as "I Am," He was telling Moses that He is the eternal God who is the same yesterday, today, and forever—He proclaims the end from the beginning and never changes. It doesn't matter how wicked and evil things are packaged by the world and the enemy; they will always be evil. What is right in God's eyes will always be the way to go!

UNDERSTANDING THE RELIGION OF HUMANISM

In this day and age it is important that we all know what we believe. There are numerous religions that we could follow, and there are even many different divisions within those religions. One of the most widely accepted but often unnoticed religions is *humanism*. Wikipedia describes humanism as "a broad category of active ethical philosophies that affirm the dignity and worth of all people, based on the ability to determine right and wrong by appeal to universal human qualities, particularly rationalism." Humanism is a component of a variety of more specific philosophical systems and is also incorporated into some religious schools of thought.

Humanism entails a commitment to the search for truth and morality through human means in support of human interests. It focuses on the capacity for self-determination and rejects transcendental justifications, such as the supernatural, divinely revealed texts (like the Bible), or dependence on faith. Humanists endorse universal morality based on the commonality of human nature, suggesting that solutions to human, social, and cultural problems cannot be narrow-minded.

In light of all this, humanism is in direct opposition to most monotheistic religions, such as Christianity. A true humanist believes man only needs himself and does not need to seek a "higher power" to know right from wrong. In fact, many humanists deny that there is a "Supreme Being" in the universe, or if there is one, he (or she) does not have, or does not want, final say in the everyday affairs of mankind.

Interestingly, humanism has been one of the driving forces behind such philosophies as the "pro-choice" movement and the fight against the Federal Marriage Protection Act, which attempts to rightly define marriage as a union between one man and one woman. Humanists are also active promoters of the theory of evolution—the false philosophy that claims we have evolved from lower life forms and that the earth and all we see around us, including human beings, came into existence totally by random chance over millions and billions of years.

In a nutshell, humanists believe man has the right to decide what is right and what is wrong, and morals may change with the times. In other words, what is considered morally wrong today may not be deemed morally wrong five years from now. Unfortunately, there are many Christians who have bought into this ungodly philosophy or who are just not passionate enough about what they believe to speak out against it.

The Truth I Believe

I certainly do not subscribe to any part of these ungodly notions. As a believer in the God of the Bible, I believe everything was created by a purposeful, intelligent God. John 1:3 states, "All things were made and came into existence through Him; and without Him was not even one thing made that has come into being" (AMP). Colossians 1:16,17 reiterates this truth declaring, "For it was in Him that all things were created, in heaven and on earth, things seen and things unseen, whether thrones, dominions, rulers, or authorities; all things were created and exist through Him [by His service, intervention] and in and for Him. And He Himself existed before all things, and in Him all things consist (cohere, are held together)" (AMP).

Since God is the great Creator and Architect of everything we see, I am confident He knows more than I do. I also believe He loves me and has my best interest in mind at all times. To help us live life to the fullest, He has given us the gift of His holy Word to teach and guide us. Indeed, He is a great God that has great plans for His children. In Jeremiah 29:11 He says, "For I know the thoughts and plans that I have for you, says the Lord, thoughts and plans for welfare and peace and not for evil, to give you hope in your final outcome" (AMP).

God is holy and there is no sin in Him. The Bible says that the wages of sin is death (see Romans 6:23). Ultimately, this death is spiritual death and separation from God. When we sin, it causes a separation between God and us. He created us for eternal fellowship with Himself, and He wants to make us the best we can be—that is, holy like Him. First Peter 1:16 says, "...Be ye holy; for I am holy" (KJV). Taking this concept one step further, because I believe in an omnipotent God who created everything and who loves me and wants a relationship with me, I also believe I can totally trust Him. He has the power and desire to do what He promises to do for me.

Mankind, in and of himself, is flawed and makes mistakes every day. We claim to be sure about one thing this year and just as sure about the opposite thing the next. For example, in the 1970s Time Magazine featured an article written by the top scientists of that day who were sure the planet was cooling off. Today, expert scientists are guaranteeing that global warming is taking place. The question is, whose report do we believe?

Unlike the mind of man, the Bible is timeless and reliable. For instance, the books of the Torah, which are the first five books of the Bible, were written between 3,500 and 4,000 years ago. They gave the nation of Israel dietary and sanitary laws that are proven to still be valid today. Indeed, "All scripture is given by inspiration of God, and is profitable for doctrine, for reproof, for correction, for instruction in righteousness" (2 Timothy 3:16 KJV). Although the Bible is thousands of years old, not one of the 5,000 prophecies of the Bible has ever been proven wrong. Only an omniscient God could provide us with this kind of changeless wisdom.

What Do You Believe?

So I ask you, *whose report will you believe*? It is important that you know what you believe and why you believe it. I choose to believe the report of the Bible because my spirit confirms it is the true Word of God, and more importantly, it has never been proven wrong. Countless prophecies of Scripture have come to pass as predicted, and none have been proven wrong. When we choose to trust in what the Lord says in His Word, and not lean to our own understanding or be wise in our own eyes, we will actually experience better health. Proverbs 3:7,8 declares:

> "Be not wise in your own eyes; reverently fear and worship the Lord and turn [entirely] away from evil. It shall be health to your nerves and sinews, and marrow and moistening to your bones" (AMP).

Are you gambling with your soul's eternal destination? If you are, do you have a good reason for believing what you believe? Don't just go with the "flavor of the day" and accept the latest philosophies and fads as truth, and don't let your morality change with the seasons. Instead, firmly plant yourself in the sound doctrine of God's holy, unchanging Word. He is the same yesterday, today, and forever (see Hebrews 13:8). He wants to share His eternal wisdom with you, His cherished creation He loves so much. He sent His Son, Jesus, to redeem us by becoming a living sacrifice and dying for our sins. "For God so loved the world, that he gave his only begotten Son, that whosoever believeth in Him should not perish, but have everlasting life" (John 3:16 KJV). Through our faith in Christ, you and I can spend eternity with Him.

The Choice Is Yours

In Deuteronomy 30:19, God says, "I call heaven and earth to record this day against you, that I have set before you life and death, blessing and cursing: therefore **choose life**, that both thou and thy seed may live." By putting your faith in Jesus Christ and His Word, you choose life.

I am very happy I chose to live life God's way after doing things my way for many years. By the grace of God, I have truly been transformed from a self-destructive street hustler to a man who is determined to help others get off the path of self-destruction. Now, instead of spreading corruption, I am spreading the Word of God to a lost generation. Instead of looking to get high from drugs, I am serving the Most High God. I went from being a man who was running from the law to a man who now fasts, prays, and reads the Word regularly. What a radical change!

I am very grateful that I chose life, and you can make the same choice if you have not done so already. I encourage you to make the choice today to believe in God passionately—make the choice to CHOOSE LIFE!

My Prayer for This Book

My prayer is that this book will be used as a tool for many people, both young and old, to avoid the pitfalls in life I have experienced. I don't want it to be about me, or my ability to overcome obstacles, or about how "holy" I have become. On the contrary, this book is about the power of the Holy Spirit to transform our lives and give us victory over whatever we may be facing. I don't want to brag about myself or my accomplishments—I want to brag about Jesus Christ and His crucifixion. He is the One who gave me the wisdom to eventually yield myself to Him and acknowledge that without Him I am nothing. If not for His grace, I would be roaming the streets as a homeless drug addict, or in jail for life, or dead. I thank God for choosing me to be able to tell of His goodness; I will sing praises to Him all the days of my life!

> Bless the LORD, O my soul: and all that is within me, bless his holy name. Bless the LORD, O my soul and forget not all his benefits: Who forgiveth all thine iniquities; who healeth all thy diseases; Who redeemeth thy life from destruction; who crowneth thee with loving-kindness and tender mercies; Who satisfieth thy mouth with good things; so that thy youth is renewed like the eagle's. The LORD executeth righteousness and judgment for all that are oppressed. He made known his ways unto Moses, his acts unto the children of Israel. The LORD is merciful and gracious, slow to anger, and plenteous in mercy. He will not always chide: neither will he keep his anger for ever; He hath not dealt with us after our sins; nor rewarded us according to our iniquities. For as the heaven is high above the earth, so great is his mercy toward them that fear him. As far as the east is from the west, so far hath he removed our transgressions from us. Like as a father pitieth his children, so the LORD pitieth them that fear him. For he knoweth our frame; he remembereth that we are dust. As for man, his days are as grass: as a flower of the field, so he flourisheth. For the wind passeth over it, and it is gone; and the place thereof shall know it no more. But the mercy of the LORD is from everlasting to everlasting upon them that fear him, and his righteousness unto children's children; To such as keep his covenant, and to those that remember his commandments to do

them. The LORD hath prepared his throne in the heavens; and his kingdom ruleth over all. Bless the LORD, ye his angels, that excel in strength; that do his commandments, hearkening unto the voice of his word. Bless ye the LORD, all ye his hosts; ye ministers of his, that do his pleasure. Bless the LORD, all his works in all places of his dominion: bless the LORD, O my soul.

—Psalm 103:1-22

Section 5
THE BUSINESS OF RELIGION AND RACE-CARD POLITICS

This final section of the book is primarily based on and devoted to the viewpoints I hold on key issues in our country, many of which I expressed during the 2008 presidential election season. I still feel they need to be shared at this point in time. During the months preceding the election, I shared many of my views concerning religion, politics, and race. These have always been a very precarious set of issues to balance, and I attempted to write about these topics with careful consideration and tactfulness from a Christian worldview. Portions of this information have been compiled and written with the help of my co-laborers who worked diligently to help me effectively express my viewpoints. To them I say thanks.

Chapter 15

Evaluating the Obama Phenomenon

I am very open and honest in telling all those who want to listen that I did not vote for Barack Obama in 2008. Not because I did not like him or thought that he was less qualified than some of our past presidents. On the contrary, Obama is a very intelligent, articulate leader who, from a natural standpoint, is actually more gifted in some aspects than many of our past presidents. So his ability, or lack thereof, had absolutely no bearing on my decision not to vote for him. The reason I did not vote for him is because my faith takes precedence over my personal feelings and desires.

As much as I would like to celebrate the concept of America having its first black president, I understand that my citizenship is first and foremost to the kingdom of God. I have been bought with a price, and once I accepted that payment, I now have a higher calling that I am obligated to fulfill. As a child of God, I must realize that I no longer look at the world through the telescope of my human understanding but through the unfailing truth of the inspired Word of God, the Holy Bible.

My natural self admires the man who became president. He is a driven, focused family man who came from humble beginnings and rose through the system to win the most powerful office in the world. His election has given many people across the globe a whole new perception of the black man in America. Indeed, it has been a long time coming—over 200 years of U.S. presidential history, to be precise. Many blacks who have passed on would have loved to have seen the day when this country would vote for a person of color to hold the highest office in the land. So as a black man, I can understand why so many black people feel refreshed to finally have a man in the White House who looks like one of us.

There are many black people who feel that none of our previous presidents could truly relate to them or their struggles as minorities. Let's face it, we live in a country that unfortunately has a history of racism that few people are proud of. I love black people and can fully relate to the unique struggles that they face. As I often remind others, I have been black all my life, and I am proud of that fact. Nevertheless, these are my personal feelings, and they must take a back seat to my faith in Christ. There are far more important things for me to feel good about than my blackness.

Once Barack Obama became president, I made a decision to respect the office he holds even though I did not vote for him. I pray for him almost every day, and I definitely want to see his administration do what is in the best interest of our country. But as a Christian, I cannot, in good conscience, support his agenda now that he is in office. My first responsibility is to Jesus Christ, not to a particular political party, race, or candidate. I am more concerned with eternal matters and with promoting biblical values that will honor God and cause our nation to flourish rather than self-destruct. As an African-American businessman who speaks to the masses, I am committed to using my platform to tell people the truth of what is really going on.

Why Do So Many Black People Love Barack Obama?

I think it is very unfortunate that many Christians vote for candidates mainly because they belong to a certain racial group or political party. Have these Christians put their loyalty to skin color or a political party above their loyalty to God's standards and values? The sad thing is that as an African-American man, I am expected by many to blindly support Barack Obama's ideologies and policies. But I do not operate like that. Again, my main agenda is speaking out on behalf of important issues that I feel are priorities to God, some of which happen to be related to pro-life initiatives and the protection of the institution of marriage.

Consequently, I have come under attack because of my writings concerning people's ideologies and philosophies. Some people have asked me, "How can you say that a person is not a Christian just because they do not follow Jesus?" I also have had people doubt my political motives for questioning Barack Obama's "Christian" faith. I assure you that I am not running for public office, nor am I on the payroll of the Republican Party. I just want to shed a little light to "white" America on what is going on in the hearts and minds of the African-American community.

I believe there are two main reasons why so many black people love and support Obama. The first reason is identification; black people in America were stripped of their identity and much of their heritage through slavery and institutionalized racism. As a result, we have been seeking to regain that identity for hundreds of years. Therefore, we sometimes grab hold of anything that we think can help us regain our culture and identity as a race. Our music, our style, and all the things that make us unique as people to the rest of the world are things we cherish.

The second big reason I believe people love Obama is reparation, or payback. Many African-Americans feel that as a country, we have never truly dealt with the horrible institution of slavery, which was legal for hundreds of years. Consequently, many blacks look for anything we can deem as a payback, or closure, for the pain and hurt that stripped us of our manhood and humanness—not only during the time of legalized slavery, but also during the "Jim Crow" era that denied us of our basic human rights. The U.S. government has given reparations to other groups that have been wronged, such as the Japanese who were compensated after World War II. Up to this point, however, blacks have not received anything of the kind, which complicates things. Therefore, many blacks see having the first black president as a sort of payback in the name of social justice.

As much as I am impressed with Barack Obama's charismatic personality and would love to support him, I can't. Yes, he has a lot of qualifications that could make him a good leader, but in good conscience I cannot support a person who is so far to the left on the issues of abortion and the radical gay-rights agenda, which is out to diminish the institution of marriage between a man and a woman. When Obama was running for office, I did my homework. I went to his official website, www.change.gov, and reviewed his radical, far-left "civil-rights" agenda. His plans focus on a few legitimate issues mixed in with a lot of pseudo-civil-rights issues, such as bogus hate crime statutes, radical gay-rights strategies, opposition to a constitutional ban on same-sex marriage, the repeal of the "Don't Ask-Don't Tell" policy, expansion of adoption rights for homosexuals, and so forth.

I believe all humans should be treated with dignity—even if we believe that their lifestyle choices are immoral. But I am opposed to the concept of celebrating destructive lifestyle choices or granting special rights—under the guise of civil rights—to those who choose ungodly lifestyles. For example, why should our nation grant special rights for gays and lesbians to adopt innocent children who have no say in the matter and will thus be forced to grow up in a home with parents who blatantly violate God's laws. It seems that the president is more interested in fighting for the rights of those who choose immoral lifestyles as opposed to fighting for legitimate civil rights issues. Regarding his pseudo-civil-rights agenda, here are some of his exact words from his 2008 open letter—released while on the campaign trail—concerning the controversial issue of gay rights in America:

> As your President, I will use the bully pulpit to urge states to treat same-sex couples with full equality in their family and adoption laws. I personally believe that civil unions represent the best way to secure that equal treatment.

> But I also believe that the federal government should not stand in the way of states that want to decide on their own how best to pursue equality for gay and lesbian couples—whether that means a domestic partnership, a civil union, or a civil marriage. Unlike Senator Clinton, I support the complete repeal of the Defense of Marriage Act (DOMA)—a position I have held since before arriving in the U.S. Senate. While some say we should repeal only part of the law, I believe we should get rid of that statute altogether. Federal law should not discriminate in any way against gay and lesbian couples, which is precisely what DOMA does. I have also called for us to repeal Don't Ask, Don't Tell, and I have worked to improve the Uniting American Families Act so we can afford same-sex couples the same rights and obligations as married couples in our immigration system.

It might sound somewhat noble for Barack Obama to use expressions like "equality" and "equal treatment," but his open letter has less to do with equality and more to do with trying to force the homosexual agenda on all of America whether we agree with it or not. A "Truth In Action Ministries" program (formerly the "Coral Ridge Ministries" program founded by the late Dr. D. James Kennedy) that aired in April 2012 reported that the Obama administration, as a part of U.S. foreign policy, is telling other countries that they must embrace the goals of gay activism. In other words, President Obama, with the help of Secretary of State Hillary Clinton and others in his administration, is on a radical mission to promote and spread the homosexual agenda worldwide as well as throughout the United States.

With all of the problems in our country and in our black communities, you would think that the first black president would have a more sensible focus regarding a "civil rights" agenda. Instead, he seems obsessed with trying to legislate immorality. Because I realize that my relationship with God and His expectations for me are paramount, I have to stand for my faith. The issues of morality, marriage, and basic human rights of unborn children are the very foundation of a civilized society, and if we do not get these correct, the economy, health care, etc. will be irrelevant.

Generally speaking, many Christians have become so enthralled with the economy and health care that we have forgotten the more important issues that are plaguing us as a nation. The condition of the economy is simply a by-product of the moral decline in America. I truly believe the ones who claim to be Christians are most responsible for the economic and moral decline in America. The fact is, many people in the Christian church have helped vote corrupt politicians into office or have not voted at all. As the old saying goes, "Evil triumphs when good men do nothing." If we continue in this direction, the economy and all the other issues will only get worse.

According to the Bible and history, whenever a nation loses its moral compass and begins to legalize and "legitimize" immoral acts, that nation begins to decline economically. This is one of the consequences of irreverent behavior and a lack of respect and reverence for God. It's true that fiscal responsibility and plans for economic recovery are crucial, and political leaders should avoid over-taxation and out-of-control spending that causes an accumulation of copious national debt. However, no amount of economic stimulus can save a nation that does not fear God!

MANY HAVE BEEN MOTIVATED BY EMOTIONS

No matter how you slice or dice it, many people voted for Barack Obama for emotional reasons. This includes people like my father and his generation who have experienced a lot of persecution and racism because of the color of their skin. As a result, many of them—not all, but many—view Obama's election as a fulfillment of a great hope and a dream come true. In their minds, it is a historical event that helps validate their equality with everyone else.

However, when we look more closely at the last election, we will see that Satan, the great deceiver, was shrewdly at work behind the scenes. Instead of really investigating what Obama believes in and stands for, many Christians, both black and white, blindly voted for him because they wanted to be a part of a historic event. I have pointed this out on the radio as well as in writing and have received quite a number of responses.

One blogger who read one of my Internet articles stated:

> It's a crying shame more blacks are not mature enough to be able to say, "This person is not the RIGHT black to vote for. But he's established a precedent, and one of these days, the RIGHT black person will come along, and we can vote with a clear conscience before God. We'll wait 'til then."

Another person resounded this idea stating:

> Mr. Green, I appreciate your view of politics. I am white and I would not hesitate to vote for a black if he or she

stood for what I believe to be the best for our country and my Christian belief.

The aforementioned bloggers both remind me that in spite of the fact that there are a lot of people who blindly support candidates because of race or political party, there are still many brave soldiers of all ethnic backgrounds who are willing to stand for what is right.

Another blogger wrote:

> Nice article Pastor Green. I just wanted to let you know that you are not alone as a black man who chooses to unashamedly declare his profession of Jesus Christ as Lord and Savior . . . on his 'ballot.' I am a 44-year-old, born-again believer in Jesus Christ. I happen to be black. Frankly, I am extremely disgusted with the African-American Christian community for their continued blind support of the Democratic Party—a party that is (generally) diabolically opposed to the will of God. I admire your grace and eloquence with which you explained your opposition to the candidacy of Barack Obama. I need to work on "sharing the truth in love." I can sometimes allow my passion to come across as hateful. Pray for me. Anyway, it just blows me away to see Christians dance, shout, and declare that God is their Jehovah-Jireh on Sunday . . . and go to the polls and vote for everything they claim they do not support. It just blows me away! When will we cast a vote for righteousness? The Proverbs declare "Righteousness exalts a nation." Do we not realize that the "blood of 52 million babies are crying out from the ground." Is our God deaf that he shall not hear? Does he turn a blind eye to the spilling of innocent blood? Keep up the good work, my brother in Christ. You are certainly a minority among minorities. But you are not alone. There are still seven thousand that have not bowed the knee to Baal. God bless you and Heaven smile upon you.

Now, I am not the only one striving to stand tall for the Christian faith. Thank God there are other brave black leaders like D.L. Foster and Bishop Harry Jackson Jr., who have not sold out to political correctness. In a pre-election, September 2008 Charisma article entitled "A Tragic Compromise," D.L. Foster expressed his concern for the way many

Christian leaders are compromising biblical principles and backing down like "wet kittens" when it comes to speaking out on issues such as homosexuality. He writes:

> Equally alarming is the way black churches have opened their pulpits to Obama despite his embrace of homosexuality. Although Obama's ascent has been due in part to African-American support, not once have I heard a prominent black pastor challenge his views on this issue...
>
> Granted, Obama is at the center of an unprecedented moment in U.S. history. But do we as black Christians put our beliefs on the back burner just to get an African-American in the Oval Office?
>
> In the last several years we've seen the advance of gay rights lead to the suppression of religious liberty. Increasingly, believing that homosexuality is a sin is being equated with bigotry.
>
> Do we reject God to get the king that we want, as the ancient Israelites rejected God's leadership for Saul? Or maybe what we're seeing is a foreshadowing of how the world will respond to Jesus during the reign of the Antichrist.
>
> I'm not endorsing any candidate, and I have no desire to tell Christians how to vote. But pastors, especially African-American ministers who have helped Obama reach this historic place, must ask the hard questions and take a decisive stand now—not just after Election Day. If the church can't depend on its leaders to uphold God's Word, we are headed for shipwreck.

In that same September 2008 issue of Charisma, Bishop Harry R. Jackson Jr., senior minister of Hope Christian Center in the Washington, D.C., area, also took a bold stand on these crucial issues. In an article entitled "The Changing Black Vote," he declared:

> I am not anti-Democrat, and I am not pro-Republican. I have been a registered Democrat since I first registered to vote...I am deeply troubled by the pro-abortion, pro-gay marriage, tax-and-spend policies of the Democrats. And a lot of people in our community feel as I do...On almost all the issues that matter most to me, I identify more

strongly with the platform issues of the Republicans... And I am not alone. More and more blacks are beginning to question their relationship with the Democrats...Voting for a party because 'we've always done it that way' is no longer acceptable.

Clearly, as people of color and Americans, it is high time we wise up and stop being moved by our emotions. Just because somebody does or says things that make us "feel" good doesn't make them worthy of our vote. We must find out the core character of the candidates we are considering casting our vote for. In other words, where do they stand on the issues? Who has been influencing their lives? How do their standards and values line up with God's Word?

True "Liberation" for the Black Community?

Back during the campaigning months of 2008, a connection between Barack Obama and Reverend Jeremiah Wright surfaced. It became known that Rev. Wright was Barack's pastor for nearly twenty years at Chicago's Trinity United Church of Christ. Knowing the extreme controversy of Wright's philosophies and negative remarks regarding race, Obama attempted to downplay the connection, calling Wright a mentor and very important person in his life. He claimed that he was not aware of Rev. Wright's view on certain controversial issues related to race in America. He then distanced himself from him as much as possible.

Being a person of faith, I found it very hard to believe that someone could attend a church for twenty years and not know what the head pastor believes. This prompted me to do some research on Rev. Wright. Before long, it became clear that the main philosophy he promotes is called Black Liberation Theology (BLT), and James Cone and Dwight Hopkins are considered the leading theologians of this system of belief.

I then did some research on BLT, and the first thing that stood out was the multiple references made on Trinity United Church of Christ's website to their African roots and their commitment to establish a type of liberation that is *not* in line with Scripture. Based on the fact that Obama attended Trinity UCC for twenty years, it would be very unrealistic to think that the basic tenants of BLT did not influence his thinking. Indeed, as Scripture warns us, "Do not be deceived: 'Evil company corrupts good habits'" (1 Corinthians 15:33 NKJV).

One of the most prevalent beliefs of Black Liberation Theology is the oppressor/oppressed paradigm. BLT is very concerned with giving power to the oppressed. However, in some cases it has distorted the category of oppressed people to include individuals who are not actually oppressed. That is, it is not exclusive to just oppressed blacks in America. When we look at Barack Obama's views on issues such as abortion rights and special rights for homosexuals and the poor and working class, they closely reflect Black Liberation Theology. They are views that try to make victims out of people who are not really victims at all. In essence, it is a pseudo-civil rights agenda.

This is the biggest problem I have with BLT—the fact that not every situation boils down to an actual oppressor against the oppressed. The issue of abortion is a perfect example. Obama has demonstrated during his time in public office that he is against limiting abortions in any way. What he has repeatedly done is to equate and associate limits on abortion as society's "oppression" of a woman's right to choose what she does with her body. During a public forum in Pennsylvania, I heard Barack Obama say that if his daughter got pregnant before she was ready, then he would not "punish" her by making her have a baby. In this case, the woman would be considered the oppressed. This thinking inherently ignores the child's right to life.

The other thing that the BLT school of thought attempts to do is to make Christians who follow the Holy Bible look like oppressors over anyone who disagrees with them. For instance, if we say that homosexuality is wrong based on what the Bible says, then we are considered as "hateful" and "intolerant." Isn't it ironic that one group of people who are supposed to be tolerant of all condemns another group of people for what they believe? Wouldn't that be considered hypocrisy?

Don't get me wrong. I am all for treating homosexuals like human beings because they deserve love and respect just like anyone else. But I am opposed to having politicians create special laws for them that are intended to punish or alienate those who believe their lifestyle is immoral and unhealthy. Similarly, I am all for helping the poor and helpless as the Bible instructs us. But I am opposed to radical politicians trying to overtax hardworking people in order to support able-bodied individuals who refuse to work because it is easier for them to get a government handout. Likewise, I am all for a woman's right to choose on many issues. But a woman's right to choose to have an abortion should not take priority over a baby's right to live. We each have a right to love others as people and still disagree with their lifestyle at the same time.

Clearly, we can see Black Liberation Theology coming through on many different levels. The philosophies and teachings that have influenced Barack Obama are now influencing American life, and the results are anything but liberating. I pray you can see from this example just how important it is to know what a person believes and what his or her standards and values are rooted in before you vote for that person.

Make no mistake about it; the last election was about a lot more than just winning the presidency or control of Congress. There is truly a spiritual battle going on in this country, and it seems that many people who call themselves Christians are fast asleep. I say it's high time we wake up!

REAL CHRISTIANS HAVE CAUSE FOR CONCERN

As a minister of the gospel I am very much concerned about what President Obama stands for. I have read his books and other writings, and I have watched videos of many of his speeches. The implications of his beliefs should seriously concern any Bible-believing Christian.

For starters, in Barack Obama's view of "Christianity," he wants to include everyone. He has repeatedly said that there are many paths to God. In his book entitled *The Audacity of Hope*, it reveals that he believes in a mixture of New Age philosophy as well as a diluted form of Christianity. New Age thinking basically denounces Christianity and Jesus Christ as outdated and primitive. It claims to be "progressive" and admonishes its followers to make God into whatever we need Him to be. Barack Obama also mentions that his mother made him read from the Bible, the Koran, and a number of other writings from the world's major religions. I believe this is why he accepts them all as valid paths to God. He doesn't really stand for any one thing morally. Instead, he feels that everyone's beliefs should be considered equally relevant.

Although Barack Obama claims to be a Christian, he openly states that he believes you can get into heaven *without* faith in Christ—that Jesus is *not* the only way. The thing that really gets me about this is that many "Christians" do not have a problem with it. Yet, it contradicts the very foundation of Christianity. Clearly, Jesus said in John 14:6 NKJV, "I am *the* way, *the* truth, and *the* life. No one comes to the Father except through Me." As a Christian, you and I must clearly understand to whom we owe our loyalty. Jesus died so that we can have eternal life. Therefore, if I proclaim to be a Christian, I have to take issue with anyone who tries to compromise Jesus' message. Since Jesus said that He is the *only* way to eternal life, to denounce that claim is to call Him either uninformed or a liar—neither of which I accept as true.

Another disturbing philosophy that is influencing Obama is his socialistic view of the economy. He admits to being mentored in Hawaii by Frank Marshall Davis, a known communist. If you look at Obama's economic philosophies, it doesn't take long to see that they stem from communism.

In a certain context, terms such as "community leaders," "transference of wealth," and empowering the "working class" are all rooted in socialism. Again, by looking at Barack Obama's mentors, you will clearly see their blueprint of how he plans to govern America.

Throughout his campaign, he ran on a platform of *change*. On the surface, we were led to believe that this change was simply referring to political and economic alterations. However, I believe the change that he is looking to implement is much deeper, as we can now see from the decisions he has made since he has been in office.

For example, he has sought to secure more taxpayer funds for abortion and remove as many limitations on abortion as possible. This should not be a surprise, seeing how he voted against giving human rights to infants that have survived abortion attempts when he was in the Illinois State Senate. President Obama has also openly supported same-sex couples and advocated giving them the same rights as heterosexual couples under law. At the same time, he has all but ignored the true Christian community, avoiding participation in things such as the National Day of Prayer, and going so far as to say that America is no longer a Christian nation.

And it doesn't stop there. Under his administration, there is a growing opposition to limit the free speech of Christians who speak out against homosexuality, abortion, and any other lifestyle that we believe is wrong according to God's Word. This means that one day it might be considered "hate speech" for me to tell my own son why I believe that homosexuality is an immoral and unhealthy lifestyle that I would not want him to get involved in. This is absolutely ludicrous.

One bill that has resurfaced since the new administration has been in place is called the Fairness Doctrine. In reality, it would be more appropriate to call this deceptive policy the **Un**fairness Doctrine because it would require conservative or Christian radio stations to offer equal air time to those with opposing views when discussing controversial issues. In other words, the ability of Christian broadcasters to share the gospel on their own Christian radio stations would be hindered. Christian broadcasters could very well be forced by the Federal Communications Commission to allow atheists or abortion activists to share their anti-biblical views on the air, even though Christian listeners would not want to hear them. To me, this would be a direct violation of religious liberties and freedom of speech. This policy was originally introduced in 1949 and abolished in 1987. Liberal radio broadcasters would love to reinstate it because they are very much outnumbered by conservative talk shows. As usual, the proponents on the far left are using language that sounds positive to try to promote their hidden agenda.

Jay Sekulow, chief counsel for the American Center for Law and Justice, a legal group specializing in constitutional law, has been preparing a litigation strategy to prevent the restoration of the Fairness Doctrine. On one of his "Jay Sekulow Live!" radio programs in February 2009, he echoed my viewpoint, stating, "Putting the federal government in control of dictating the content of what's aired would effectively muzzle Christian broadcasters and is an unconstitutional attempt to stifle free speech."

Because the mission of a Christian broadcaster is based on building the faith of the listeners, entertaining opposing viewpoints is counterproductive to the mission. If the Christian broadcaster is trying to encourage listeners to have faith in what the Bible teaches, then broadcasting opposing views undermines that objective. It would be like forcing Ford Motor Company to promote Mercedes Benz products along with theirs. This would put Christian radio in a precarious position, and from a business standpoint, it would not make sense. Undoubtedly, it would cause many Christian listeners to stop tuning in.

These are just some of the kinds of things we are up against under the new administration. Clearly, Barack Obama is the most liberal president this country has had in recent times, and he will be very persistent in pushing the liberal, far-left agenda. I sincerely believe that we are about to face some very trying times in the near future. As Christians living by the standard of God's Word, we are now facing a serious, uphill battle, and if we do not stand up for Christian values, we will be silenced forever.

Now, I am not out to just pick on the president. I am praying for him and those in authority as the Bible directs us, and I urge you to do the same (see 1 Timothy 2:1-3). In addition to praying, there are plenty of scriptures that let us know we also need to speak out and shine the light of truth in a culture of corruption and immorality. Indeed, as Christians, this is the hour we must stand strong and fight for our values and morals.

Franklin Graham Under Fire

The Rev. Franklin Graham, a prominent evangelical leader and CEO of the international relief organization Samaritan's Purse, came under fire and sparked a lot of controversy on more than one occasion when he seemed to indicate that he did not know whether or not President Barack Obama is really a Christian.

It was on a panel on MSNBC's "Morning Joe" show on February 21, 2012, that Franklin Graham was asked if he believes President Barack Obama is a Christian.

"I think you have to ask President Obama," Graham responded.

Some of the panelists, seemingly frustrated by Graham's ambiguity, pressed him insistently for a more direct answer.

Throughout the interview, Graham repeatedly tried to point the panelists back to President Obama's own confession of faith.

"He has said he is a Christian so I just assume that he is," said Graham.

One of the panelists continued to interrogate Graham: "You've said in the past that the President is Christian in as much as he goes to church on Sunday. But you don't know if he's accepted Jesus Christ. Do you still believe that?"

"I mean I don't know," Graham replied. "I asked him when he was running—when he was a senator—I asked him how he came to faith in Christ. He said that he was working in the South Side of Chicago in the community and they asked him—the community—asked him what church he went to. He said 'I don't go to church.' They said, 'If you're going to work in the community, you have to join one of our churches.' And of course, he joined Reverend Jeremiah's church. So that's what his answer to my question was."

"So therefore, by your definition, he's not a Christian," the panelist stated.

"You have to ask him. I cannot answer that question for anybody," said Graham.

Responding to a panelist's inquiry about Obama's family connection to Islam, Graham stated that because Obama's father was a Muslim, "under Islamic law, the Muslim world sees Barack Obama as a Muslim."

During the interview Graham was also asked, "Is there one candidate who shares your beliefs more than another?"

"I would say on moral issues Rick Santorum. He's a very sharp guy and as far as the Christian faith, more in line," Graham explained.

When the panelist asked Rev. Graham if he believed that Rick Santorum is Christian, Rev. Graham stated that he believed Santorum was a Christian because "His values are so clear on moral issues. No question about it."

A panel member then accused Rev. Graham of having a double standard regarding his opinion about the faith of Santorum versus the faith of Obama.

Franklin Graham then countered by saying that you have to look at what a person does with his life because anyone can say he's a Christian. The panelists expressed their frustration and continued to challenge Franklin Graham's concept about who or what is a Christian. And by the time the interview was over, a whirlwind of controversy was in the air.

In the upcoming days and weeks following this controversial MSNBC interview, black church leaders were among many who openly expressed their displeasure regarding Franklin Graham's comments. More than a dozen members of a religious subgroup of the NAACP implied that Graham was "bearing false witness" and contributing to racial division. The open letter from these NAACP faith leaders stated:

> As Christian denominational leaders, pastors, and, most importantly, followers of Jesus Christ; we are greatly troubled by recent attempts by some religious leaders to use faith as a political weapon. We were disturbed and disappointed by statements made by Rev. Franklin Graham during an interview on MSNBC that questioned whether President Obama is a Christian. Rev. Graham also seemed to imply that the President may be a Muslim, despite the fact that the President has repeatedly expressed his faith and belief in Jesus Christ. By his statements, Rev. Graham seems to be aligning himself with those who use faith as a weapon of political division. These kinds of comments could have enormous negative effects for America and are especially harmful to the Christian witness.

One day after NAACP faith leaders issued the open letter to Rev. Franklin Graham, on February 28, 2012, the evangelist offered an apology stating the following:

> I regret any comments I have ever made which may have cast any doubt on the personal faith of our president, Mr. Obama. The president has said he is a Christian and I accept that (and have said so publicly on many occasions). I apologize to him and to any I have offended for not better articulating my reason for not supporting him in this election—for his faith has nothing to do with my consideration of him as a candidate.
>
> In fact, Article VI of our Constitution strictly prohibits any religious test for public office. I believe we should consider a candidate's values and competence above anything else when considering whom to support for public office. I even reject the idea that we should only vote for a candidate of our own particular faith, for oftentimes that is not an available option.
>
> My objection to President Obama is built on his policy positions on a number of important moral issues, and not on his religion or faith. For example, I believe his positions on abortion and on traditional marriage are in direct

conflict with God's standards as set forth in Scripture. I have determined I cannot and will not vote for him or any candidate in either party whose policy positions on such critical issues violate biblical truths and standards.

Graham further stated that he would personally vote for a politician who was affiliated with either political party or who was of a different faith than his own as long as the politician upheld certain values that were important to him. Graham closed his response to the NAACP faith leaders by stating that he is praying for our country and for those who lead it in this election season and challenging economic time.

Months prior to his conflict with NAACP church leaders, Graham also came under fire and was openly criticized by popular black TV preacher T.D. Jakes for questioning the faith of President Obama on another occasion. When Roland Martin interviewed Bishop T. D. Jakes on the May 15, 2011, Washington Watch television program, Martin asserted that President Obama is on record as saying that he walked down the aisle and gave his life to Christ, yet Rev. Franklin Graham has questioned his faith. Martin asked Bishop Jakes, "So what do you say to folks like Rev. Graham, who frankly are muddying the water, and other people who are questioning the Christianity of this President?"

Bishop T. D. Jakes responded:

> I find it insulting. We didn't question the Christianity of President Bush when he said he accepted Christ and I'm disappointed in Rev. Franklin Graham in that regard. I wish he had the diplomacy of his father who brought the gospel to people without being nuanced by politics, because when you do those things you offend people that you are actually called to save and to serve. And I would hope that he would see the rationale in apologizing for such statements because if the President's faith is suspect then all of our faith are suspect because the Bible is quite clear about what it takes to be saved. And the President has been quite open about his accepting Christ and him openly confessing it before men. And if it's good enough for the Bible it ought to be good enough for the rest of us.

Just as Bishop T. D. Jakes finds it insulting that President Obama's Christian faith was questioned by Rev. Franklin Graham, I find it insulting that a man like Jakes who is supposed to stand on biblical truth, along with the NAACP church leaders, would insinuate that it is not biblical to question a leader's faith at times. Do men like Bishop T. D. Jakes understand that there are times when we should question a man's faith if he is using his confession of faith to deceive himself or to mislead the gullible? Jim Jones, for example, was a cult leader who claimed to be a gospel preacher, yet he led hundreds of his followers to suicidal death. Are we allowed to question the "Christian" faith of imposters like Jim Jones? The answer is obviously *yes*. I am not saying that Barack Obama is Jim Jones, but I am simply bringing out the point that T. D. Jakes is not properly representing the Bible by implying that it is not really right to question a person's faith just because the person professes to be a Christian. Jesus clearly stated, "Beware of false prophets, which come to you in sheep's clothing, but inwardly they are ravening wolves. Ye shall know them by their fruits...Not every one that saith unto me, Lord, Lord, shall enter into the kingdom of heaven; but he that doeth the will of my Father which is in heaven... And then will I profess unto them, I never knew you: depart from me, ye that work iniquity" (Matthew 7:15, 16, 21, 23 KJV).

The Apostle Paul also warned us about those who deceive others by misrepresenting the true gospel of Christ: "I marvel that you are turning away so soon from Him who called you in the grace of Christ, to a different gospel, which is not another; but there are some who trouble you and want to pervert the gospel of Christ. But even if we, or an angel from heaven, preach any other gospel to you than what we have preached to you, let him be accursed [condemned to destruction]" (Galatians 1:6-8 NKJV).

Concerning those who promote perverse ideologies that are clearly contrary to the biblical value system, Paul also said, "Now I urge you, brethren, note those who cause divisions and offenses, contrary to the doctrine which you learned, and avoid them. For those who are such do not serve our Lord Jesus Christ, but their own belly, and by smooth words and flattering speech deceive the hearts of the simple" (Romans 16:17-18 NKJV). Wow! Does it sound like these verses could even be applied to some of our crafty politicians who claim to be "Christians" for their own personal gain?

All of the preceding verses prove that it is not only a true Christian leader's right, but it is also his responsibility to question another so-called Christian leader who is deceiving and misleading others by espousing a corrupt value system that misrepresents true Christianity. It seems to me that so-called Christian leaders who believe you should not question another person's faith—even when that person's value system is totally opposite of biblical values—need to go back to Bible school and take a few courses in basic Bible doctrine.

I respect the fact that Franklin Graham, the son of evangelist Billy

Graham, was humble enough to offer up an apology to those who were offended when he questioned the President's Christian faith. But I personally feel that there is no need for him to apologize, unless, of course, he simply did it because he felt he could have expressed his opinion in a better way.

It seems racist to some that Graham, being a white evangelist, would feel confident that a white Republican like Rick Santorum is a Christian, but would express reservations or doubts about Barack Obama's Christianity. To me there is nothing racist about this. Rick Santorum has a track record of supporting policies that foster a pro-life culture along with traditional marriage, true faith, and family values. Barack Obama has a radical track record for supporting a culture of death through abortion on demand and he supports perversion that is contrary to traditional family relationships. In other words, many of his policies and values clearly do not match his confession of faith.

It is unfortunate that Bishop T. D. Jakes could not acknowledge the validity of Graham's questioning of President Obama's faith, especially in light of the fact that Obama's value system and policies regarding polarizing social issues like abortion and gay adoption are in greater opposition to biblical values than any other President in the history of the United States. Are ministers like T. D. Jakes standing for God's value system or are they standing for the value system of the first black President?

I do appreciate the fact that Franklin Graham does seem to understand that issues of religion and race-card politics are so emotional and polarizing that we must be very careful about the timing of our statements as well as how we say things. In Graham's apology, he seemed to indicate that he felt he may have gone too far with some of his comments. It is obviously unrealistic for Christians to expect every politician to be a devout Christian or to only vote for Christian candidates. And Graham did a good job in expressing the need to be open-minded regarding these issues when he gave his apology.

On the other hand, a Christian leader like Franklin Graham has a right to speak out if he feels a candidate's values and policies blatantly contradict biblical principles to the detriment of the culture. For this reason, I encourage some of the white evangelical leaders like Franklin Graham to stand tall and strong when you know you are speaking the truth with wisdom and tact and do not be intimidated by some of the liberals or black religious leaders who will sometimes try to use the race card to cause you to back down from biblical truth. Black and white leaders who are true preachers of the gospel cannot allow themselves to be held hostage with race-card politics. Let the truth be told!

Chapter 16

The Issue of Life

In this chapter I am going to primarily address the issue of abortion. Abortion is one of the most heinous atrocities that a civilized society has ever done, and God hates it! Proverbs 6:16,17 says, "These six things doth the LORD hate: yea, seven are an abomination unto Him. A proud look a lying tongue, and **hands that shed innocent blood.**" Without question, abortion is the shedding of innocent blood.

I personally had to repent for being a part of four abortions in my life. For many years, I was under the deception that it was a person's right to decide whether or not to discontinue a life. This is a lie straight from the pit of hell. The only choice we have in this matter is whether or not we engage in sexual activity. When we have sex with a person of the opposite gender, there is always the possibility that a baby will result. This is where our "freedom of choice" ends. God has never given us the choice to kill an innocent baby, whether born or unborn. The Word of God tells us that.

In Jeremiah 1:5 God says, "Before I formed thee in the belly I knew thee; and before thou cameth forth out of the womb, I sanctified thee, and I ordained thee a prophet unto the nations" (KJV). Clearly, each of us is a person with an identity and purpose from God. Our life begins the moment we are conceived, and no one other than God himself has the right to end it.

We have turned murder into a form of birth control, and I know that God is not pleased with it. I used to think that because I was not directly performing the abortion of the unborn child I was absolved of any wrongdoing, but God also requires us as believers to speak out against injustice and to defend the innocent. I thank God often for revealing to me the error of my thinking.

In the Political Ring

One of the things that grieves me is the fact that many people who profess to be Christian will sometimes blindly vote for a political candidate who is a big supporter of abortion just because the candidate happens to belong to their preferred political party. This unfortunate trend is all too common among many black and white voters who profess to be Christians. It is also quite disturbing to see a lot of blacks who profess to be Christian blindly vote for a candidate only because the candidate happens to be black or Democrat. A Christian should cast votes based on a candidate's value system, not based solely on the candidate's race or party affiliation. In my younger years, because of my work in the community, I was given the opportunity to do advertising for the Democratic campaign. At that time, I believed the Democratic Party truly had the best interest of the African-American community, as well as the best interest of the middle- and lower-class people of the country. The Republicans, on the other hand, represented more of the "Old Boy Network." From what I could see at that time, they were primarily the party of the rich and upper-middle to upper-class white people. Although that was the impression I had then, I now believe this school of thought is in error.

Without getting into a long political discourse, I will simply say that my views have changed. I have worked closely with people on both sides of the political aisle, and I will say without fear of contradiction that getting wrapped up in whether a person is a Democrat or a Republican will lead you to be deceived. You must look at the individual candidates and what they believe in. No party cares more for any race than the other. We have to vote on issues and not be fooled into blindly believing that one party is all *right* or that one party is all *wrong*.

Unfortunately, there are many minorities who register to vote, but they never actually go out and vote. As a result, they cheat themselves out of being a part of the political system. The powers that be do not know who we vote for, but it is public record whether or not we vote. The bottom line is if you don't vote, the politicians who are looking to keep their jobs will ignore you because you are not helping them get reelected. It would actually be better if you went in and voted for Mickey Mouse than for you to not participate at all. This is a tough fact that many people have a hard time grasping, which is why I stressed not only registering to vote but also being actively involved.

One thing is for sure: I made a lot of money doing ads for the Pennsylvania State Democratic Party. It was nothing compared to the large amounts of money the parties spend for presidential elections. I was basically thrown some "scraps" because of a push from some influential friends who forced the State Democratic Party to spend some money with a minority company. It is a shame to say it, but the powers that be still have to be told that minority businessmen should have equal consideration when it comes to spending public money.

From this experience and seeing exactly how the political system works from the inside, I realized that money and power are the driving forces behind the political system. In this day and age, racism is not really as much a color thing as a socioeconomic thing. There was a song from the rap group the Wu-Tang Clan called "C.R.E.A.M.," which stands for "Cash Rules Everything Around Me." And from what I experienced in the political ring, there is a lot of truth in this statement.

The Truth About the Abortion Industry

Since 1973, there have been over 50 million babies aborted in America. That is nearly 4,000 infants a day, and approximately 35 percent of all these abortions were performed on black mothers. Keep in mind, blacks make up only about 12 percent of the population in America. At current rates, a black baby is *three times* more likely to be aborted than a white baby.

To have a better understanding of the abortion issue, we need to take a look at one of the major proponents of this culture of death and corruption. I am referring to Margaret Sanger (1879 -1966), the founder of the American Birth Control League, which eventually became the largest abortion chain in America—Planned Parenthood.

Margaret Sanger dedicated her life to controlling and eliminating people she felt were inferior—especially blacks. She carried out her plan in a number of ways, including segregation, sterilization, and various other methods of birth control. But her primary tool to accomplish her task was abortion. Tragically, Planned Parenthood has ended the lives of nearly 15 million African-Americans in the United States through abortion.

To this day, Sanger remains a controversial figure because of her racist views and the fact that she embraced and spoke to radical organizations like the Ku Klux Klan. As a result of her racist ideologies, the abortion industry has targeted the black community for decades for the purpose of keeping the black population from expanding in the U.S. Today, 80 percent of Planned Parenthood clinics are located in black and Hispanic neighborhoods. Worst of all, Planned Parenthood receives millions of dollars from the federal government every year to continue their "work."

Margaret Sanger was an extreme advocate of the negative eugenics movement. *Eugenics* is defined as "belief in the possibilities of improving the qualities of the human species or human population, especially by such means as discouraging reproduction by persons having genetic defects or presumed to have inheritable undesirable traits." In other words, Sanger viewed eugenics as the means by which to create a master race by controlling who has children and who doesn't. As Michael Hichborn of the American Life League stated in a YouTube video, "Margaret Sanger was a racist. She was responsible for the millions of babies that have been ethnically cleansed from our country..."

Here are some more startling facts about Margaret Sanger from the American Life League website (www.all.org) that you may not be aware of:

- Margaret Sanger, the founder of Planned Parenthood, was an adulteress, racist, and bigot; she was a supporter of Hitler's Nazi party and a believer in eugenics—the purification of a particular race of people by selective breeding. Her magazines and journals were filled with writings and articles by well-known eugenicists and members of Hitler's Third Reich.

- Instead of helping the poor, she considered them slum dwellers (particularly blacks, Hispanics, and Jewish immigrants) who would soon overrun the boundaries of their slums, contaminating the better elements of society with their diseases and inferior genes.

- Sanger's brand of prejudice was based on what author John L. Keller labels "Scientific Racism"—the belief that as long as people demonstrated "a good quality gene pool," they were esteemed a valuable part of society. On the other hand, if a group, including whites, demonstrated undesirable traits, their fertility had to be curbed along with other "inferiors and undesirables."[1]

- In his book *Grand Illusions*, George Grant states: "In her book *Women and the New Race*, she [Margaret Sanger] asserted that the 'most merciful thing a large family can do to one of its infant members is to kill it.'"[2]

- On October 19, 1939, Sanger outlined a plan for stopping the growth of the black community. She predicted that "the most successful educational approach to the Negro is through a religious appeal. We do not want word to go out that we want to exterminate the Negro population, and the minister is the man who can straighten out that idea if it ever occurs to any of their rebellious members."[3]

The above-mentioned quote from Sanger regarding her desire to "exterminate the Negro population" shows how shrewd she was in accomplishing her mission to murder black babies. She knew that if she could mislead black ministers into thinking that her mission was harmless and in the best interest of the black community, she would have a better chance of accomplishing her treacherous task. Sounds a bit like some of the far-left politicians of our day, doesn't it?

AN EYE-OPENING INTERVIEW WITH ALVEDA KING

When it comes to the issue of life, I know few people who are more involved and outspoken than pro-life activist Alveda King, the niece of the late Dr. Martin Luther King Jr. In August 2008, I had the privilege of doing a radio interview with her. She offered some powerful insights regarding abortion, civil rights, and the organization of Planned Parenthood. For starters, she said:

> Abortion is *not* a civil right. Pro-life is a civil right because every person has a right to life, liberty, and the pursuit of happiness—or should. And so a baby in the womb of his or her mother, which has 46 chromosomes like you do and I (we get 23 from our dad and 23 from our mother at conception)—that person has civil rights. Even as Dred Scott was told, "You're not a human being because you are colored or black…and so therefore you are less that human. We will not allow you personhood…," to say that to a tiny little baby, "You're not a person because of your size," …is taking away the civil rights of that person.
> My uncle, Dr. Martin Luther King Jr., said "The Negro cannot win if he is willing to sacrifice the future of his children for immediate, personal comfort and safety." And he said, "Injustice anywhere is a threat to justice everywhere." …I've had abortions myself in ignorance without being aware; I was told by Planned Parenthood that it [the baby] was a blob of tissue and that it wouldn't hurt. Well, it hurt me and it hurt my body, and it certainly hurt my child. And so, civil rights belong to *every* person, and science now agrees with the Word of God—that a little baby with the 46 chromosomes at conception is a human being.

Interestingly in 1966, Planned Parenthood Federation of America gave its "Margaret Sanger Award" to Dr. Martin Luther King Jr. They did this in order to continue their deceptive public relations practices. Alveda King explained to me that Dr. King, like so many others, accepted the award due to his lack of knowledge. In a passionate plea to proclaim the truth on the issue of life and reveal Planned Parenthood's true agenda, Alveda said:

> ...In not fighting for the child, we've been deceived and we've been fooled in various communities across America. And we've been told by one of the greatest and most racist enemies of life in America—Planned Parenthood—that the little babies are not real; that's a blob of tissue.
>
> They gave our leaders like Martin Luther King Jr. and Rosa Parks and others awards and said, "We want to help you build your community." Dr. King accepted that award just like I accepted their lies as his niece. But the time has come for us to be educated, informed—to not perish for lack of knowledge and to tell the truth.

Later in my interview with Alveda King, I brought up the issue of Barack Obama's views on abortion. I was very concerned that many people were being deceived by the rhetoric being broadcast by the media. Clearly, Obama is very crafty at parsing words in order to avoid giving direct answers to difficult questions. For instance, he at first claimed that he believed marriage should only be between a man and a woman, but he has always openly supported gay-rights activists who are trying to pervert the institution of marriage as we know it. He also claimed that we should do all we can to eliminate unnecessary abortions. Yet, he has a political track record of being one of the most radical supporters of abortions at all stages. Alveda King concurred, stating:

> ...Senator Barack Obama is pro-abortion...he voted against the Born Alive Infant Protection Act—that means if a baby is in the process of being aborted but lives, then Senator Obama said, "Do not give that baby medical treatment...just let the baby die because the intent was to kill the baby." And then he supports legislation that is anti-procreative marriage. And so, if you tear down marriage, you tear down family—and I mean marriage between a man and woman. If you tear down family [and] you abort babies, your society is going to suffer. Actually, the people that need to be born that can solve some of

the problems that we have today have been aborted, and that's very tragic.

I also asked Alveda King why so many black church people, including clergymen, seemed to be giving Barack Obama blind support for the presidency. She responded by explaining that not only were many people blindly supporting him, but also a number of others were supporting him who were *fully aware* of his radical political track record. She revealed:

> And, I would like to say that people don't know [about his track record]…but even sometimes when we share that information with people, they say, "Well I don't wanna hear that. I wanna vote for Barack Obama. Shut up. Don't tell me that. You gotta be lying anyway." And of course we're not. And so, I believe that we have to continue to pray. The major answer to having people's hearts available to receive truth is prayer. And we really do have to pray for people.

Finally, I made the comment that a lot of misguided black people were supporting Barack Obama simply because they saw the opportunity for him to become president as sort of a payback for all the years that blacks have suffered in America. To this, Alveda King responded:

> The problem with doing that—that says, "God, we don't trust You, because You can't deliver us and make things right for us. And I don't want to submit to You anyway. So I'm just going to vote for this person because they're black, and that's gonna fix it."
>
> What we really need to do is what the Bible says in 2 Chronicles: *If My people, who are called by My name, will humble themselves and pray, and turn from their wicked ways, and seek My face, then I will hear from heaven and forgive their sins and heal their land.* And so that's what we're gonna have to rely on—the power of the living God and His love for us. And then we'll see deliverance.

The bottom line is, if all of the liberal politicians were really concerned about helping the black community, they would not be such big supporters of the abortion industry that has exterminated millions of black babies. In spite of the fact that blacks helped to build this country with free labor when they were exploited as slaves, blacks are becoming a smaller and less powerful minority in America—largely due to the abortion industry that has targeted them for decades.

Please understand, I am not only concerned about the millions of black babies that have been aborted, but also the millions of babies of all races that have been destroyed. As Alveda King said, "Abortion is not a civil right. ...The woman has a right to choose what she does with her body, but the baby is not her body."[4] I am very grateful that there are brave individuals like Alveda King on the front line who understand and can articulate the difference between legitimate civil rights and pseudo-civil rights.

EXPOSING AND STANDING FOR THE TRUTH

Within the past few years, undercover investigators have exposed the shocking truth of how Planned Parenthood representatives often cover up statutory rape cases and are also willing to accept donations specifically earmarked for the racist practice of aborting black babies. And they have the recorded conversations to prove it!

In a 2008 *Breakthrough* television broadcast entitled "Life's Greatest Enemy: Planned Parenthood Exposed," Pastor Rod Parsley of World Harvest Church clearly pointed out that Margaret Sanger, founder of Planned Parenthood, detested black people. He also revealed that Planned Parenthood is using our tax dollars for the purpose of committing black genocide.

Gary Bauer, president of American Values, was also on the program that day. He stated that "When the U.S., in 1973, started abortion on demand, the nation enshrined in our Constitution that it's OK to take the life of an innocent, unborn child." I agree with Mr. Bauer and would also add that the Roe vs. Wade decision has created a culture of death in the U.S., so much so that many people do not value life the way they should. Bauer also pointed out that George W. Bush, to his credit, was willing to sign the ban on partial birth abortion. He further stated that abortion does not empower women—it empowers sexually irresponsible men who want sex without a price. Furthermore, he pointed out that many women who have abortions suffer from post-abortion syndrome—a fact that the mainstream media frequently fail to acknowledge, if they acknowledge it at all.

Another program guest that day was Dr. Johnny Hunter, founder and president of Life Education and Resource Network (L.E.A.R.N.). Dr. Hunter stated that even if Roe v. Wade is not overturned, "The hearts and minds of this nation must be overturned. Churches must have the guts to get out of the pulpit and rise up and speak against this thing...to stand right…to show love and compassion to those that have already made the mistake…[and] forgive them for their sins…The church needs to rise and be the church and not sit back while this is going on."

Where does God stand on all this? He says in His Word that He "*hates hands that shed innocent blood*" (see Proverbs 6:16,17). I cannot think of a more innocent life than that of an unborn child. It is clear throughout Scripture that God watches how we care for people less fortunate than us. He requires us to look out for the widows and orphans of the world, identifying this duty as a major part of "true religion" (see James 1:27). And in Matthew 25:40, Jesus tells us that whatever we do to even the *least of those* around us, we have done to Him. Indeed, **all life is precious**. I am amazed at how we as a country have a welfare system that helps make provision for people who cannot provide for themselves. We also give a lot of money in aid to those in need around the world. We even have organizations like People for the Ethical Treatment of Animals (PETA) that fight for the rights of animals. But why aren't more people fighting for the "least of these"—the unborn child? Why is it that the people who protest about how dogs and cats are treated or who have huge rallies to save the planet aren't more boisterous in speaking out against the murder of innocent, unborn babies?

Yes, I believe people have a certain amount of "choice" with what they do with their bodies—but only a certain amount. Even that is limited. Think about it. Our society in general considers suicide as something that is illegal or wrong. Therefore, if we can tell someone not to take their *own* life, why is it OK for them to end the life of a child?

Worst of all, not only do we allow for babies to be murdered in the early stages of pregnancy, but also in the late stages. This procedure, known as partial birth abortion, takes us to a new low level of depravity. In one common late-term abortion procedure, the mother has her labor induced. Once her cervix is dilated enough, the physician performing the procedure uses forceps to pull the baby's body out of the mother, leaving the head just inside the birth canal. The abortionist then jams scissors into the base of the baby's skull, making a hole large enough to insert a suction tube. The child's brains are then sucked out, causing the skull to collapse. The dead baby is then removed. How in the world can we think that this is okay with God?

If I were to witness a person beating a two-year-old child to death, everyone would expect me to do something or at least say something to stop it. If it were the child's parent doing the beating and they said it was their "choice" to do it and that no one else had a right to tell them what to do, we would all balk at that answer—and rightly so. My point is, I believe that anyone who shares the view that life begins at conception has an obligation to speak out against these horrible and barbaric practices that we have allowed to take place for decades in our country.

In the book of Genesis when Cain killed his brother Abel, God said that Abel's blood was crying out to Him from the ground (see Genesis 4:10). Can you imagine what the sound of over 50 million unborn babies crying out from the ground must sound like in God's ears?

I am unapologetically pro-life, and I believe a baby should be considered a human being at conception. When we put a woman's right to "choose" over a baby's right to live, we create a culture of death and corruption in which individuals grow more and more desensitized and callous to the value of a precious life. There are a lot of women who received abortions out of ignorance because they were misinformed by a system that has made snatching a baby out of the womb into a multibillion-dollar industry. If you are a woman who has had an abortion, you do not need to live under condemnation. All you need to do is to ask God to forgive you, receive His forgiveness, and avoid repeating the same act again.

I encourage you to check out the issue of life for yourself. Go online and do some research on abortion procedures. A couple of good places to consider looking are the National Right to Life organization, www.nrlc.org, and Concerned Women for America, www.cwfa.org. Once you see some pictures of aborted babies, there will be no doubt in your mind that an aborted fetus is a life that should be valued.

(1) Grant, George: *Grand Illusions* (Brentwood, TN: Wolgemuth & Hyatt, 1988), pp. 98-99. (2) Grant, p. 59. (3) Drogin, Elasah, *Margaret Sanger, Father of Modern Society* (New Hope, KY: CUL Publications; [Rev.] edition, 1986) p. 33. (4) Alveda King stated this in an August 2009 televised interview with CBN (Christian Broadcasting Network).

CHAPTER 17

MURDER IN THE BLACK COMMUNITY

I have often wondered about the factors that allowed me to go so easily from a basically good life to a drug dealer and criminal. It took a lot of soul searching, but I believe that I came up with a few answers. I began to really look at the black community and what it has become. Why has our culture evolved into what seems to glorify many bad human traits? Our music and our neighborhoods exalt drug dealers and thugs over husbands, fathers, and factory workers. We call our women the "b" word and some of the men brag about being pimps and thugs. My grandparents' generation would never have bragged about being participants in such lowly ghetto activities. I remember using bad grammar as a young man and being told that I was not to act as though I was uneducated. Most of the people that I knew who used improper grammar did so because they didn't know any better, not because they thought it was something of honor as many do today.

    I am torn about the black community. I love my people but I sometimes hate what we have become. I have always admired the fact that even though we are a people that were stripped of our identity, robbed of our language, and taken from our original land through slavery, we still have survived as a people. We have excelled in many of the things that we have put our minds to. In the face of some of the worst demonstrations of cruelty and inhumanity, we have continually celebrated our humanness. Black people are passionate, creative, beautiful people. From the Moors of North Africa that had a heavy influence on Europe to the Ancient Egyptians that have astounded the rest of the world with their architecture and such, we have a rich history that has constantly affected and shaped the rest of the world.

    I obviously have a true love for black people, and I have been black all of my life! Many of my closest family members are black. My wife is black and so are my children. I grew up with black people. I believe that the descendants of Africa living in America are some of the greatest people on the earth. My reason for making these statements is so that people will realize that everything I say about black people is said out of love. I come across hard at times because I know how much potential we have. I have been able to accomplish things in my own life because I have been very frank with myself and sometimes pretty hard on myself. In Psalm 51 King David recognized that God requires us to have "truth in the inward parts"—meaning we have to be honest with ourselves first in order to live this life in the correct manner. I also make that statement because I may be accused of harboring some type of hatred towards my people. I am not one who is suffering from self-hate; I simply have an honest heartfelt desire for African Americans to reach the full potential that God has placed inside of them.

Seeking Answers About a Declining Culture

At one point I began to get disillusioned with my black culture. Around the same time that God began to heal me and to bring me back to wholeness, I started to look at the factors that allowed me to get so far away from the true path that God wants for us. I was a lawbreaker, a liar, a fornicator, a failure, a bad parent, and very selfish. No one would have mistaken me for a positive role model by any stretch of the imagination. When I looked at my overall life, I was very disappointed at what I had become. I was a bad example of a man and it only took me a few years to get to that place. I lacked integrity, accountability, and only cared about myself. I knew that this is not how God wanted anyone to live.

Unfortunately I was not an uncommon example of many men in our society. I am speaking more so in regards to the black community, but I must also say that these negative characteristics are all too common in people of all racial and ethnic backgrounds in our nation. The Bible talks about the dangers of calling evil good and calling good evil. It also demonstrates more than once what happens when humans seek evil instead of good. Turning away from the ways of God never ends up positive.

There are many different factors that I believe are prevalent in the demise of the morals of too many men in the black community, but I want to discuss a few that I think are the most prominent:

1. The psychological bonds of slavery
2. The Stockholm Syndrome (believing the lie)
3. Allowing hate to be your god

The Psychological Bonds of Slavery

The negative impact that slavery has had on the psyche of the black man truly should not be discounted or minimized in any way. It has been almost 150 years since the Emancipation Proclamation was signed, and there is still a negative residue left in the black community from the unjust institution of slavery. Many of the negative habits reflect what was instilled in the race during the more than 200 years that black people were enslaved here in the U.S.

Think about how the black male was used to breed with the black women to make the biggest and strongest children and to produce more good slaves. The men were not permitted to stay and help raise their own children, but were shipped from one master to the next like a piece of property. It is no wonder why some black men wear fathering many children to different women as a badge of honor. Also, think about the divisiveness that has plagued the black community over "light skinned" blacks versus "dark skinned" blacks. I believe these are direct results of the things that were impressed upon the race through the institution of slavery.

Many of the slave traders obviously developed intentional and systematic ways in which to keep the slaves in a form of mental bondage that was also intended to keep them enslaved for generations to come. It caused a breakdown of the family structure, fed distrust between blacks, and also fostered competition for the slave master's approval as a form of manipulation and control.

I don't believe that any of this should or can be used as an excuse for failing to achieve whatever you desire to accomplish. I write this simply to acknowledge that these things do exist and they have left a lasting impression in the black community. Knowledge is power, and once you have the knowledge that these societal concepts exist, then you also have the power to overcome them.

The Stockholm Syndrome—Believing the Lie

The Stockholm Syndrome is another concept that I want to point to as a reason for the decline in the black community. It is a psychological phenomenon in which people who are taken into captivity eventually begin to sympathize with and even defend their captors. The Stockholm Syndrome is named after a bank robbery in Stockholm, Sweden, in which several bank employees were held hostage in a bank vault from August 23-28, 1973. During this situation, the victims became emotionally attached to their kidnappers, rejected assistance from government officials, and even defended the robbers after the victims were freed six days later. I know that I am probably using this term rather loosely, but I believe this dynamic is similar to a mentality in our community. In essence, those who are being oppressed by social inequities or various forms of institutional racism begin to believe that somehow they deserve the injustices they endure. They accept their position, and the desire to rise above their circumstances disappears. They agree with society's stereotypical assessment of them, and they begin to act in accordance with the negative labels that have been placed upon them.

Think about the use of the "N" word. I stopped using that word around the same time that God convicted me of cursing. For many years I was a champion curser. I grew up in the hood where everybody thought it was cool to cuss. I played sports, which gives you an open outlet to express yourself through using profanity. I was in the military; in the military profanity is so natural that if you don't cuss, no one thinks you are serious about what you are saying. Also, the culture at large encourages bad language through the media and music.

The Bible tells us that blessings and curses are in the power of the tongue. In the biblical culture it was so important to realize the power of the spoken blessing that Esau even wanted to kill his brother Jacob for stealing his father's blessing that was meant for him.

Taking that into consideration, imagine how much damage we do to each other by calling ourselves pimps, thugs, the "N" word, the "B" word, or all the other horrible names we "affectionately" call each other. It is no wonder that some blacks perform so many self-deprecating acts, due to the ignorance and horrible influences that surround them. They have had an excessive amount of negative words and images imparted to them all their lives.

Many blacks have embraced all the harsh words or curses that have been spoken over them and their community, and we see the manifestation of it through high crime rates and high teenage pregnancy rates among inner-city blacks. It is a national tragedy that black-on-black crime ranks as the fourth leading cause of death for black men. In the age group of 15 to 34, black-on-black crime is the number one killer of black men. Some years ago I read statistics stating that one out of every four black males living in the inner city would die before reaching their twenty-fifth birthday. And most of the deaths would come at the hands of another person who looks just like them. According to the FBI's Uniform Crime Reporting Program, blacks accounted for 49 percent of all homicide victims in 2005. Statistics also indicate that black victims of homicide were more likely to be male (85 percent) and between ages 17 and 29 (51 percent).

The following statistics on African American males are from www.morehousemaleinitiative.com, a Morehouse College website dedicated to the study of "personal, academic, and leadership development of African American males." These statistics remind us that many of the problems in the black community are self-inflicted, while some are attributed to lack of opportunity and institutional racism:

- One in three black men between the ages of 20 and 29 is under correctional supervision or control.

- Blacks account for only 12 percent of the U.S. population but also account for 44 percent of all prisoners in the United States.

- The black male homicide rate is seven times the white male rate.

- The Justice Department estimates that one out of every 21 black men can expect to be murdered, a death rate double that of U.S. soldiers in World War II.

- Sixty-seven percent of black children (up from 17 percent in 1967) are born out of wedlock.

- White males with a high school diploma are just as likely to have a job, and tend to earn just as much as black males with college degrees.

- Light-skinned blacks have a 50 percent better chance of getting a job than dark-skinned blacks.

- Blacks are rejected twice as often for small business loans than whites of comparable credit.

Allowing Hate to Be Your God

The third point I want to discuss is what happens when we allow hate to become our god. I recall getting into a discussion about "Black Liberation Theology" in the fall of 2008. The discussion started from an article I wrote concerning then-Senator Barack Obama's former pastor, Jeremiah Wright. In the article I outlined the basic tenets of BLT and why I felt that it was not based on biblical concepts. The responses that I received and the open dialogues that came from it were eye-opening.

From a secular standpoint it is understandable why the world would say that it is OK to get revenge for wrongdoing and to dwell on past injustices perpetrated against us. The world would tell you it is OK to look out only for those people in your respective race and not care about individuals of other races. It is undeniable that the institutions of slavery and racism plagued us for hundreds of years, and the residue still haunts the black community even today. I have experienced both overt and covert racism in my life, and I know that I have been denied certain opportunities because of my race.

I sympathize with my father's generation and my grandfather's generation. They had to endure many things that no group of people should ever have to endure. I admire how they stood up in the face of being treated as less than human and lived normal lives for the most part. I think it would have been difficult to survive that type of inhumane treatment without going totally insane.

The beautiful thing about the God that I serve is that He promises that if I trust in him, not only will He exact vengeance against those who have wronged me, but He will also heal my heart. My responsibility is not to hold grudges and wish hurt on those who wronged me. My job is to release them through praying for them and loving them regardless. The first rule of thumb with God is that if you want something, you have to be willing to give the same thing out. Since we all need mercy and forgiveness, then we have to give it to others.

I believe that forgiving someone is one of the most difficult things to do. It is very easy to hold animosity against someone that you feel has wronged you. But God does not allow this. The biggest thing that Jesus did was to provide us with forgiveness, because we wronged God through sin and disobedience. Because He has freely given us the gift of forgiveness, we must give it to everyone else. Unforgiveness hinders our relationship with God. It also hinders us from having the proper relationship with our fellow man. But more importantly it hurts us. Unforgiveness is like a poison that eats away at our insides. It has been said that harboring unforgiveness towards someone is like drinking poison with the hope that the other person will die.

Because of all the pain and hurt that have been inflicted against African Americans for so many years, many people of color still harbor hatred against whites. You can see the effects of it in the community. As I stated earlier, blacks have internalized such negative feelings for so long that some of us subconsciously destroy ourselves. Most of the crimes perpetrated in the inner cities against blacks come at the hands of other blacks.

Think about the 1992 race riots related to the Rodney King incident in Los Angeles; the 1968 race riots in Washington, D.C., related to the assassination of Martin Luther King Jr.; the 1965 Watts riots in Los Angeles; and other riots throughout the years. Blacks were angry about injustices committed against them, so they tried to destroy communities. They looted stores and set houses on fire, showing their bitterness against whites by hurting themselves with cancerous hatred.

The Sure Path of Self-Destruction

I think about my years of rebellion and how I ultimately did more harm to myself than to anyone else. The drugs, the dealing, and the alcohol put me in danger more than anyone else could have. It was as if I wanted to kill myself but I was just too chicken to go ahead and do it, especially since killing yourself is still considered a sign of weakness in the 'hood.

That is what harboring hate does to a person. Some of us have gotten so overwhelmed with feeling hatred against whites that it causes us to fail. There are actually some young black kids in some schools that don't want to seem too smart because it makes them seem like they are acting "white." Acting real "ghetto" or just pretending like I don't care about anything are signs of the nonconforming attitude caused by hate. We ultimately cause our lives to fail because we don't want to seem to be conforming to the white man's world.

Dealing with a person who is controlled by hate can be a very difficult thing—especially when that person has been "disenfranchised." When a person begins to have hatred and combines that hatred with a feeling of hopelessness, it leads to the sure path of self-destruction. This reminds me of the time when I hung out with some real "gutter guys" who didn't fear going to jail. The environment that they came from seemed so treacherous that jail just didn't seem all that bad to them.

Materialism Is Not the Answer

Then there is the challenge of low self-worth in the black community that often leads to the path of materialism. And we see young people using material possessions as a false indicator of self-worth. They begin to feel as though having a fancy car, expensive clothes, and more money determines whether or not they are somebody in life. Since many young people from the inner city have been given the impression that they can never accumulate such things by legitimate means, they pursue illegitimate shortcuts in their quest for "success."

It is a tough sell to tell a young black boy from the 'hood that if he works hard, gets good grades, and keeps himself clean, he can become wealthy in a legitimate way. Many of them have never seen or personally met anyone financially independent who looks like them or has come from their neighborhood. As a matter of fact, in some neighborhoods, they don't even see many men who live long lives. In those situations, many adopt the mind-set to get all they can as quickly and as easily as possible through illicit affairs such as drug dealing or robbery.

A Self-Deprecating Culture

The Notorious B.I.G. had a song about wealth that states: "Either you're slingin' crack rock or you got a wicked jump shot." The rapper 50 Cent had a very popular CD entitled *Get Rich or Die Tryin'*. These themes and much more of popular black culture glorify a lifestyle of wealth over character or morality. This mentality suggests that in order for you to gain wealth you must either become a talented rapper, you must grow to be 6'8" and play in the NBA, or you must become a street hustler. Self-hate has brought many of us in the black community to the point of feeling as though the only self-worth we will have is through excessive material gain. We perpetuate this sentiment through our culture, our music, and our behaviors.

When radio personality Don Imus called the Rutgers women's college basketball team "nappy-headed hos" in 2007, it understandably sparked major controversy. When he said it, he did it in the form of a joke. It was a slang term that is used in this day and age more than it should be. I was at home talking with my wife shortly after that incident, and for effect I said "I am not mad at Imus; maybe he didn't know any better." Without any words, her look told me that she disagreed with me. I then turned the television channel to BET and there were young black women dressed very scantily and they were dancing on table tops. Watching all this was a group of young black men, covered with tattoos, draped in gold chains and gold teeth, throwing money at the girls and pouring expensive champagne on the floor. Obviously I knew Imus was totally wrong for what he said. But my point is that if we treat our young women like strippers and allow them to be disrespected by us, then how can we expect anyone else to respect them?

Those young women—whom the music and videos treat as though their butts and breasts give them value—are daughters, sisters, wives, or someone's mother. We will never have the respect that we need or desire as long as we allow women in general to be treated simply as objects for men to lust after.

As a Christian, I have come to the realization that my self-worth comes from God. God created me intentionally the way I am. He implanted destiny in each one of us, and He gave each and every one of us the talent and the ability to achieve great things. I came to the conclusion that sexual prowess, materialism, or rebelling in excess is not the path to choose. Living my life in agreement with what God calls me to is the only truly honorable thing in life.

Being married and raising godly children is one of the most honorable things a man can do. Being sexually pure or saving yourself for your spouse is a noble thing to accomplish. Getting educated while being able to articulate your thoughts and feelings without cursing or using bad language is also the type of thing that leaves a legacy for your children and your community. It should be considered a greater accomplishment to achieve a worthwhile education and to make a positive difference in the world than to own a fleet of luxury cars. A school teacher, a fireman, a community businessman, or a police officer is much more of a hero than a drug dealer or a man with multiple children and multiple women. Unfortunately, the current culture does too much to uphold the bad and ignore the good.

I cannot honestly say that this is simply the black community's problem, because our nation has been experiencing a dramatic increase in moral decay across the board—regardless of race. But in this chapter I am primarily addressing the serious problems in the black community.

This country's moral decline is also becoming very evident based on the amazingly low moral values that are reflected in popular entertainment. While flipping through the cable channels I am alarmed at how horribly degrading and immoral many of the shows have become. On networks like BET, so many videos are about sex, drugs, and materialism. The women act like strippers—mere sex objects—and the men wave wads of cash, showing off massive amounts of tattoos. And everyone has a very expensive car and a mansion. Is that the extent of what we are about?

Just think about shows like the Sopranos that made a Mafia crime family look like the all-American family. It was a show about a crime family that did illegal activity and murdered people, yet they were treated like heroes. This series was considered one of the best shows of all time. There are also shows on cable television about a friendly serial killer and a male prostitute that is well endowed. This is what we call entertainment.

We meditate on corrupt things day and night. We focus on sexuality, materialism, and accepting bad choices. We glorify stars that jump from one relationship to another. We think it is chic for women and men to be considered bisexual. We see the negative fruit of that meditation coming out in the lives of those that focus on them. For as he thinks in his heart, so is he (Proverbs 23:7 NKJV).

The problem with all this is that it seems to have hit the black community the worst. We still have the lowest life expectancy in the country. Our average household income is still well below that of whites. We also by far are incarcerated at an alarmingly high rate in comparison to whites. And 35 percent of all abortions are done on African American women even though we make up only about 12.5 percent of the population. The last time I checked, the statistics showed that as many as 9,000 African Americans are murdered annually in the United States, and 93 percent of these murders are perpetrated by other blacks. If that is not a problem then what would you call it?

Just as these statistics are disturbing, it is also disturbing to see some of the high-profile black leaders constantly using the race card to indict white people, while failing to utilize their influential platforms to properly address the self-destructing trend of murder in the black community that is caused by black-on-black crime.

True Identity, Forgiveness, and Full Responsibility

There is a hope for the better tomorrow that God has promised. The first thing we have to do is to take full responsibility for our own failures in the black community, while forgiving those who have wronged us. Once you forgive others and take full responsibility for your own actions, it frees you from the heavy burden of anger and hatred. We have to love others in order for us to love ourselves. Forgiving people means that you cannot hold onto the burden of hatred towards them, no matter what they have done. It does not mean that you ignore mistreatment, racism, and unfair practices; it just means that you cannot harbor hatred or anger against the perpetrators. The cancer of bitterness or hatred will keep you in bondage and will also prevent you from growing or maturing as a person. In Matthew 6:15 Jesus said, "But if ye forgive not men their trespasses, neither will your Father forgive your trespasses."

The next step is to accept that our identity comes from God and not man, realizing that we are precious creations of the Heavenly Father. God created each of us intentionally as we are. He has wonderful plans for your life, and therefore you must shun the world's definition of value. Your value is great in the kingdom of God, and no material possessions or man-given status can replace the identity that we have as God's people.

I must also acknowledge that once I am saved and redeemed through the blood of Christ, then my kingdom identity takes precedence over my earthly identity. The family of God takes priority over the biological family that I was born into. I see too many black people allowing their blackness to be more important than their identity in Christ. Putting culture above Christ keeps some of us in bondage, because many cultural habits contradict God's Word. Unfortunately, many Christians from all races place their cultural heritage or race above God's Word.

CHOOSING LIFE OVER DEATH

The final and most important point to make is about choices. No matter what your past is, you can choose to do the right thing. We know that there is a right way to live, yet many of us choose the wrong path and wonder why we have such distress in our lives. I consciously made wrong choices in my life. I knew it was wrong to sleep around, yet I did it because it felt good. The results were a divorce, a fractured family, and a host of other negative consequences. I knew it was right to stay away from drugs, but I used them anyway. I recognize that bad choices caused me to end up in a bad place, until I finally found redemption through the Lord.

I see many people in our communities making bad choices. There are parents who don't want to discipline their children and then wonder why they end up in jail. We glamorize sexual promiscuity over purity and holiness, yet we wonder why there is such a high level of unwed pregnancies, sexually transmitted diseases, and broken relationships along with a high abortion rate in the African American community. When you start out on the wrong path, you will end up in places you do not want to be.

You have a choice. Right choices bring us blessings, peace, and prosperity. Once we start making right choices, then God will strengthen us to keep making the right choices. The right choices are often hard to make, but they save us a lifetime of despair and hurt that bring negative consequences on ourselves, our children, and other loved ones. If you are not sure what choices to make, I would like to suggest a great book for you to read and apply to your life—the Holy Bible!

Deuteronomy 30:19 declares, "I call heaven and earth to witness this day against you that I have set before you life and death, the blessings and the curses; therefore choose life, that you and your descendants may live (AMP)."

Chapter 18

Justice Is the Main Issue

The Trayvon Martin Tragedy

The killing of Trayvon Martin is an example of how issues of race and politics can distort the thinking of individuals on both sides of the political aisle if we fail to keep the focus on the main issue. And in the Trayvon Martin case, the main issue should be *justice* rather than race or politics. The case has stirred up Sanford, Florida, the Orlando suburb where 17-year-old Trayvon was shot to death on February 26, 2012, by George Zimmerman, a 28-year-old neighborhood watch volunteer who became alarmed when he spotted Trayvon walking through the gated condominium complex that he patrolled. A national outcry erupted due to the fact that Zimmerman hadn't been arrested weeks after the murder, claiming self-defense under Florida's Stand Your Ground law or the Justifiable Use of Force statute.

Although millions of people are attributing the tragedy to racial prejudice, the main issue here is not whether or not George Zimmerman, the son of a white father and Hispanic mother, was motivated by racism in the shooting of Trayvon Martin. Neither is the main issue whether or not Trayvon Martin, the 17-year-old black kid, was being racially profiled by Zimmerman. The latter are possibilities worth considering, but the main issue is not related to race. And we should also avoid being distracted from the main issue due to the misuse of the race card by some of the prominent black leaders or the liberal media in their attempts to have Zimmerman arrested immediately.

The main issue should be to seek justice in a case where a gun-carrying neighborhood watch volunteer seemed to act irresponsibly in his quest to protect his community. As he drove his car through the Retreat at Twin Lakes townhouse complex while wearing a holstered Kel Tek 9mm semiautomatic handgun, the saga began when Zimmerman got out of his vehicle and pursued Trayvon on foot because he thought the kid looked suspicious. Zimmerman did have a concealed weapon permit.

While simply walking from the store to the home of his father's fiancée with a can of Arizona iced tea and a bag of Skittles candy, Trayvon Martin, a young, unarmed black kid, was followed by a man he did not know who perhaps frightened or annoyed him. Trayvon's girlfriend said he called her on his cell phone while he was being stalked by Zimmerman, worried because a strange man was following him. She told him to run away. A few minutes later, neighbors heard a scuffle and a shot, and 17-year-old Trayvon was dead. When Zimmerman called 911 shortly before the shooting occurred, even the 911 dispatcher advised the neighborhood watch volunteer that it was not a good idea to follow the kid, telling him "We don't need you to do that."

Just the Facts Please

As of this writing, there are still discrepancies regarding the facts in terms of not being sure about who threw the first punch during the altercation or not being sure if Zimmerman was actually being beat up by the kid. That said, there seems to be enough information to at least determine that Zimmerman provoked the situation and was a bit reckless in carrying a gun while stalking the kid who apparently was not causing any problems. Following a person with a firearm is the type of thing that only a trained and fully authorized police officer should be doing when there is reason to do so.

Why have some of the conservative talk show hosts decreed that there is a "rush to judgment" simply because the parents or Trayvon and some of the civil rights leaders or lawyers have requested that Zimmerman be arrested immediately? One conservative talk show host even challenged Martin family lawyer Jasmine Rand to repudiate the request of certain civil rights leaders who were vying for Zimmerman's immediate arrest. To see this conservative talk show host acting as if the shooter was being treated in an unfair manner seemed like a "rush to judgment" at the other extreme.

Trayvon's father, Mr. Tracy Martin, and his mother, Sybrina Fulton, shared their hearts at rallies around the country, requesting that Zimmerman be arrested. At one particular rally, family attorney Benjamin Crump made it clear that Trayvon's parents "are not asking for an eye for an eye. They just want justice." At a New York rally held in March 2012, Trayvon's mother proclaimed, "This is not about a black and white thing. This is about a right and wrong thing,"

During media appearances and rallies, Trayvon's mother has simply stated that she felt that there was enough evidence to arrest George Zimmerman right away and he can later have his day in court to get a fair trial before a judge and jury. What is so repulsive or outrageous about a broken-hearted mother who simply wanted to know why her unarmed son could be shot dead while the person who did it is still a free man in spite of his apparent recklessness? This has less to do with race and more to do with justice. Even if there is "another side of the story" and even if Trayvon was not the "perfect kid," it does not seem that it is a "rush to judgment" to feel that Zimmerman should have been arrested immediately. Based on various media reports, there seems to be sufficient evidence to prove that neither George Zimmerman nor Trayvon Martin were choirboys. But the burden of proof should be on triggerman George Zimmerman because he is the one who initiated this incident in a rather careless and irresponsible manner. And it is not difficult for a rational individual of any race to understand why Trayvon Martin's parents wanted Zimmerman arrested immediately.

He Said She Said

Upon observing statements from various witnesses or neighbors, it seems evident that this incident might not be as clear-cut as some would make it out to be. Reportedly, just within the past year there were several crimes—mostly robberies and thefts—that took place in Zimmerman's neighborhood. And in a Miami Herald interview, neighbor Ibrahim Rashada, a black man, indicated that the perpetrators of the crimes were usually black. This information helps us to understand why Zimmerman might have been a bit zealous in his quest to follow Trayvon, with the simple intent of protecting his community. This does not necessarily make Zimmerman a racist or a racial profiler. Concerning witnesses, some seem to be implying that Zimmerman acted in self-defense, while others seem to be implying that he had no valid reason to shoot Martin. One particular witness allegedly stated that George Zimmerman was on the ground screaming and yelling for help while Trayvon Martin was on top of him, punching him and slamming his head to the ground. Reportedly, police also arrived to find Zimmerman with blood on his face and his head. It has also been reported that Zimmerman had a broken nose. Are all of the witnesses reporting the facts truthfully? Are the police reporting all of the facts truthfully? Unfortunately, some of the individuals on the Sanford police force seemed biased and indifferent and failed to conduct a solid investigation from the very beginning.

An April 7, 2012, Miami Herald article also reports that two witnesses have said they saw the encounter, but their stories contradict each other. "One man interviewed by a local Fox news station, who asked to be identified only as John, said he saw the man wearing a red jacket—Zimmerman—on the ground, being beaten by someone on top of him—Trayvon," wrote Frances Robles. "But last week another unidentified man told CNN that he saw a larger man on top and a boy underneath. There wasn't much movement, he said."

Mary Cutcher, a witness who resides in Zimmerman's gated community, heard the neighborhood watch volunteer shoot 17-year-old Trayvon Martin in her backyard while she was in her home with her roommate. Sanford police said that shooter George Zimmerman claimed self-defense in the killing. But in an interview conducted by Central Florida's WFTV reporter Daralene Jones, Mary Cutcher stated that she feels the person crying for help was Trayvon. She also said that even if Martin got the best of Zimmerman, it's no excuse to kill an unarmed teenager who is half his size. "I assumed he's going to be arrested. Common sense will tell you, and he wasn't," Cutcher said, referring to Zimmerman.

In the WFTV interview, Cutcher shared her account of what happened when she and her roommate approached Zimmerman after hearing the gunshot: "We said, 'Is everything OK? And he just looked at us. Selma [another witness] asked him again, "What's up, what's going on, everything OK? And he just said, 'Call the police,' kind of nonchalantly, kind of like, 'Leave me alone,'" Cutcher said.

According to a partial police report, the Sanford police took a statement from Cutcher and five other witnesses. Cutcher said the statement police took from her was very short and that police never questioned her in detail until after she tried to reach them on several occasions.

"Blew us off, and I called him back again and I said, 'I know this was not self-defense. There was no punching, no hitting going on at the time, no wrestling,'" Cutcher said. But the Sanford Police Department denied the claims that her witness testimony was ignored, stating that there were some inconsistencies with her statement and what was aired on the news report.

Cutcher told the WFTV reporter that she believes whatever confrontation there was, it ended before they got to her backyard. She also said she believes Zimmerman continued to chase Martin as he tried to get home. It is also relevant to point out that although Mary Cutcher did not witness everything, she is a white woman who admitted to being afraid to come forward at first. But she apparently came forward because she is interested in justice being served.

Contrary to what Mary Cutcher believes about Zimmerman continuing to chase Trayvon, the Miami Herald reports that Zimmerman told police that Trayvon approached him from behind as he was returning to his car, knocked him to the ground with a punch to the nose, then, he says, Trayvon started punching him and slamming his head on the concrete.

In sharing his son's account to an Orlando TV station, George Zimmerman's father Robert, a magistrate in the Virginia court system from 2000 until 2006, stated that as his son was being beaten the gun his son kept in a holster on his waist was exposed. The father claimed that Trayvon continued to beat his son George and also told his son that he was going to die. "At some point, George pulled his pistol; and did what he did," Robert Zimmerman said.

On the 911 recorded call, George Zimmerman also says that it was him screaming for help as he was being attacked by Trayvon Martin. Some voice analysts, however, say that they believe it was Trayvon Martin who was yelling for help. Who was screaming for help? From my vantage point, even if Zimmerman was the one yelling for help, this still does not exonerate him because you could argue that the altercation was started in the first place due to Zimmerman's reckless and unwise actions.

Trayvon Martin's girlfriend, who chose to remain anonymous, spoke to ABC News about her last conversation with Trayvon. She reported that he actually called her on his cell phone as he was being chased by Zimmerman. "He said this man was watching him so he put his hoodie on," she said to ABC News. She went on to explain that suddenly Trayvon was confronted by Zimmerman. "Trayvon said, 'What are you following me for?' Then the man said 'What you doing around here?' Then somebody pushed Trayvon 'cause the headset just fell." Trayvon's girlfriend says the line then went dead. Shortly thereafter, Zimmerman shot Martin.

Since the accounts or opinions from the witnesses differ, the best thing to do is to stick to the simple facts that we are sure about. Even though witness Mary Cutcher obviously cannot know the whole story, what she experienced perhaps provides evidence that some of the individuals on the police force who did not return her calls were as careless in their investigation as Zimmerman was in initiating the events that led him to shoot this unarmed kid. At the very least, it shows that there was perhaps an indifference towards the killing of this unarmed black kid even among certain individuals on the police force.

A Rush to Judgment?

Quite frankly, it was rather disheartening to see some of our prominent conservative talk show hosts go the extra mile to prove that many people were "rushing to judgment" against the shooter when these talk show hosts should have been focusing on the concept that, based on the facts that we do have, it is not unreasonable for a heart-broken mother and father to request the immediate arrest of the man who killed their unarmed son.

Truly, it is a sad commentary that on broadcasts and blogs all across the nation, blacks and whites are spewing venom and attacking one another, making this into a race war. I personally do not like it when the national media or certain prominent leaders misuse the race card in a case like this. This misuse of the race card, however, does not nullify the possibility that racism might very well have played a part in this tragic situation—especially from the standpoint of the indifference or negligence displayed by some of the Sanford law enforcement members. Unfortunately, some of our conservative talk show hosts seem to be trying too hard to prove that race is no longer a real issue in America. And in their attempt to do so, they sometimes make themselves look like racists. The lesson to be learned is that in our efforts to combat those who misuse the race card, we should be careful not to deny that racism is still a legitimate problem that still rears its ugly head at times in our great country. When conservatives are not willing to admit this, they simply appear to give more credence to the exaggerated claims of some of the "race-baiters" who have made a handsome living from the misuse of the race card. This ultimately hurts the cause of those who want to positively influence the culture with conservative values.

Some of my fellow conservative leaders whom I have a lot of respect for seem to be outraged by the fact that some of the "race-baiters" are making the Trayvon Martin case too much about race and politics. Obviously, these "race-baiters" should not try to take the law into their own hands, inciting hateful riots or other types of lawless activities. But instead of just showing selective outrage about the "race-baiters," I think some of my conservative colleagues need to put themselves in the shoes of the parents of Trayvon. They would then be more outraged about the fact that two broken-hearted parents are mourning the death of a son who would still be with us if a gun-toting neighborhood watch volunteer would have acted more responsibly. My plea to some of our well-meaning black and white conservatives is *please do not make yourselves look obstinate and insensitive with your unbalanced attempts to be "fair and balanced."*

During Sean Hannity's Great American Panel segment, on a March 29, 2012, edition of the Sean Hannity Show, Hannity started addressing the Trayvon Martin case by mentioning that there is such a rush to judgment against Zimmerman by the New Black Panthers who are putting a bounty on his head and also by people like Spike Lee who tried to expose Zimmerman's address by re-tweeting it.

Guest panelist Deirdre Imus, wife of syndicated radio personality Don Imus, stopped Hannity in his tracks and challenged him, saying "OK Sean, you're jumping way ahead here…What would you do if this was your kid? Wouldn't you want that person to be arrested and put through the court system? If this was my child, I want him arrested."

Hannity responded to Deirdre's remarks by mentioning that Zimmerman had lacerations and an eyewitness who saw Trayvon on top of him beating him up, and Zimmerman had a broken nose.

"How do you know all this?" Deirdre Imus refuted.

"We have eyewitnesses," Hannity responded.

Deirdre continued to challenge Hannity, asking him *how did he know all this and how did he know that the eyewitnesses were telling the truth*?

Throughout the discourse, Deirdre Imus firmly stood her ground and pointed out that we should let a jury determine these things because that's what court is for.

In reference to those who seemed to be going the extra mile to share unsubstantiated information in defense of Zimmerman, Deirdre Imus remarked, "This is unbelievable, everybody is saying all this," while she and one other panelist agreed that based on the facts we do have, the police should arrest Zimmerman and then allow him to have his day in court.

Just a few seconds before Hannity had to close the program, Deirdre challenged Hannity, slipping in one final remark: "Sean, this is thirty-three or [thirty] four days later. Again, if this was your kid?"

Suddenly time ran out and Hannity could not respond. What a fitting way for a program to end—"If this was your kid?" I think Deirdre Imus hit the nail right on the head and did an excellent job in sticking to the simple need for justice based on the facts available at that point and time.

As much as I respect Sean Hannity, I think he missed it on this issue. And Deirdre Imus was right on target. I am sure Hannity had good intentions in his attempt to keep people from "rushing to judgment," but he was jumping way ahead just as Deirdre implied. Obviously the New Black Panthers and Spike Lee should not be taking matters into their own hands. But the focus should not be on the New Black Panthers and Spike Lee. Instead of focusing too much on how others are reacting to the tragedy, the main focus should be to seek justice in a case where an unarmed kid was shot to death.

In Hannity's "fair and balanced" attempt to expose the flaws of some left-wingers who are "rushing to judgment" against Zimmerman, could it be that Hannity was giving Zimmerman and his defenders too much credibility—which in and of itself is a "rush to judgment"? With the evidence we have so far, why should the dead kid who cannot speak for himself be on trial, while the instigator who stalked and shot the unarmed kid with a loaded gun is portrayed as a credible victim when he has every reason in the world to stretch the truth in order to save his own neck? Talk about a rush to judgment! Just as many on the far left are biased and unbalanced in their reporting of these highly charged issues; where is the balance in this type of reporting?

On The O'Reilly Factor, which aired right before Sean Hannity's show on March 29, 2012, Trayvon Martin family lawyer Benjamin Crump rightly stated that "There is a big difference between an arrest and a conviction." In other words, it is sensible to want Zimmerman to have a fair trial with an opportunity to be exonerated in a court of law if he is truly not guilty of any wrongdoing. Until a trial takes place, however, it is not a "rush to judgment" for the parents to want to see Zimmerman arrested based on the facts available at the point of the O'Reilly Factor interview. We know for a fact that the gun-toting Zimmerman was not an authorized police officer, and his unwise act of stalking a kid led to a confrontation and shooting of a 17-year-old who was only armed with a can of Arizona iced tea and a bag of Skittles candy.

Does Race Really Matter?

We must all look beyond the anger and accusations long enough to understand that what happened is a real tragedy that has negatively impacted the lives of Trayvon Martin and his family along with George Zimmerman and his family. As we rightly desire true justice, we should still realize that both of these families need our prayers in the midst of such a tragedy that only God can help them through.

Based on the information that we do have so far, it is difficult to prove that Zimmerman was motivated by racial hatred in the killing of Trayvon Martin. George Zimmerman apparently had some close black friends, and it is reported that he tutored black kids on a volunteer basis. Based on the excessive amount of calls on record that he made to the police in his attempt to protect the neighborhood over the past several months, Zimmerman, a married insurance underwriter who studied criminal justice at Seminole State College, was apparently an overzealous, wanna-be cop who was over-the-top in his quest to protect his neighborhood. Consequently, all of the individuals of all races who are pressing to have him arrested because they feel he is a racist who maliciously killed a helpless black kid in cold blood are inciting people unnecessarily and setting up a riotous atmosphere. At the other extreme, as previously pointed out, there are some so-called conservative individuals and media personalities who have gone out of their way to try to bring out the point that perhaps Zimmerman shouldn't be arrested because he was possibly defending himself against an angry, murderous black youth who was going to beat him to death with his bare hands or kill Zimmerman with his own gun.

Even if Trayvon Martin was kicking Zimmerman's butt, I think it is very unfair and insensitive for people to make the above assessment of a kid who is not alive to defend himself for the following two primary reasons.

Reason number one: Since Trayvon did not know that Zimmerman was a neighborhood watch volunteer, Trayvon could have been simply "standing his ground" and reacting out of fear, if indeed he was verbally threatening and physically beating up Zimmerman, a stranger who was stalking him with a gun. This leads to the following simple fact; if Zimmerman was not stalking an unarmed kid with a gun in the first place, the tragic killing would have never occurred.

Reason number two: Even if the unarmed Trayvon was playing tough by threatening Zimmerman and kicking his butt, it is very difficult to prove that the unarmed kid actually had the intent or ability to kill this grown man with his bare hands or take his gun and kill him. Should law enforcement take the word of the man who pulled the trigger over the unarmed kid who is no longer around to tell his side of the story?

The aforementioned two reasons alone were enough to arrest—but not necessarily convict—Zimmerman immediately. Then he could have his day in court and get the chance to exonerate himself in front of a judge and jury. In other words, instead of focusing on a lot of speculative issues like whether or not this was a racially motivated hate crime or whether or not Trayvon intended to kill Zimmerman, the focus should be on the simple facts. It is a fact that Trayvon Martin was simply coming from the store and heading to the house of his father's fiancée with a can of Arizona iced tea and a bag of Skittles in his hand. It is a fact—validated by the recorded 911 call—that George Zimmerman accused Trayvon of looking suspicious, admitted to following him, and was told "We don't need you to do that" by the 911 operator. It is a fact that George Zimmerman admitted to pulling the trigger on the gun that killed the unarmed Trayvon Martin, claiming that he did it in self-defense because his life was threatened (which at this point is not a proven fact). It is a fact that Trayvon Martin would not have been shot and killed by Zimmerman if the watch volunteer would not have initiated the incident by following the kid with a loaded gun. It is a fact that Zimmerman walked around the neighborhood with a loaded gun but was not an authorized and identifiable police officer with a uniform or a badge. And based on these simple facts alone, it is not hard to understand why Trayvon Martin family members and millions of others called for the immediate arrest of George Zimmerman and have accused the Sanford Police Department of conducting a shabby and biased investigation. Although the primary focus of this investigation should not be about race, it does make one wonder if Zimmerman was let off the hook so quickly because it was "just another angry and dangerous black kid that he shot and killed."

According to ABC News, multiple sources told them that the lead homicide investigator in the shooting of unarmed teenager Trayvon Martin recommended that neighborhood watch volunteer George Zimmerman be charged with manslaughter the night of the shooting. According to the article on the ABC news website, Sanford lead investigator Chris Serino was instructed not to press charges against Zimmerman because the state attorney's office headed by Norman Wolfinger determined there wasn't enough evidence to lead to a conviction, the sources told ABC News. Based on the controversy that erupted over the handling of this case, Sanford Police Chief Bill Lee also "temporarily" stepped down on March 22, 2012, and eventually was terminated.

"Race Matters. That is Reality." That's the title of an April 6, 2012, article Geraldo Rivera wrote for the Fox News Latino website, where he stated:

> Because George Zimmerman has not been arrested, the Trayvon Martin case continues to generate enormous attention and outrage. Half the nation, generally younger and more minority, believes a grave injustice has been done. The other half, generally older and whiter, believes that a mob led by professional agitators is trying to railroad Zimmerman for their own political purposes. The case has fractured the country along the undeniable racial fault line that is always there, but is most apparent in charged cases like this and Rodney King, Amadou Diallo, Ramarley Graham, Sean Bell and a hundred others.
>
> What almost everyone agrees on, is that had the roles in the Trayvon case been reversed, and had the shooter been the black kid and the dead victim the white guy, there would have been an arrest for manslaughter or even murder on the spot. That dichotomy is as deplorable as it is undeniable. Given the evidence and the outrage, Zimmerman will inevitably, if not imminently, be arrested and charged.

Rightly so, Geraldo Rivera did not imply in his article that there is proof that George Zimmerman, a man of white and Hispanic heritage, was filled with racism against blacks when he shot Trayvon Martin. Rivera pointed out that the main point which should not be obscured "is that an unarmed kid was killed by an armed civilian who had no business behaving like super cop."

"Trayvon Martin Case: Does Race Play a Role, Though Zimmerman's Not White?" This was the title of another Fox News Latino website article written on March 21, 2012, by Chantilly Patiño. Patiño says that she believes race does play a role because "Trayvon Martin wasn't committing a crime when he was pursued. Then there is the issue of a young boy's death that has not been fully investigated. Why wasn't the investigation thoroughly conducted? Why was Trayvon Martin tested for drugs and alcohol following his death, while Zimmerman (the shooter) was not?"

Patiño believes that more than likely racial privilege and criminal justice community connections played a large role in Zimmerman's release, and that these potential biases were overlooked by Sanford officials. The fact is that George Zimmerman, an aspiring law enforcement officer who studied criminal justice at Seminole State College, became somewhat of an ally to the Sanford Police Department. He also has a white father who was a magistrate in the Virginia court system. That is, he was a judicial officer. Although the Sanford Police have claimed that a "fair and impartial investigation" was conducted, Patiño disputes their claim and asks the question: "Now, how could that be, when a killer is walking free and the evidence clearly shows that Zimmerman pursued and killed an innocent teen?"

Justice Is What Matters Most

Franklin Graham was on point when, in an April 2012 Huffington Post article titled "When the NAACP Came to Lunch" he wrote:

> After speaking about the religiously motivated slaughter in Sudan over the past decade, I had to admit I didn't know much about the cold killing of an unarmed teenager in Florida last month. I do now, and hope and pray a thorough investigation will resolve what went wrong during a rainy-night Neighborhood Watch patrol—and that justice will carry the day. It will likely take more time and information to determine if there was a racial injustice that February 26 night, but it takes no time to conclude there was an injustice, one that snuffed out the earthly life of Trayvon after 17 short years.

Making reference to an enlightening meeting he had with twenty NAACP representatives at the Billy Graham Library in Charlotte, N.C., Rev. Franklin Graham also wrote:

> I expressed outrage at the killing of Christians in South Sudan; they were indignant about the killing of Trayvon

Martin in Sanford, Fla. I said I couldn't support a candidate of any party who supported the right to abortion and same-sex marriage; they urged white evangelicals to expand our objection to these two issues to include opposition to injustice, racism, the plight of the poor, and other very real social problems."

Graham also pointed out that while the meeting with the NAACP representatives wasn't exactly a "Sunday picnic," it was a remarkable and important experience that helped him to better understand areas where they differed and agreed, along with a commitment to work together on important challenges in our country.

I salute the Rev. Franklin Graham in his efforts to have intelligent dialogue with individuals of another race—dialogue that focuses on the issue of what it takes to really achieve true justice for all of God's children in all types of circumstances.

Los Angeles Times writer Sandy Banks, in her March 24, 2012, article titled "Anger Over Trayvon Martin's Slaying Transcends the Issue of Race," wrote about the public outcry related to the Trayvon Martin case. "It's a response that seems to transcend race and age and politics," she said. "Locally, it even had KFI-AM radio talk show hosts John Kobylt and Ken Chiampou lining up on the same side as the Rev. Al Sharpton, their perpetual target." Banks was correct in stating that "the furor is not just about skin color, it's about justice."

More than six weeks after the death of Trayvon Martin, on April 11, 2012, special prosecutor Angela Corey made the announcement that a second-degree-murder charge was filed and George Zimmerman was arrested for the killing of Trayvon Martin. Many in the black community feared that Corey, a white prosecutor, would not file charges against Zimmerman due to racial bias. Now that the charges have been filed, there are many in the white community accusing Corey of filing the charges because she caved in to public pressure. Angela Corey was actually selected for the case because she has an iron-clad reputation as a tough prosecutor who does not fold under pressure from public opinion. It is unfortunate that this case has been so racially charged and politicized that millions of people are missing the point that the focus should always be on the simple facts. And so far, there are enough facts to justify the arrest of George Zimmerman. Why then do some polls suggest that the overwhelming majority of blacks believe that Zimmerman is guilty of wrongdoing while the overwhelming majority of whites believe he is not? A simple answer to this question is that a lot of Americans (black, white, and other) are still racially biased. In the case of Trayvon Martin, a lot of blacks are making the mistake of making it too much of a racial issue and decreeing that this is definitely a racially motivated hate crime. On the other hand, a lot of whites are making it too much of a racial or political issue, decreeing that Zimmerman is an innocent man being "lynched" by race-baiters and far-left liberals. At both extremes, a lot of whites and blacks are race-baiting or politicizing this case instead of focusing on the basic facts as outlined in this chapter. Whether or not one agrees with the second-degree-murder charge, the basic facts seem to point out that Zimmerman should have definitely been charged with something and arrested.

On the day of the arrest during an April 11, 2012, "On The Record With Greta Van Susteren" Fox News program segment, criminal defense attorney Ted Williams made a valid point when he said "I think it's a great day, specifically for the mother and father. I got to tell you, Greta, as a black man who has followed this case, it is my firm belief that if it would have been Zimmerman lying down on that ground and Trayvon Martin would have been standing over him, we would not have to be here tonight. There would have actually been an arrest."

"There should have been justice a lot faster," Greta responded.

"Absolutely. And I think the police department down there screwed this case up," commented attorney Ted Williams.

During the interview on Greta Van Susteren's program, another criminal defense attorney, Bernie Grimm, stated that he never had a homicide in 25 years where his client got his gun back.

Attorney Williams replied, "Not only did he get the gun back, but they didn't take his clothes that night."

This leads us to believe that if certain individuals on the Sanford police department would have conducted the investigation properly, it would have never gotten to the point where there needed to be a media circus before Zimmerman got arrested.

Following the arrest, Martin family attorney Benjamin Crump says that he and the parents of Trayvon Martin were very disappointed that Zimmerman was released on bond on April 23, 2012—and a relatively low bond of $150,000 at that. Zimmerman had to put up 10 percent, or $15,000, to make bail while he awaited trial on the second-degree murder charge.

The family was also outraged that Zimmerman did not disclose the fact that he had received about $135,000 from various donors through his website's PayPal account before the bond hearing.

Prosecutors had asked for a bond of $1 million, but Judge Kenneth Lester Jr. made it $150,000 after Zimmerman's attorney, Mark O'Mara, said his client was "financially indigent," in arguing for a lower bail. The Zimmerman family also testified that they did not have the resources necessary to pay the cost of a higher bail.

At the April 21, 2012, bond hearing, George Zimmerman surprised many when he apologized to Trayvon's parents, saying, "I wanted to say I am sorry for the loss of your son. I did not know how old he was. I thought he was a little bit younger than I am, and I did not know if he was armed or not."

Attorney Crump felt that the apology was disingenuous and dishonest, especially since the 911 tape from the night of the killing recorded Zimmerman saying that Trayvon Martin looked like a teenager, contradicting the 28-year-old Zimmerman's bond hearing statement that "I thought he was a little bit younger than I am."

Attorney Benjamin Crump further stated that Zimmerman's failure to reveal that he had the money shows that he is being dishonest.

"If his testimony at the bond hearing is any indication of what is to come, then the lying has already begun," Crump said. "This is going to say a lot about whether Trayvon Martin can get a fair trial," he told CNN's Erin Burnett. "If he [Lester] doesn't revoke his bond, the court should severely sanction him so George Zimmerman understands you cannot lie to the court."

On Friday, June 1, 2012, Circuit Court Judge Kenneth Lester revoked George Zimmerman's bond and ordered him back to jail within 48 hours after prosecutors showed he and his wife Shellie Zimmerman had lied about his personal finances during his original bond hearing in late April. The judge scolded Zimmerman, saying he does not properly respect the law.

Based on a conversation between George Zimmerman and his wife that was recorded by jail officials, prosecutors also said that Zimmerman intentionally failed to disclose a second passport. This violated the conditions of his release that required him to be monitored by GPS and surrender his passport.

Following the judge's order, Zimmerman surrendered to Seminole County Jail in Florida and was locked up again on June 3, only to await a second bond hearing that would take place on June 29. His wife was arrested June 12 on suspicion of perjury.

These shady events call to question George Zimmerman's credibility all the more. Before Mark O'Mara started representing him, George Zimmerman's original attorneys stated in a May 2012 press conference that they would no longer be representing him. Attorneys Craig Sonner and Hal Uhrig explained that they were quitting on Zimmerman because he repeatedly ignored their legal advice, and that they had lost contact with him. Could it be that Zimmerman ignored the legal advice of his first attorneys in the same manner that he ignored the advice from the 911 dispatcher who told him he didn't need to follow Trayvon Martin?

From the time Zimmerman stalked Trayvon Martin until the time he and his wife perjured themselves, the former neighborhood watch volunteer has shown consistent signs of impulsive, bullheaded behavior—the same kind of behavior that apparently led him to stalk and get into a scuffle with the unarmed Trayvon Martin. In spite of his repeated pattern of disorderly behavior, Zimmerman was still released on bond for a second time—most likely using $100,000 of the money he lied about to come up with the 10 percent security to pay the bail after Judge Kenneth Lester set the bond at $1 million. And his attorney, Mark O'Mara, reported that since Zimmerman had been released on bond for the second time, supporters were still sending in donations. Reportedly, Zimmerman had over $200,000 in his account when he needed to post bail the second time around. It is unfortunate that an unarmed kid can be shot and killed, the killer and his wife can perjure themselves in court, and the killer can get out on bail a second time using the money that he lied about in court to pay his bail. Is this justice?

On the ABC news website, one blogger stated, "Only in America, a 28-year-old adult killed an unarmed teenager, and he is profiting from it and getting rich from this tragedy. That's sickening and despicable."

Stop the Race Wars

In pointing out that there has been too much race-baiting, this should not lead one to believe that race could not have played a role in this tragic event. It could very well be that Trayvon was less likely to be shot if he were a white kid. In this particular case, many whites don't know why a lot of black people justifiably felt that if Zimmerman wasn't arrested it would be a miscarriage of justice based on the simple facts we do have. Unfortunately, a lot of our white colleagues are looking at this case through the eyes of the "dangerous black male" syndrome. In other words, some of these individuals believe that perhaps Trayvon should have been shot and killed by Zimmerman because he is probably just another dangerous young black male fully armed with Arizona iced tea and Skittles! This type of thinking gives credence to those who are focusing on the racial profiling issue to an extreme. Let's stop focusing on the fringe groups and peripheral issues and show some compassion for the dead black kid who was unarmed. Based on the circumstances, the unarmed and deceased Trayvon Martin should be the one who is innocent until proven guilty. And the burden of proof is on Zimmerman to try to prove he was justified in shooting an unarmed kid who apparently was minding his own business.

On too many occasions I have seen a well-meaning conservative talk show host acting like "a white man who has no clue"—contributing to the escalation of the hate talk rather than helping to diffuse it in the midst of this tragedy. At one point during the Trayvon Martin controversy, Sean Hannity talked about the threat looming from the New Black Panthers so much on his program that it seemed to promote the concept of fear instead of focusing on the concept of seeking true justice. Why do some of these program hosts seem to be going out of the way to tell Zimmerman's side of the story as if it is their goal to exonerate him? Can these broadcasters let the judge and jury handle that in a court of law, since the evidence so far shows that Zimmerman acted irresponsibly? I concur that someone needs to speak out at times against the race-baiters and the liberals who work so hard to politicize this tragedy, but the majority of time should be focused on making sure that the family of the unarmed kid who was killed will truly get justice. Just as criminal defense attorney Ted Williams said on Greta Van Susteren's program, if Trayvon Martin were the one with the gun and Zimmerman ended up dead, Martin would have been arrested immediately.

For those of you who don't know, I've got an announcement: we still have race problems in our country! Just like I get on the cases of a lot of my black colleagues for voting for some of our corrupt politicians just because they are Democrat or because they are black, I am going to get on a lot of my well-meaning white colleagues who want to act as though racism is still not a problem at times. It's time to wake up so that we can become part of the solution instead of part of the problem.

This nation needs a lot of prayer. Quite frankly, it is disturbing to see how racially charged this case has become and how people are stirring up hate more than ever before. The New Black Panthers are threatening to kill "the whities" and many whites in America are buying guns in case they have to kill some radical "darkies." Then you've got men like Harvard Law Professor Alan Dershowitz decreeing that the Zimmerman arrest affidavit was "irresponsible and unethical." In an appearance on MSNBC's Hardball, Dershowitz was extremely critical of special prosecutor Angela Corey's decision to charge George Zimmerman with second-degree murder. On "The Conservative Review" website, Marcus Porcius implied that "the second-degree-murder charge was a victory for George Zimmerman race-baiters," stating "If Professor Dershowitz is correct that the 'affidavit does not even make it to probable cause,' then Angela Corey does not have the authority to charge, arrest, or otherwise prosecute George Zimmerman. By doing so, she is violating his rights under the Stand Your Ground statute. Angela Corey should be behind bars, not George Zimmerman."

What have we come to when a man seems to be outraged that the shooter of an unarmed kid is charged with murder, and based on the evidence, does not even appear to consider that Zimmerman might be guilty of wrongdoing. May God help us all! George Zimmerman and his attorney will have their day in court to try to prove that the charges are unfair.

When George Zimmerman did an exclusive interview on Sean Hannity's July 18 show after he got out on bail the second time, he basically made it sound as if Trayvon Martin ambushed him for no real reason and then tried to kill him with his own gun.

In reference to the incidents that caused him to kill Trayvon, Hannity asked Zimmerman if he regretted getting out of the car or having a gun and also asked, "Is there anything you would do differently in retrospect?"

"No, sir," was Zimmerman's thoughtless reply.

Although Sean Hannity did ask a few good questions that put Zimmerman on the spot, Hannity's somewhat soft interview failed to ask one very important question: why should we believe your version of the story, Mr. Zimmerman, especially from the standpoint that you already perjured yourself and might be stretching the truth again just to save your own neck?

I just did not think it was fair for Hannity to sit there and give Zimmerman the benefit of the doubt when Trayvon Martin isn't alive to tell his side of the story. The next day after the exclusive interview, in a follow-up program, Hannity and a couple of his guest analysts almost seemed to be a bit too impressed with Zimmerman, commenting on how he seemed like such a nice guy and even trying to explain away some of Zimmerman's more controversial comments. In fact, on the same program, Hannity seemed to be tougher in grilling the Trayvon Martin family lawyer than he was when he questioned Zimmerman. Is this fair and balanced reporting?

I can understand how Hannity and his guest analysts would question the media for making Zimmerman out to be a racist monster or how they would question the second-degree murder charge. Perhaps it might be difficult to make this charge stick. But to seem to imply that Zimmerman is the one being railroaded and is justified in killing Trayvon based primarily on Zimmerman's side of the story is lopsided reporting.

A Call for Civil Discourse

To my black colleagues, I say please do not see everything through the racially tarnished eyes of an "angry black person." To my white colleagues I say, please do not act like "a white person who has no clue," acting as if racial injustice is only in the imagination of "the angry black person" because it is only "a thing of the past." These types of attitudes only foster a lot of bitterness and resentment on both sides of the fence. We must get to the point where we can have factual, intelligent, passionate, compassionate, and civil discourse about these highly charged, polarizing issues.

My plea to decent Americans like Sean Hannity is...stop taking the bait from the race-baiters. Stop fighting the wrong battle. Some of you have taken the bait—hook, line, and sinker—and the race baiters are reeling you into their misguided battle. As far as I'm concerned, many people in liberal and conservative media have acted rather irresponsibly in the reporting of this event. Many of the liberals are spouting out rhetoric about the need for hate crime prosecution, turning it into too much of a racial issue. On the other hand, many of the conservatives are focusing so much on what the liberal media has done wrong that they have failed to acknowledge that perhaps the police did mess up and perhaps an injustice has taken place in this investigation in part due to Trayvon's race. So I offer up my rebuke to the liberal and conservative media for helping to stir up a potential race war due to a lack of balanced reporting.

Too many people on all sides of the fence—so-called liberals, conservatives, and race-baiters of all persuasions—have been spouting out inflaming rhetoric that can ignite a race war. Things are going out of control and gun sales are through the roof because so many are in fear. What we need are more leaders and media personalities who will simply state the need for simple justice while also stating the need for us to pray that God will help us to avoid a senseless race war.

CHAPTER 19

THE STARTLING TRUTH ABOUT DEMOCRATS & REPUBLICANS

In this chapter I will share with you some startling facts about the roles that Democrats and Republicans have played to either obtain or obstruct civil rights for blacks in America. This chapter will also unveil the truth about the often misunderstood three-fifths clause. It will provide evidence as to whether or not the Constitution was an anti-slavery document. And you will gain real facts about whether or not the Republican Party has truly been the racist white man's party, while determining whether or not the Democratic Party has always represented true freedom and equality for blacks.

The history of blacks in America began with slavery in 1619. But the political history of blacks in America began in 1787, the year the Constitution was written. Black abolitionist Frederick Douglass researched the Constitution carefully only to conclude that the Constitution was not a pro-slavery document as he was originally taught. Douglass discovered that the Constitution was actually an anti-slavery document. He also discovered that the three-fifths clause referred only to representation. It did not imply that a black person was less than human or only three-fifths human as was erroneously believed and taught by some critics of the Constitution. The three-fifths clause had nothing to do with the worth of a person but simply implied that only three-fifths of the slave population—only 60 percent of slaves—would be counted to calculate the number of Southern representatives to Congress, thus greatly reducing the number of representatives to Congress from states with extremely large slave populations. In other words, the three-fifths clause had nothing to do with the worth of any individual but was actually an anti-slavery clause. One of its purposes was to actually limit the number of pro-slavery representatives in Congress. For this and other reasons, Frederick Douglass emphatically declared that all of the Constitution was anti-slavery.

In 1808 Congress abolished the slave trade. Although slavery was not totally abolished in America (as some states were free while others permitted ownership of slaves), the fight for freedom was making progress and the number of free states were increasing.

By 1820, Thomas Jefferson's party, the Democratic Party, had become the majority party in Congress. In 1820, a Democratic Congress passed the Missouri Compromise which reversed some of the freedoms gained for blacks and increased slavery to almost 50 percent of federal territories. For the first time since the Declaration of Independence, slavery was being officially promoted by congressional policy. And slavery was supported by Democrats—the party that so many blacks today are blindly loyal to because so many don't know the real story. Please understand that my intent is not to demonize Democrats in general. My intent is to call to question why so many blacks or liberal whites tend to demonize Republicans, labeling them as racists, without knowing the full history of Democrats and Republicans in the United States. In other words, we should not bash or support either party solely because of blind tradition.

In 1850, the Democratic Congress also passed the Fugitive Slave Law, which allowed Southern slave-masters to capture and abuse free Northern blacks, turning them into slaves.

In May of 1854, a number of Democrats who were against slavery, along with anti-slavery protestors from other parties, formed the new Republican Party primarily for the purpose of standing against the institution of slavery and to acquire equal rights for black Americans. The Republican Party entered and lost its first presidential election in 1856 with a strong emphasis on abolishing slavery and acquiring equal rights for blacks while the Democrats ran on a platform that promoted slavery and demeaned blacks. Democratic presidential candidate James Buchanan and his constituents declared that attempting to end slavery would ruin the happiness of the nation as a whole. In 1857, a Democratic-controlled Supreme Court delivered the Dred Scott Decision, declaring that blacks were not persons but property, and therefore had no rights.

In the 1860 presidential election, Republican candidate Abraham Lincoln ran against Democratic Senator Stephen Douglas of Illinois. While Lincoln and his constituents criticized the Fugitive Slave Law and the Dred Scott Decision and proclaimed their intent to end slavery, Democrat Stephen Douglas praised the Fugitive Slave Law and the Dred Scott Decision.

In 1860, Republican Abraham Lincoln was elected President of the United States and Republicans also took control of Congress, which gave them control of the law-making process for the very first time. Southern and Northern Democrats were in support of slavery, while Republicans in general were for equal rights and anti-slavery. From 1860 to 1861, eleven Democratic states seceded from the union to have a slave nation—that's what the Civil War was all about. In 1862, Republicans abolished slavery in Washington, D.C. And in 1863, the Emancipation Proclamation was issued, freeing all slaves in the Southern states. Republicans continued making forward progress by introducing a great number of civil rights bills to protect the rights of blacks. On the other hand, Southern Democrats were attempting to formulate an entire nation on the notion of white supremacy. Some Southern Democratic leaders also accused the Republican Party of having too many colored people in it.

The Civil War, which started in 1861, finally came to a close in 1865. The nation of slave-holding states had been defeated. The party of Abraham Lincoln called themselves the Republican Party because they wanted to go back to the original intent of the founding fathers of our nation. The original intent was to have representative government ruled by law (the Constitution)—a Republic—rather than direct government ruled by the majority (mob rule)—a Democracy.

Remaining true to their convictions, the Republican Party took a radical stance by creating numerous laws and amendments to protect the rights of blacks against a Democratic Party that wanted to rule in a mob-like fashion. Consider the compelling fact that when the 13th Amendment was passed in 1865 to abolish slavery, there were 200 members of Congress at that time, and 137 of these individuals voted to abolish slavery. All 118 Republicans in Congress were in favor of and signed the 13th Amendment for the purpose of abolishing slavery. Of the 82 Northern Democrats who were still in Congress (after the Southern Democrats left to start their own slave-holding nation), only 19 voted to end slavery by signing the 13th Amendment. In other words, only 23 percent of the Northern Democrats in Congress voted to end slavery, while 100 percent of the Republicans voted to end it. So why are many people demonizing the entire Republican Party and also acting as if the entire history of the Republican Party is steeped in racism, when in actuality, history shows that the Democratic Party was the racist party from the very beginning? The Southern Democrats, who referred to slavery as the cornerstone of the Confederacy, were the ones who decided to break off from the United States to form their own slave-holding nation.

After the Civil War ended, in order to get back into the Union, the 11 southern states that broke away to have a slave nation had to take an oath of loyalty that consisted of swearing before Almighty God that they would obey the laws pertaining to civil rights and anti-slavery and that they would uphold the Constitution of the United States along with the 13th Amendment. Blacks were free because of the Emancipation Proclamation but racist Southerners were ignoring it, which is why the Republican Party proposed a constitutional amendment. Now, with the addition of the 13th Amendment, blacks were truly free. Consequently, blacks started registering to vote, electing black officials, and forming political parties across the South. And it is a historical fact that nearly every Southern Republican Party was started by blacks, not whites.

On July 4, 1867, 150 blacks and 20 whites rallied together to formulate the Republican Party of Texas, along with starting other state Republican Parties throughout the South. Many blacks became Southern legislators. Regarding Black Republicans in state legislatures, in Texas, the first 42 blacks elected were Republicans. In Louisiana, the first 95 black representatives and first 32 black senators were Republicans. Also, in Alabama, the first 103 blacks elected to the state legislature were all Republicans. In Mississippi, the first 112 blacks elected to the state legislature were all Republicans. In South Carolina, the first 190 black legislators were Republicans. In Virginia the first 46 black legislators were Republicans. In Florida the first 30 black legislators were Republicans. In North Carolina the first 30 black legislators were Republicans. In Georgia the first 41 black legislators were Republicans.

Even in Democratic states there were not only Republicans who fought for the cause of racial equality, but there were also black Republicans. Because the 14th Amendment was passed, blacks could be elected to the Federal Congress.

The first 23 blacks elected to the Federal Congress were all Republicans, many of whom were ex-slaves. Among them were men like Hiram Rhodes Revels of Mississippi who was the first black U.S. senator, Benjamin Turner of Alabama, Robert De Large of South Carolina, Josiah Walls of Florida, Jefferson Long of Georgia, and Joseph Hayne Rainey of South Carolina, who was the first black elected to the House of Representatives who served as Speaker of the House, and Robert Brown Elliott of South Carolina, who later became Speaker of the House of the state legislature. These were the first 7 of the 23.

Between the fourteen-year time period from 1861 to 1875, these men joined with white Republicans to pass 23 civil rights laws. The next time Congress passed another civil rights law was 89 years later in 1964.

In 1876, Democrats regained partial control of Congress. Prior to this, when the Republicans had the House and the Senate and the Presidency, Republicans were passing an abundance of civil rights laws. But in 1876, Democrats put a halt to much of this civil rights legislation when they regained control of the House. Henceforth, the South started to get more racist and more violent.

It was during this period in history that a violent group was started nationally to keep Republicans out of office in order to stop the forward progress that blacks were making from a civil rights standpoint. This violent and racially prejudiced group was started by Democrats in 1866. And can you guess what the name of this group was? It was the Ku Klux Klan and its original purpose was to destroy Republicans so that Democrats could gain control and perpetuate a racist society. Obviously, many blacks were victimized by the Klan because blacks were Republicans back then. The Klan also terrorized white Republicans as well for the purpose of furthering their racist agenda. The Klan promised relief from terror if their victims vowed not to vote Republican. And the Klan considered the Republican Party dangerously radical because it was a biracial party that allowed blacks to vote and hold public office. Primarily blacks were lynched by the Klan, but it is a fact that many whites were lynched as well. It is on record that 4,800 Americans were lynched—1,300 were white and 3,500 were black. The Klan was a partisan group that was actually an entire wing of the Democratic Party.

The Civil Rights Movement

Because slavery was referred to as the cornerstone of the Confederacy, the Southern Democrats who came back to the Union to reunite with the Northern Democrats after losing the Civil War did not want to grant civil rights to free slaves in spite of the passing of the 13th Amendment. Consequently, Congress came up with the 14th Amendment which declares that a free slave is a citizen of the state in which he lives. The public records state that in 1868 not a single Democrat in Congress voted in favor of the 14th Amendment, which was designed to grant civil rights to former slaves. To further protect the civil rights of blacks, Congress also passed the 15th Amendment in 1870 which declared that a person cannot be deprived of the right to vote on the basis of color, thus guaranteeing the right of blacks to vote.

Contrary to what some believe, the Voting Rights Act of 1965 was not the landmark legislation that first granted the right for blacks to vote. That right was first granted way back in 1870 with the 15th Amendment. The Voting Rights Act of 1965 was actually a piece of national legislation designed to help enforce the 15th Amendment by outlawing discriminatory voting practices such as the requirement of unfair literacy tests as a prerequisite to voting.

The year 1892 was the first time the Democrats regained everything (the Presidency, the House, and the Senate) and they repealed every civil rights law, developed illegitimate literacy tests to keep blacks from voting, and came up with all types of other bogus means of suppressing blacks.

In was not until 1944 that the U.S. Supreme Court struck down the

Democratic policy that declared that blacks cannot be elected to public office as Democrats. In 1972 Barbara Jordan and Andrew Young were the first Southern Democrats elected to Congress because of a Supreme Court ruling that demanded that the Democratic legislature of Georgia and Texas redraw lines so that blacks could be elected.

It is important for me to point out here that neither party is totally blameless of wrongdoings and it is not my goal to glorify one party over another. My goal, however, is to show you that it is best to be a values voter by supporting the party that has foundational principles that more closely match biblical values. Frederick Douglass declared that we must vote righteously because "Righteousness exalteth a nation: but sin is a reproach to any people." In the *Frederick Douglass Papers, Volume II*, the famous abolitionist declared that this scripture from Proverbs 14:34 constitutes his politics. An individual should not cast a vote only on the basis of party affiliation, but should examine the values of each candidate to avoid putting the wrong person in office. In his *Lectures on Revivals of Religion*, famous American revivalist Charles Finney implied that voters will answer to God for their votes and "He [God] will bless or curse this nation according to the course Christians take in politics."

Because the Republican Party was on the right side of the issue in the 1960s, the Civil Rights Act of 1964 and the Voting Rights Act of 1965 were passed. After decades of oppression, the 1964 Civil Rights Act and the 1965 Voting Rights Act were both introduced by Democratic President John F. Kennedy because of the racial tension that resulted from the riots in Birmingham, Alabama. These would be the first Civil Rights Acts passed by Congress in 89 years! Both of these acts were previously introduced by Republican President Dwight D. Eisenhower but were both killed in the Senate by the Chairman of the Senate Judiciary Committee—a Democrat. At that point, with the extreme level of racial tension, Democratic President John F. Kennedy decided that it was time to re-introduce these bills, so he approached the Republicans and asked them to help him pass the bills.

During this time, President Kennedy was assassinated, and his successor, President Lyndon B. Johnson, continued where Kennedy left off and moved forward with the Civil Rights Act and Voting Rights Act. When these acts went into the Congress for a vote, two-thirds of Congress were Democrats in the House and the Senate with a Democratic President.

Although the majority Democratic Congress only needed a simple majority vote, they failed to pass the Civil Rights Act of 1964 and the Voting Rights Act of 1965. According to the records of Congress, Democrats had it totally in their power to pass these acts, but did not even come close. The two-thirds Democratic Congress only needed 269 votes from 315 Democrats, but they only came up with 198 votes on the Civil

Rights Act. The overwhelming help to pass these acts actually came from the Republicans—an overwhelming 83 percent of the Republicans voted to pass those two acts while only 62 percent of Democrats voted to pass them.

In short, if it had not been for Republicans, these two acts would not have been passed. But because Democrats were in control, it appeared that the Democratic Party was primarily responsible for the passing of the 1864 Civil Rights Act and 1965 Voting Rights Act.

Do Not Sell Your Soul for any Political Party

The goal of sharing the information in this chapter is to simply tell history accurately and to help people to think more rationally with facts. The moral of the story is this: *do not sell your soul for any political party*. If a political party (Democratic, Republican, or any other) begins to promote ungodly values, then you need to stand up for what is right by withdrawing your support or by speaking out. The Republican Party is supposed to be the party of morality and family values, yet there are even some corrupt Republicans in this day and time who believe that the party needs to focus primarily on economic issues and forget about standing against injustices such as abortion. It is obviously very important to focus on economic issues at times. But some of these more "moderate" Republicans feel that their constituents need to loosen up and get more liberal regarding social issues like abortion and same-sex marriage so that the Republican Party can compete better against the Democrats. This type of "if you can't beat 'em, join 'em philosophy" should be protested and is not worthy of support whenever it is suggested. I have determined in my mind that I am not going to vote for a person with corrupt social or moral values just because he calls himself a conservative or a Republican.

Again, do not sell out for any political party if it starts going too far off course. Your number one loyalty should always be to please God and not to please man. In my quest to uphold biblical values, my conscience will not allow me to vote for far-left liberal Democrats. Therefore, I unapologetically give the majority of my support to Republican candidates because I believe this party's value system is more closely aligned with the biblical values that made this nation great in spite of the obvious imperfections of some Republicans in general.

In spite of the fact that the Republican Party has such a rich historical heritage of helping blacks to acquire equal rights, why is it often perceived by many blacks as the racist party that is not concerned about the black community? I do need to first make it very plain that there are actually some racist Republicans who are not at all concerned about the black community at large. But this is obviously not the case for many Republicans. Then there are those well-meaning Republicans who just don't have a clue about the fact that some racism still exists in our American culture. Many black people are insulted when the Republicans who fall into this category always want to act as if racism is only a thing of the past. Overall, however, I think there are three basic reasons why the Republican Party in general is often perceived by many blacks as the racist party that is not concerned about the black community at large.

First of all, I think that our educational system has largely kept students in ignorance concerning these matters, allowing history to be taught with gross inaccuracies and imbalances. Second, I think the liberal media has done an effective job of distorting the facts to unfairly demonize the Republican Party as a whole. Third, I feel that the Republican Party in more recent years has not done enough to reach out to the black community in general. It has become a party that espouses a lot of good rhetoric about taking full responsibility, working hard, and pulling yourself up by your bootstraps, but I think many Republican leaders need to take more action to help overcome some of the problems or inequities in the black community that are an indirect result of America's infamous legacy of slavery and racism. Though many Republican leaders espouse good rhetoric, many of these leaders have failed to reach out to the black community at the grass roots level with real programs and activities (not hand-outs) that can actually provide a sensible form of restoration to some of these disenfranchised black communities. It is true that some of the problems that plague black America in general are a direct result of the irresponsibility of some black Americans. On the other hand, if more Republican leaders would admit the simple truth that some of the disenfranchisement in present-day black America is the indirect result of a generational trickling-down effect from centuries of slavery and institutional racism, this would be a good starting point for the bridging of the gap.

Let me make it very clear that blacks in America should not have an entitlement mentality coupled with a "blame the white man" ideology. Blacks must take full responsibility for their own lives in this great land of opportunity known as the United States of America. On the other side of the coin, should whites who have benefited for centuries from the spoils of slavery and institutional racism (even without realizing it at times) not feel the need to take some of the responsibility to help to create a more level playing field in some of our communities that have been disenfranchised at least in part due to racism?

Some of our present-day Republican leaders have oversimplified the race issue by simply decreeing that "black people just need to get over it, forget the past, and take responsibility." Consequently, some liberals have capitalized on this type of Republican rhetoric, citing a lack of black community involvement from the Republican Party in general, and unfairly labeling virtually all present-day Republicans leaders as intolerant racists or Uncle Toms. It could very well be argued that the Republican Party of our day often projects an image that is "too white" and does not do enough to reach out to the black community at the grassroots level. In all fairness, however, it is important to bring out the point that a biased liberal media and many misguided blacks who have unfairly demonized Republicans make it very difficult for some good Republican leaders to bridge the gap even when they desire to do so.

It is not difficult for any sensible person to see that Democrats and Republicans have missed it at certain times throughout the course of our nation's history. But Bishop E.W. Jackson, a black pastor in Virginia, is convinced that the present-day Democratic Party is so morally bankrupt that real Christians should totally disassociate themselves from the party.

In August of 2012, ChristianPost.com reported that Bishop Jackson has taken a radical stance against the radical left by calling Christians to leave the Democratic Party over what he describes as a "cult-like devotion" to abortion and what he terms as a "rejection" of the traditional family.

Christian Post reporter Paul Stanley reported that "Bishop E.W. Jackson, a veteran of the Marine Corps and Harvard Law graduate, says the Democrats' enslavement of some Americans, most notably black Americans, is the modern-day equivalent of slavery, and his focus is to lead an exodus, similar to what Moses did in the Old Testament."

"Let God's people go," Jackson told The Christian Post in a telephone interview.

"Clearly, the Democratic Party is the anti-Christian party in this nation. They reject the Bible, what Bible-believing Christians embrace, and they encourage the growth of what we call a 'non-traditional' family. That is morally wrong and a disgrace to our nation and our Lord," said Jackson.

In reference to the NAACP, Jackson further stated that "What was once an historic and honorable civil rights organization is now nothing other than a left-wing apparatus of the Democratic Party. I will say that some of the local chapters still advance civil rights, but in my opinion the national chapter no longer cares for the average black person. That is a shame too."

Rather than defect from the Democratic Party, some individuals are of the mind-set that more true Christians should align themselves with the Democratic Party to fight against the immorality from within. Whether the battle is fought from the inside or the outside of the Democratic Party, Christians who want to be true to biblical values need to take a stand one way or another.

CHAPTER 20

IS THERE A CASE FOR POLARIZED POLITICS?

Before he suspended his campaign in April 2012, some Republicans were terrified at the prospect that Rick Santorum, the supposedly unelectable social conservative, might actually win the GOP presidential nomination for 2012. In his book titled *The Case for Polarized Politics: Why America Needs Social Conservatism*, Jeffrey Bell makes the case that social conservatism has a winning track record for the Republican Party. Consequently, a candidate like Rick Santorum could very well be much more electable than the pundits think. Bell, who worked on Ronald Reagan's presidential campaigns in 1976 and 1980, stated "Social issues were nonexistent in the period 1932 to 1964. The Republican Party won two presidential elections out of nine, and they had the Congress for all of four years in that entire period. . . . When social issues came into the mix—I would date it from the 1968 election . . . the Republican Party won seven out of 11 presidential elections."

Bell also points out that the Democrats who won, including Barack Obama in 2008, downplayed social liberalism in their campaigns. In two of the past six presidential elections (1988 and 2004), social issues have come to the forefront on the Republican side. "Those are the only two elections since Reagan where the Republican Party has won a popular majority," Bell says. "It isn't coincidental."

Bell also explains that social conservatism is not the Republican Party's initiation of aggression, but rather a response to the aggression from the left. In other words, conservatives don't like far-left liberals trying to force things on them that violate their moral beliefs and family values.

In the 2012 race for the Republican nomination, Rick Santorum was considered the most socially conservative candidate, but Bell rejects the common claim that Santorum places too strong an emphasis on social issues: "I think that's unfair to Santorum. He goes out of his way to say that he has an economic platform; he isn't just about social issues."

He notes that on a February 2012 segment of NBC's "Meet the Press," host David Gregory opened his interview with the candidate by asking a series of questions about social issues, one of which he prefaced by saying that such issues "have come . . . to define your campaign."

Santorum disputed the premise: "It's not what's defining my campaign. I would say that what's defining my campaign is going out and talking about liberty, talking about economic growth, talking about getting manufacturing jobs back here to this country, trying to grow this economy to make sure that everybody in America can participate in it."

Bell believes that although liberals have tried to create the narrative that Santorum has too much of a focus on social issues, Santorum has ultimately benefited from their narrative, which could perhaps be one reason why—before he suspended his campaign—he suddenly skyrocketed to second place behind Romney in the race for the 2012 Republican nomination.

Jeffrey Bell makes the point that even voters who are not big on social issues might still be willing to vote for a social conservative as long as the candidate is not trying to force his moral or social agenda on everyone. "The key thing along that line is the issue of coercion," Bell says, and "Who is guilty of coercion? I happen to think it's the left." Bell further pointed out that if Santorum were to win the Republican nomination, President Obama and his supporters would "imply that Santorum wants to impose all the tenets of traditional morality on the American population. He doesn't. He just doesn't want the opposite imposed on Middle America."

David Shedlock also shines some light on the compelling case for polarized politics. In his book titled *With Christ in the Voting Booth*, the author states:

> The conventional wisdom is wrong that wise presidential candidates run to the base during the primary and to the center in the general election. The theory, in actual practice, has been proven wrong so many times to the detriment of the Republicans that it is secretly being promoted by Democrats. When the GOP falls for it, they lose. My theory is that the closer the two candidates are perceived to be on the political spectrum by the general public, the more likely it is that the Democrat will win. I disagree with those that say social conservatives must downplay their true views in order to win.

If the assessment of men like Jeffrey Bell and David Shedlock holds true, then Mitt Romney might have a more difficult time trying to beat Barack Obama in the 2012 presidential election than Santorum would have had. And now that Santorum is no longer in the 2012 race, Romney might not prove to be as electable as the pundits thought.

One of my colleagues, a socially conservative, devout Christian who is also a rather politically astute black man—who will not vote for Barack Obama or Mitt Romney—explained that Romney might very well lose to Barack Obama in the November 2012 general election primarily due to a lack of contrast among the two candidates. He did say, however, that Romney would only be likely to win if there were an overabundance of anti-Obama voters who will only vote against Obama rather than for Romney. My colleague also feels that Santorum would have had a better chance of beating Obama in a presidential election because of the dramatic contrast between the two and because of the level of trust Santorum has built over the years. In contrast, he points out that Romney, a very liberal Republican, has had a track record of disregarding socially or fiscally conservative values all too often. Romney has a solid track record as a multimillionaire businessman, but my colleague points out that it takes much more than just a good businessman to be a good president (or else someone like Bill Gates would be the best candidate for president). Rick Santorum, he feels, is one of the few candidates who understands the profound impact between morality, faith, family values, and the economy—understanding that when a nation dishonors God and devalues family, the economy of that nation will be negatively impacted. My colleague notes that Santorum had to suspend his 2012 campaign in large part due to a lack of support from the highly influential Republican pundits and media elites who made Romney the establishment candidate from the very beginning. My colleague further points out that both of the previous elections that were won by President George W. Bush (2000 and 2004) were won primarily because of the reasons stated in *The Case for Polarized Politics*. And the evangelical Christians concerned about social values were the group that played a huge role in pushing George W. Bush over the top by a narrow margin against contender Al Gore.

Is it fair that a leader with Santorum's record has been disregarded by so many of the Republican elites or political pundits of his own party? With a very consistent track record in terms of standing for faith, family values, free enterprise, and social conservatism, Santorum has some very good ideas regarding fiscal and economic matters as well. For those who argue that he is a Republican who would not be electable in a presidential race, it is important to point out that as a Republican state representative for one term and senator in Pennsylvania for three consecutive terms, Santorum had a track record of defeating many of his opponents in highly populated Democratic districts. And during the 2012 campaign season, the political analysts pointed to poll results showing that in comparison to his opponents, Rick Santorum had the highest positives and the lowest negatives.

I want to make it very clear that I am not campaigning for Rick Santorum, but I am simply using him as an object lesson in this chapter, giving a tangible example of what I am referring to in regards to a politician who stands by his value system. In other words, the principles he supports make him worthy of our support.

As a minister of the gospel, I make it a point not to endorse candidates, but rather to endorse the principles spelled out in the Scriptures. This is not to imply that a minister should never endorse a candidate. I am simply sharing my personal conviction, because I think pastors or ministers in general need to be very careful with the concept of going all-out to endorse political candidates. Some church leaders have become so enamored with powerful political personalities to the point that they have compromised biblical values in order to brush shoulders with them. Politicians can often be very deceptive in order to get the church vote, and some well-meaning church leaders have been bamboozled into endorsing corrupt politicians. Therefore, I feel that my primary responsibility as a minister of the gospel is not so much to endorse the man or woman, but to endorse the principles the man or woman stands for. My focus is more about teaching people to become values voters who are discerning enough to vote for the politicians whose public policies will reflect the value system that is most pleasing to God Almighty.

The Cutthroat Business of Politics

In one debate during the 2012 primary, Republican Ron Paul said Santorum was a phony because Paul felt that Santorum was a big government spender. It is perfectly acceptable for Ron Paul to respectfully disagree with some of Santorum's actions as a politician, but to say that Santorum is a phony was a cheap shot based on Santorum's overall conservative track record. This type of unsubstantiated rhetoric is nasty business and bad for the Republican Party as a whole. Likewise, the Mitt Romney Super PAC also ran a lot of negative ads that created a false narrative about Santorum's track record. When Santorum confronted Romney about this, Romney basically passed the buck by saying that he had no control over the ads his Super PAC ran—even if the ads contained lies about Rick Santorum.

In the midst of all this cutthroat activity during the 2012 Republican primary, Mark Levin, author of *Ameritopia*, expressed the viewpoint on Sean Hannity's program that out of all the remaining Republican candidates at the time (which included Rick Santorum, Mitt Romney, Newt Gingrich, and Ron Paul) Rick Santorum was the truest conservative with the best track record. The *Ameritopia* author also pointed out that the type of nit-picking that the other candidates were doing in an attempt to discredit Santorum as a big-spending, big-government type of guy created a false narrative about Santorum. Whether you are a fan of Mark Levin or not, you have to admit that this constitutional scholar, lawyer, and author whom Sean Hannity refers to as "the great one" has a very good understanding of the Constitution and the freedoms that made this nation great. And Levin pointed out on Hannity's program that Santorum is the truest conservative in reference to standing for freedom and constitutional matters, and in terms of his conservative viewpoints in general.

On the other hand, Ann Coulter, a very influential "conservative" author and a Romney supporter, has tried to discredit Rick Santorum, accusing him of not being as conservative as he claims to be, stating that Santorum is simply creating a false narrative about being the most conservative candidate. Yet Coulter, who is a big supporter of the very liberal Mitt Romney, made it seem as though she was the one creating the false narrative on the Fox News channel in April of 2012 when she picked a couple of things she claimed Santorum supported that were not reflective of a true conservative. Even those who are not Santorum supporters can easily see through his track record that he has been much more conservative than Romney over the years. The truth is, you can nitpick just about any politician, Democrat or Republican, and create a false narrative. But the way to know the real deal about any candidate is to evaluate his or her overall track record over an extended period of time.

Michelle Malkin, conservative author of *Culture of Corruption,* said of Santorum, "He didn't follow the pro-bailout GOP crowd—including Mitt Romney and Newt Gingrich . . . and unlike Romney and Gingrich, Santorum has never dabbled with eco-radicals like John Holdren, Al Gore, and Nancy Pelosi. He hasn't written any 'Contracts with the Earth.' . . . Santorum is an eloquent spokesperson for the culture of life. He has been savaged and ridiculed by leftist elites for upholding traditional family values—not just in word, but in deed. . . . And at this point in the game, Rick Santorum represents the most conservative candidate still standing who can articulate both fiscal and social conservative values—and live them."

I have resided in Harrisburg, the state capital of Pennsylvania, for many years—the same state where Santorum served four years in the U.S. House of Representatives and twelve as a U.S. senator. And I know firsthand that Santorum has constantly fought for a culture of life, faith, freedom, fairness, and family values in the midst of much opposition, ridicule, and harsh criticism. Even in terms of helping to provide equal opportunities to minorities, Santorum is the only Republican I know of who has made special efforts to speak at events for the United Negro College Fund so that many of the underrepresented traditionally black colleges could get much needed financial support. Santorum has been one of the few politicians who has shown the courage to stand up for a lot of the values that many politicians choose to ignore, so it is rather surprising to see those in his own Republican camp accusing him of being a phony or accusing him of creating a false narrative.

I would expect the far-left liberals on the other side of the camp to create false narratives about Santorum by falsely accusing him of being against women (because he is anti-abortion), of being hateful towards homosexuals (because he simply believes that God made man for woman and marriage should only be between a man and a woman), and of racism (simply because he desires to help all classes of people without creating crippling entitlement programs). But it is interesting to see him get attacked in certain ways by those in his own Republican camp. These attacks are reminders of the type of disingenuous and vicious activity that creeps into politics at all levels on both sides of the aisle. And it is also a reminder that we can't put too much trust in politicians in general due to the cutthroat nature of politics among Democrats and Republicans.

To further illustrate the disingenuous aspect of politics, one-time rivals Santorum and Romney united after Romney became the Republican frontrunner to deny President Barack Obama's reelection. This "unity" came after Santorum referred to Romney as the "worst Republican in the country to put up against Barack Obama" during their bitter contest. After being criticized by his own party for making the comment, Santorum explained that he primarily meant it in the context of Romney's position on health care. Nevertheless, after all of the warfare, former presidential hopeful Rick Santorum would later urge his supporters to back fellow Republican Mitt Romney's presidential campaign. This obviously brought on some backlash that has worked against Santorum.

Santorum has also taken some heat for endorsing "liberal" Republican Senator Arlen Specter in 2004, explaining that he endorsed his fellow Pennsylvanian because Specter assured him he would support then-President George W. Bush's judicial nominees as the head of the Judiciary Committee. Santorum's support of the pro-abortion Specter has become a source for campaign trail attacks, causing some critics to accuse Santorum of putting party politics above his professed principles. These are the types of seemingly contradictory actions that can cause some to wonder if anyone in politics is totally sincere.

Whether you believe Santorum's endorsements of men like Arlen Specter and Mitt Romney were gross contradictions or something he felt necessary to do for the good of the Republican Party, it is a clear example of the cutthroat and contradictory nature of politics in our day and time. This is the ugly side of politics that can cause people to become cynical to the point of not believing in any of our fellow politicians. How could the same Santorum who said in Wisconsin that Romney is "the worst Republican in the country to put up against Barack Obama" later say "Gov. Romney will be that nominee, and he has my endorsement and support to win this—the most critical election of our lifetime." I am not implying that Santorum is not real, but I am asking the question, "How can anyone be totally real in today's cutthroat political environment?" I guess it takes a rather unique individual to have the ability to cut a man's throat on Monday and then bandage him up and work with him on Tuesday. Does this simply go with the territory for those who choose to be politicians in our day and time? One thing I do know for sure is that we currently have a vicious political system with flawed men and women working in it. While we need to hold these men and women to a certain standard, we are setting ourselves up for disillusionment if we expect them to be totally flawless in the midst of a very cutthroat political environment. In short, even the most upstanding political leaders are subject to inconsistencies, contradictions, and shortcomings at times due to the nature of the beast. This is why we must be quick to pray for those in authority—not letting them off the hook so easily for blatant transgressions, but showing them some grace for those irritating inconsistencies or flaws that are difficult to eliminate in such a cutthroat environment.

In spite of some of Santorum's inconsistencies for the sake of "party unification," I still agree with my previously mentioned colleague's opinion about him being one of the best candidates out there—even though many have attempted to portray him as an extremist, a racist, and a hatemonger. In the midst of all the criticism, however, highly influential leaders like Christian talk show host and Focus on the Family founder James Dobson spoke highly of Santorum, saying, "While there are other GOP candidates who are worthy of our support, Senator Santorum is the man of the hour."

For the most part, Rick Santorum has gained a reputation among many of his peers as one of the few men who is on the level about his mission to uphold true conservative values. Rush Limbaugh, probably the most influential and polarizing conservative radio talk show host on the planet, said, "everybody is guilty of some transgression somewhere against conservatism…except Santorum."

The former U.S. senator of Pennsylvania was elected to the U.S. House of Representatives in 1990 at the age of 32, and from 1995 to 2007, served in the U.S. Senate. In spite of his overall success as a senator, Rick Santorum lost overwhelmingly to Bob Casey in his reelection bid in 2006 by 18 points. Why he lost by so many points has been the subject of much discussion over the years. One probable reason is that the 2006 election took place at the height of the unpopular Iraq War, and Santorum could not escape the negative wave that struck George W. Bush and the Republican Party. In addition, Santorum's opponent, Bob Casey, had already established a track record as the biggest vote-getter in state history when he won the state treasurer's post in 2004. Bob, a pro-life Democrat, is also the son of the highly celebrated former Pennsylvania Governor Bob Casey. In short, the Democrats could not have run a stronger candidate against Santorum. And to add to Santorum's challenges during that time, Bob Casey was very effective at raising questions about whether or not Santorum was an absentee state resident because he owned a home in the D.C. suburbs. All of these factors led to the biggest defeat by an incumbent U.S. senator in state history.

Capitol Hill Point Man

Every politician under the sun has given us some reasons to wonder whether he or she is really worthy of our vote. It is no secret that Santorum, a Catholic, has become well-respected and truly endeared by many Protestant evangelicals who feel that he has truly earned their support. While serving as a public official, the former chairman of the Senate Republican Conference Committee became the standard bearer of social conservatives on the Hill, speaking out against issues like gay marriage and abortion rights. His method of operation entailed listening closely to the concerns of evangelical leaders, speaking with them monthly, and keeping them abreast of the status of legislation. Santorum's staff was also very astute at networking with evangelical broadcasters and activists for the purpose of mobilizing support for their causes.

During his time in elected office, the former senator—who in 2005 was named by Time Magazine as one of the 25 most influential evangelical leaders—also authored the original Federal Marriage Amendment, led the fight for longer sentences for child predators, and wrote legislation to protect children from Internet predators. If he is one day elected president, he declares that he will defend the Defense of Marriage Act in court, ban military chaplains from performing same-sex marriage ceremonies on military bases or other federal properties, call on Congress to reinstitute Don't Ask/Don't Tell, and veto any bill or budget that funds abortion or funds any organization that performs abortions, including Planned Parenthood. Santorum has stated that he will also call on Congress to reinstitute 2008-level funding for the Community Based Abstinence Education program and advocate for a federal law permitting schools to allow prayer at graduations, football games, and other school functions.

He has been a champion of traditional American values who has fought to protect families and the unborn. Rick Santorum believes that to have a strong national economy, we must have strong families, and he has been a consistent proponent of preserving traditional marriage. As stated on his campaign website, when activist judges took it upon themselves to redefine marriage, Rick Santorum spearheaded the debate in favor of the Federal Marriage Amendment in 2004 even though he knew he would be labeled a bigot or worse by members of the liberal elite. Rick understands that our freedom to practice our faith is not just under attack through the redefinition of marriage, but in nearly every facet of the popular culture. As a member of the United States Senate, Rick authored the "Workplace Religious Freedom Act" to ensure individuals of all faith could not be discriminated against while on the job.

Santorum became known as one of the most conservative senators in Pennsylvania's history in part due to the battles he waged to maintain fiscal sanity in Washington, fighting for a balanced budget and a line-item veto. In terms of his accomplishments on the social front, Senator Santorum wrote and championed legislation that outlawed the heinous procedure known as partial-birth abortion, as well as the "Born Alive Infants Protection Act," the "Unborn Victims of Violence Act," and the "Combating Autism Act" because he believes each and every individual has value and the most vulnerable in our society need to be protected.

In summary, Rick Santorum has earned a reputation as a fighter for traditional values and an advocate for smaller government, less wasteful spending, a strong national defense, simpler tax codes to promote free enterprise, and a return to our country's founding principles with a healthy respect for the Constitution and Declaration of Independence that propelled this nation to greatness. While campaigning, Santorum has stated that his vision for America is to restore America's greatness through the promotion of faith, family, and freedom. He believes that at its core, America is a moral enterprise, but that foundation is quickly eroding. As a result of the values he expressed throughout his campaign, Santorum came from far behind and soared to co-frontrunner status with Romney in 2012.

Willing to Lose to Do What Is Right

Just as he values his ability to make changes through his role as a public official, Rick Santorum is quick to point out that he relishes his role as a husband and father. Married to his wife Karen for 21 years, they are the parents of seven children: Elizabeth, John, Daniel, Sarah Maria, Peter,

Patrick, and Isabella. And it was Rick's wife Karen who truly believed that it was God's will for her husband to run for president, stating in a Fox News interview that initially she had "totally closed the door to the idea" of her husband joining the Republican nomination race for president, but "in the end, despite my resistance, when God asks something—you will do it." Karen says Rick was running as a calling and he prays daily, telling God, "Lord here I am. I'm your servant. What do you want from me today?" Regarding their faith, she said, "Our Christian faith is everything to us. It's so important to pick a leader who comes to the table with strong Christian principles." However, she made it clear that, "he's not going to make people do things they don't want to do."

While he was on the campaign trail, Santorum hypothetically asked the question, "Are you willing to lose to do what is right?" Could it be that in spite of the fact that Santorum had to suspend his 2012 campaign, God's primary purpose was for him to resurrect himself as a major political figure so that he can look at the possibility of entering the race again with an even brighter future? Could it be that all of America needed to see Rick Santorum lose the Republican nomination the first time around—without resorting to the cutthroat tactics of some of his Republican opponents—in order to see that Santorum is one of the few who is willing to lose to do what is right? Time will tell the story.

To address those who attempt to portray Rick as an extremist, in an interview with CNN's Piers Morgan, Karen Santorum made it clear that although her husband personally opposes the use of contraception, he will not do anything to try to force this personal belief on women. Regarding the issue of protecting religious freedom, he is just concerned about making sure that the government does not try to force religious institutions to violate their conscience concerning the issue of handing out contraceptives as a health care requirement. So "women have nothing to fear when it comes to contraceptives," Karen says. Rick does firmly oppose legalized abortion, however.

Where Will You Put Your Trust This Time?

After Santorum—Romney's main rival for the GOP nomination—suspended his campaign on April 10, 2012, Romney became the presumptive Republican nominee. Santorum ultimately fell far behind Romney in March 2012 in the battle for delegates and also said a lack of finances was one of the reasons he ended his bid for the White House.

Based on the political climate, now that a solid conservative like Rick Santorum is out of the race for the 2012 presidential election, it seems that the only way a "liberal" Republican like Mitt Romney will defeat Barack Obama is if enough people are desperate enough to get Obama out. Other than that, a lot of devout Christians, social conservatives, and Republicans in general don't really trust Romney. They point out that throughout his political career, Romney has changed positions on the abortion issue. The health care law he passed while governor of Massachusetts (known as Romneycare) is also viewed negatively and is labeled by many as the pilot program for Obamacare due to certain similarities. Then there is the issue of Romney's religion. Some people of faith view the Mormon religion as a cult and not as just another brand of Christianity. A lot of people aren't saying this publicly, but these are the types of concerns some people have. In an October 2011 Associated Press-GfK poll, 21 percent of respondents said they would be less likely to cast a presidential vote for a Mormon. Four percent said they would be less likely to vote for a black person. These findings seem to be to the advantage of President Barack Obama, but an AP poll during the 2008 campaign did find that nearly 40 percent of white Americans had at least a partially negative view of black people.

To complicate matters all the more about Romney and his religion, Glenn Beck, a Mormon himself, has publicly stated that he does not trust Romney and that he trusts Santorum more than any candidate out there. The popular talk show host once stated, "I don't endorse candidates . . . People ask me all the time, 'who is out there?' I tell them the same thing, I don't trust any of them, but if I had to trust the reins of power with one person that is currently in this field . . . If there is one guy out there that is the next George Washington, the only guy that I could think of is Rick Santorum. I would ask that you would take a look at him."

There are also those who feel that Romney is not a true fiscal conservative because he supported some of the government bailout programs. In short, many true conservatives and people of faith do not really view Romney as a principled man, but he is viewed as a man who sort of blows with the wind of public opinion and says what people want to hear for the moment. For example, let's examine some of the things that influential Christians like Bob Enyart, Bill Keller, and Tricia Erickson are saying about Mitt Romney.

On the May 24, 2012, edition of the Bob Enyart Live radio program, the Christian conservative host suggested that presidential candidate Mitt Romney may be just as bad as Barack Obama, or that he might even be worse. He asserts that Mitt Romney has been deceiving Christians from Day One by claiming to be pro-marriage, pro-life, and Christian. Enyart pointed out that his assessment of Romney is based on the fact that Romney authorized abortion-on-demand through Romneycare and has already done more to kill babies with tax dollars than Barack Obama and Hillary Clinton have dreamed to do, even after claiming to be a "pro-lifer." Enyart further stated that Romney forced Catholic hospitals to administer chemical abortions on demand, including late term, and also placed Planned Parenthood in a permanent seat on the advisory board of Romneycare.

In reference to the gay marriage issue, Enyart and his guest agreed that Romney is "the godfather of gay marriage" who willingly imposed same-sex marriage on the State of Massachusetts by constitutional fiat, and then lied to us, making it seem as if he was forced to do so. Enyart says Romney made and fulfilled a number of promises to homosexual activist groups; illegally, unconstitutionally, and perversely supporting homosexual marriage and turning restrained judges into activist judges.

Enyart then posed the quandary of voting for the lesser of two evils, making a very good case that there is a time when it is best not to vote for either candidate when both exemplify deplorable values. Concerning this issue of voting according to values, Enyart also pointed out that there are millions of people in churches in America who no longer know right from wrong, and the Christian leaders are a part of this problem.

Making mention of a Romney Abortion Fairytale TV ad that was aired during the primaries, Enyart pointed out how he produced and used this ad to show how Romney flip-flopped in his own words. He was pro-choice in 1994, 2002, and 2005 and was pro-life in 2001, 2004, and 2006 and then contradicted himself again by funding abortion through Romneycare the same year. As he closed out his radio interview, Enyart boldly challenged his guest, asserting that if he votes for Romney he is not just voting against Barack Obama but he is also voting for a child killer.

Bill Keller, the world's leading Internet evangelist and the founder of LivePrayer.com, with over 2.4 million subscribers worldwide, states that a vote for Mormon cult member Mitt Romney will insure at least 1 million souls will end up in hell. Keller went on, "The Republican choice will be a member of the satanic Mormon cult who will never have to say a word for his cult to take advantage of their ultimate goal since they were founded 200 years ago, and that is to gain mainstream acceptance, giving them all the ammunition they need to aggressively seek converts to their cult's beliefs.... Any 'Christian leader' who supports Romney obviously cares more about politics than souls!"

In her book entitled *Can Mitt Romney Serve Two Masters? The Mormon Church Versus the Office Of The Presidency of the United States of America*, author Tricia Erickson states that "If the American people knew what he truly believed, they would surely not place him in the highest office in the land." As a former Mormon bishop's daughter and Mormon wife, she shares how she went through "the cultic, violent, and bizarre Mormon secret temple ceremonies of which Mitt and Ann

Romney continue to attend to this day." Erickson goes on to explain that Mitt Romney truly believes he will become a "god" in the afterlife (equal to Jesus Christ), Satan is Jesus' literal brother, and Jesus was *not* born of a virgin birth. Mitt also believes in a religion with a history that is full of racism against black Americans, Native Americans, Jews, and more, she says. Furthermore, she states that there is a *Mormon Plan For America.* Tricia Erickson also makes it clear that she is not a supporter of Barack Obama. She believes that both candidates are equally dangerous to the American people because there is not much difference between Obama and Romney. Their policies and records are very much alike.

These are some of the core issues that could cause Romney not to get support from a lot of evangelical Christians, Republicans, and independents. I already know of conservatives who have said that they definitely will not vote for Obama in 2012, but neither will they vote for Romney. The general thinking of some true conservatives is that the conservative elites and Republican pundits have made Romney the establishment candidate because they have allowed style to trump substance. This was supposed to be the year that substance would trump style, but it seems that a man of substance like Rick Santorum was never really given a chance by the establishment against the "illustrious multimillionaire businessman who will save the economy." Even though Romney's Super PAC outspent Rick Santorum by millions of dollars, Santorum still gave Romney a run for his money for the 2012 Republican nomination. But Santorum just could not seem to get enough support from the overall Republican establishment in order to have a real chance to win the race for the nomination for president.

From the very beginning, Romney was heralded by the liberal and conservative media, the pundits, and party elites as the most experienced and the most electable—the establishment candidate and the dynamic businessman who will save America by defeating Obama. But many true conservatives see this as a false narrative and do not believe that Romney is the true conservative who has what it takes to win the 2012 presidential election. Also, it is not hard to see that the conservative media covered for Romney the same way the liberal media covered Obama's back by failing to give balanced reporting about his checkered background. The lesson we can learn from all this is that we must stop letting the Democratic or Republican Party push their establishment candidates on us. Midway through the primary in April, all of the Republican elites and pundits suddenly came out of the woodwork to endorse Romney and to declare that Santorum should get out of the race. Santorum did step down shortly thereafter, and the so-called conservative elites and Republican pundits got their wish. Although I am not making a prediction, if Romney actually loses to Obama in November 2012, this will make the case for polarized politics even stronger. Based on the feedback I'm getting from a lot of true conservatives, Romney will have to depend on getting a lot of votes from people who really don't trust him but are extremely desperate to get Obama out, because Romney just doesn't seem to have enough true believers to defeat Obama. This is because so many voters—Republicans and independents—feel that he is too much like Obama.

Regardless of who wins the 2012 presidential election, I have made up my mind that I am not looking for a Democrat or a Republican to be my savior. In God I trust! What about those who ask me if they should vote for Romney to get Obama out of the White House even though they don't like Romney? I tell them that you have to look at the facts and then pray that the Lord will speak to your conscience and give you wisdom so that you will obey Him and will not do what seems to be right in your own eyes. Is it right to vote for a Republican presidential candidate with atrocious values in order to kick out a Democrat with atrocious values? Who do you vote for in a case like this? Some have expressed to me that, as a matter of conscience and obedience to God, they feel that not voting for Romney or Obama is the right thing to do. Some spiritual leaders also believe that a Romney-Obama match-up is a sign that God might be judging this nation by allowing many of the citizens of America—Democrats and Republicans—to reap the consequences of their immoral choices for leadership. Consequently, the greatest hope for America is to repent of our sins and turn back to God.

What to Do No Matter Who Wins the Next Presidential Election

The general consensus among some conservatives is that Barack Obama has enforced his far-left agenda in such a radical fashion that a "liberal" Republican like Mitt Romney is not conservative enough to reverse the tide if he becomes the next president.

On the other hand, if Barack Obama is elected as President of the United States for a second term, this will mean that America simply got what it wanted based on the choices that Democrats and Republicans have made. The writing is on the wall. Even those who are not politically astute can easily see that Barack Obama is one of the biggest supporters of the abortion industry, a big supporter of same-sex marriage, and a supporter of useless special interest groups who waste billions of dollars from taxpayers. He also has a track record as a tax-and-spend politician who is helping to put this nation in greater debt than ever before. Furthermore, he is a big supporter of the type of hate crime laws and health care system that is a threat to freedom of speech and free enterprise as we know it.

With all these negatives, how could Barack Obama possibly win another election? He actually has a chance of winning a second term, in part, because the Republican Party as a whole was not wise enough to select an opponent who is conservative enough to have a stark contrast against Barack Obama's far-left agenda. In short, Obama could only win if the majority of voters—Democrat and Republican—allow him to win by putting him back in office again. Whether Barack Obama or Mitt Romney wins, Americans who are opposed to the respective value systems of both men have to face the reality regarding how far this nation has declined morally and spiritually. It is a sign of the times, and the only means of hope is for true people of faith to look to God for personal guidance so that we won't go down with a sinking ship. I am not trying to be a doomsday prophet, but the reelection of Barack Obama or the election of Mitt Romney is a sign that Americans in general are more spiritually bankrupt and government dependent than ever before, and are totally ignorant or apathetic regarding our constitutional rights and the Judeo-Christian values that made this country great.

The best advice I can give you if Barack Obama is reelected or if Mitt Romney is elected is to implore you to trust in God Almighty and live by His principles, even if the world system seems to be collapsing all around us. This might seem like overly simple advice, but in Jeremiah 17:5-8 the Bible promises that God can cause us to prosper in days of recession or depression (famine) if we trust in His ways. But this particular passage also lets us know that we are cursed if we put too much confidence in man or if we put our trust in the world system. So my advice to you is to find shelter and hope in Christ so that you can escape a lot of the calamity that this nation might very well face due to the consequences of many bad choices that have been made. Regardless of who holds the office of president, this is the wise thing to do from a biblical standpoint.

If you are personally disgusted with both candidates, I implore you to pray that those who put too much trust in politicians with charisma and style will get desperate and discerning enough to actually elect a presidential candidate with real substance to hold office after Obama and Romney are off the scene. Although a single president cannot save our nation, having the right person in office could help to turn the tide or bring the type of recovery that can save America from being totally diminished.

In the next and final chapter, I will share some additional concepts that will encourage you to continue to fight regardless of who holds the office of president. As long as God is on the throne, there will always be hope and we should never stop fighting the good fight of faith!

CHAPTER 21

YOUR CALL TO ACTION

More and more, the message of Christianity has been greatly diluted in today's society. The level of compromise that has taken place within the realm of Christianity is appalling. So many people want to call themselves Christian, yet they don't want to follow the tenets of the Christian faith based in Scripture. This seems to be especially true of politicians during election year. Why is this the case? I believe the primary reason is because it attracts votes for them from the religious community.

Few things annoy me more than to see some of our black leaders call themselves "reverends" (I call them imposters), yet they do not stand for anything that is moral or biblical. All they do is chase after every possible opportunity to gain television publicity through the illegitimate use of race-card politics. At the same time, there are high-profile individuals who are professing to be Christians living perverse lifestyles that are totally contrary to biblical standards. What is our country coming to?

God hates compromise! In the Old and the New Testaments, God's judgment was most severe on those who said they were people of God, yet made a mockery of true biblical values. Jesus harshly condemned certain religious leaders saying, "This people honors Me with their lips, but their heart is far from Me" (Mark 7:6). These are the same kind of people Jesus termed as "wolves in sheep's clothing" that lead many people astray (see Matthew 7:15).

These descriptions remind me of men like Bishop Gene Robinson—the professed homosexual who also proclaims to be a "Christian" minister and also opened President-elect Barack Obama's inauguration with a prayer. He and others like him are attempting to hijack Christianity and to turn it into something that is convenient for them. They want the title of Christian, but they do not want to be inconvenienced or hampered by the lifestyle. This makes me want to say, "Bishop Robinson, if you don't follow the Bible, then why do you want to have the title 'Christian'? And if you don't believe in what you profess, then why bother professing it at all?"

Being a Christian is not about being in a club or a social organization. It is a way of life that is based on faith. The Bible says that our salvation starts with our confession of faith—faith in Jesus Christ and faith in the Word of God. You demonstrate your faith by being obedient to God's Word—not by just proclaiming to be a Christian. Without faith it is impossible to please God, and faith without works is dead (see Hebrews 11:6; James 2:26). Being called a Christian will not get you into Heaven; conforming to biblical standards will.

In this day and hour, God is sounding a call to action to those who call themselves Christians. What is this call? It is a call to repent of our sins, take a stand for what is right, and put our trust in Him and not in the frailty of man.

While it is my intent to encourage Christians to live according to biblical virtues, I also want to encourage Christians not to feel condemned if they are sincerely trying to follow God while still giving in to the temptation to sin at times. So that no one is misled into thinking that a person has to be perfect or sinless in order to be a real Christian, I want to make it clear that real Christians can struggle with sin. But a real Christian will not willfully embrace and profess a lifestyle of sin without making any effort to repent or change. Whenever an individual has an unrepentant attitude about sin which enables the person to embrace a value system that condones sin, the Bible declares that such a person is walking in darkness and shall not inherit the kingdom God (see 1 Corinthians 6:9, Galatians 5:21, and 1 John 1:6). Therefore, any politician who wants to use his or her platform to condone or legislate gross immorality is not worthy of your vote.

On the other hand, if we only sought to vote for politicians who have no sin in their lives, then no politician would be worthy of our votes. We should still, however, avoid voting for politicians whose values are in direct opposition to biblical values. I have heard Christians make lame excuses for voting for politicians who openly live immoral lives and openly profess or even legislate ungodly values. Christians who support such candidates say things like, "I know this politician supports abortion and same-sex marriage, but all politicians have sinned and I have to vote for somebody, so this is the one I chose to vote for." This is faulty logic and wrong thinking. It is true that all politicians sin at times, but it is not true that all politicians have a value system that supports, justifies, or legislates sinful practices. When a politician wants to use his or her platform to promote unrighteousness or use the dollars of taxpayers to support sin and legislate immorality, this type of politician should not get support from godly individuals.

Clean Out the Closet

It is clear to me that many "Christians," and I use that term loosely, are lazy and complacent. They don't take the time to really study the Bible and understand what God requires of them as a follower of Christ. Instead, their aim is to make an "image" of God that is convenient to the lifestyle they want to live. However, God doesn't work that way.

In our morally loose, politically-correct culture, more and more people are coming out of the closet and parading their immoral lifestyles. But God's Word teaches that we should not be boasting about our sins. Instead, we should be "cleaning out our closets" and repenting of them. We cannot live in open rebellion to God's Word and still have a relationship with Him. Many people do not want to hear or accept this truth, but the Bible is very clear on it.

As a minister of the gospel, I don't preach against sin to be mean or hateful. Ministers are required by God's Word to preach repentance from sin out of love for people. Because God loves us, He corrects us (see Hebrews 12:6). He calls preachers to openly warn others that the result of living in sin is eternal death, but the gift of God is eternal life (see Romans 6:23). Yes, we make mistakes and sin against God, but if we repent for our sins, He is faithful to forgive us and wash us clean from all wrong (see 1 John 1:9). There is, however, no forgiveness for intentional, unrepentant sin....period! Scripture declares,

> Do you not know that the unrighteous and the wrongdoers will not inherit or have any share in the kingdom of God? Do not be deceived (misled): neither the impure and immoral, nor idolaters, nor adulterers, nor those who participate in homosexuality, nor cheats (swindlers and thieves), nor greedy graspers, nor drunkards, nor foulmouthed revilers and slanderers, nor extortioners and robbers will inherit or have any share in the kingdom of God.
> **—1 Corinthians 6:9-10 AMP**

These are not my words; they are directly from the Word of God. It seems very clear that if we live our lives openly and willfully sinning, we cannot have a relationship with Him. First John 1:7 AMP says, "If we [really] are living and walking in the Light, as He [Himself] is in the Light, we have [true, unbroken] fellowship with one another, and the blood of Jesus Christ His Son cleanses (removes) us from all sin and guilt...." Without being connected in vital union with Jesus, we are not true Christians. Again, this is not my opinion. It is what the Bible says. So don't get mad at me...I am just the messenger.

The reason I tend to talk more about sins like homosexuality and abortion is *not* because I am a religious zealot who likes to harp on certain sins more than others. I do it because the media, the educational institutions, and other organizations in the world system are constantly working to desensitize people to the depravity of these particular sins. That is, they are continually bombarding our minds and our children's minds with the false notion that abortion and homosexuality are normal and acceptable, which is totally contrary to the Word of God.

If you hear a lie long enough, you will begin to believe it—especially if you are not rooted in the Word of God. This is why I and many other Christians who are concerned about restoring our nation's moral fabric are regularly pointing out that these immoral acts are *not* right in God's sight. We are combating the enemy's constant barrage of lies with a constant barrage of truth in these areas in order to keep our nation from being brainwashed. In other words, we are putting forth a greater concentrated effort to bring the healing cure where the "cancer" of sin is growing most.

God loves all people, but He hates all sin because sin hurts and destroys lives. It breaks His heart to see cities hold parades for people that are living in a lifestyle that He calls "detestable" (see Leviticus 18:22).

God despises it even more when we ignore wrongdoing and accept, or make excuses for, sin. If you are a Christian who is deliberately living a lifestyle that glorifies what God says is unacceptable, you are mocking Him, and He will not be mocked (see Galatians 6:7,8).

Jesus said, "If you [really] love Me, you will keep (obey) My commands" (John 14:15 AMP). Jesus did not die on the cross so that we can live in sin yet claim to be His followers. He is a Holy God and will lovingly but firmly deal with those who bear His name and choose to live a life of sin. Indeed, judgment begins with the house of God (see 1 Peter 4:17). With the condition that many of our American churches are in, we need to make some drastic changes so that we do not continue to slide down the slippery slope of compromise.

The good news is that God has promised to forgive us and deliver us, if we are willing to humble ourselves and fully turn to Him. The Scripture says,

> If my people, which are called by my name, shall humble themselves, and pray, and seek my face, and turn from their wicked ways; then will I hear from heaven, and will forgive their sin, and will heal their land.
>
> **—2 Chronicles 7:14 KJV**

Based on this Scripture, we can see that *true liberation* for any ethnic group or nation can only come from taking personal responsibility for our actions, turning away from our corrupt ways, and turning to God. His merciful help is our only hope of change!

True Hope and Change Cannot Come from Man

As black people, we cannot be so desperate for "hope and change" that we allow someone to sell us a bill of goods just because they happen to be black, a Democrat, or a good public speaker. There are a lot of political and church leaders who specialize in getting people of color all riled up into thinking that they are going to be "saved" by a liberal political party or by a "Messianic" black man who happens to be charismatic. Consequently, many black people run to the polls and cast their vote solely based on a person's race or political party rather than on his or her true character and values.

It is as if people in the black church are saying, "If I am going to be led down the highway to hell, at least I am going to be led there by an eloquent black man who will give me 'social justice.'" Unfortunately, too many black people have allowed a "free government cheese" mentality to dupe them into a false sense of hope regarding promises that will never come true. The government alone will never raise up the black community. The people in the community must take a certain amount of personal responsibility themselves. I am all for social justice—as long as it is the kind of justice that lines up with sensible, biblical values.

I am amazed at the number of people I have talked with about these key issues who say, in essence, that they don't care about the politician's ideologies, values, or policies. As long as he or she is a black or a Democrat, that's all that matters. Sadly, many people in the black community have been hoodwinked and bamboozled into thinking that anyone who is a Republican is intrinsically evil, and anyone who is a Democrat will take them into the Promised Land. The truth is, there are corrupt Republicans and there are corrupt Democrats, and it is the responsibility of the Christian voter to become informed enough to know what is the right way to vote on Election Day, based on the values of the candidates who are running for office. More importantly, Christians need to take personal responsibility and stop putting so much trust in the system alone to take care of all our problems.

Consider what God says in Jeremiah 17:5-8 KJV about people who trust in man versus those who trust in the Lord:

> Thus saith the LORD; cursed be the man that trusteth in man, and maketh flesh his arm, and whose heart departeth from the LORD. For he shall be like the heath in the desert, and shall not see when good cometh; but shall inhabit the parched places in the wilderness, in a salt land and not inhabited.

> Blessed is the man that trusteth in the LORD, and whose hope the LORD is. For he shall be as a tree planted by the waters, and that spreadeth out her roots by the river, and shall not see when heat cometh, but her leaf shall be green; and shall not be careful in the year of drought, neither shall cease from yielding fruit.

This Scripture is right on target for our present culture because it lets us know that putting false hope in a politician or any other person is a sure-fire way to disillusionment and failure. On the contrary, Scripture also informs us that putting our hope and trust in the Lord is the sure-fire way to succeed—even in the midst of recession or drought.

Sometimes disillusionment can be a healthy thing. Perhaps all of the people who are looking to mere mortals like Barack Obama to be their "Messiah" will be gravely disappointed when they find out that he cannot truly bring the hope and change they long for. The Republicans have had their opportunity, and a lot of people have been disappointed. Now it's the Democratic Party's turn, and after many more people are disappointed by these far-left liberals, perhaps we will finally decide to seek real hope and change from the Lord above. It's been a long time comin', but a change is gonna come!

You Can Make a Difference!

You might see yourself as just an average citizen, but you have a lot more power than you think. Politicians are generally obsessed with getting votes; therefore, they will pay attention to your letters, emails, faxes, and phone calls protesting some of their policies. If they get bombarded from concerned citizens like you, then some of them will begin to change their minds about instituting some of these ungodly policies that are being proposed.

George W. Bush was not a perfect president, but many people in the Christian community gave him credit for supporting our basic religious liberties and freedom of speech, as well as upholding certain moral values, such as the sanctity of life and marriage. Consequently, they rewarded him by going to the polls and voting for him. If it were not for the votes and prayers from the evangelical Christian community, I am sure that George W. Bush would have never defeated Al Gore by the skin of his teeth. I believe this is why every politician under the sun is now trying to pretend to be a Christian—because they realize that the Christian vote can be the deciding factor in many elections.

Similarly, Barack Obama probably would not be president today if he had not gotten a large number of votes from the black church community and the African-American community at large. Even many white churchgoers voted for him. Again, the reason I am saying this is to pound home the point that your vote as an individual makes a huge difference, and our collective votes as the church community carry great weight on how an election is decided.

With this in mind, what would happen if more Christians became more politically savvy and decided to call these politicians on the carpet on certain issues? What if we became more informed and responsible voters and told them they could not earn our votes as long as they supported things like abortion, extreme gay rights activism, same-sex marriage, bogus hate crimes legislation, the fairness doctrine, excessive taxing and spending, and the like? This would force some of the wrong politicians *out* of office and help get more righteous politicians *into* office.

I am not implying that we should put all of our hope in getting the right politicians in office. But we do need to do our part in terms of voting for and supporting people whose policies are closest to the biblical values we profess to believe. This is especially true when it comes to policies related to the sanctity of life, the sacredness of marriage between a man and a woman, freedom of speech, religious liberties, and free enterprise.

As a black man I reserve the right to make a choice. I am not telling you who to vote for in the future, nor am I telling you to vote Republican. What I am saying is that I put a high priority on my belief in the sanctity of life, the institution of marriage, and my personal and religious liberties. They are the very foundation upon which civilization rests. My vote will reflect what the most important issues of the day are. I will not allow color, gender, or political party to overshadow the issues that must be dealt with in accordance to the will of my Creator. I will not vote for a candidate who does not share my same views on these vital issues. That is a personal thing with me; you have the right under our Constitution to not only differ with my opinion, but to vote for whomever you like. But keep in mind, if you are a believer, your first allegiance is to God.

So use your voice—it makes a difference! Be aware of what your candidate believes in *before* you cast your vote, and don't give in to the pressure or manipulation of religious and race-card politics. No matter what anyone tells you, it is foolish to not find out what a person believes before you vote for them. Call the candidate's office or "google" his or her name and check out his or her website to find out where the candidate stands on key issues. Then share what you find out with your friends. If we ignore the very core beliefs of the candidates that are running for office, then we might as well just put names in a hat and choose the presidency that way. As a Christian, you should look to vote for the person who most closely reflects your morals and values. We cannot, nor should we, separate our vote from our values.

And by all means, **pray** for God's mercy on America. As Daniel did for Israel in the days of old, repent for the sins of our nation and ask Him to forgive us and heal our land. Pray that people's eyes would be opened to the truth and that their hearts would be softened and turned back to Him. Just as you should not underestimate the power of your vote, never underestimate the power of your prayers. As Scripture says, "…The earnest (heartfelt, continued) prayer of a righteous man makes tremendous power available [dynamic in its working]" (James 5:16 AMP). Although turning things around may seem impossible to us, *nothing is impossible with God!*

About the Author

Joseph L. Green was born in Washington, D.C., but grew up in Harrisburg, Pennsylvania. He is a 1985 graduate of Harrisburg High School and attended the University of Pittsburgh and Towson University. He graduated with a Bachelor of Science degree in communications and also spent four years in the U.S. Navy as an electronic technician.

In January 2005, Joe started his radio career as a production engineer and on-air personality for radio station WWII 720 AM "THE ROCK" in Shiremanstown, Pennsylvania. In June of 2007, he purchased 720 AM and became the first African-American to ever own an FCC licensed radio station in central Pennsylvania. Before parting with 720 AM, he partnered with Bruce Collier in 2008, using licensee name Trustworthy Radio, to acquire WHYL-960 AM, at that time his second AM station in Pennsylvania's centrally-located capital market, Harrisburg-Lebanon-Carlisle.

While acting as co-owner of WHYL-960 AM in Carlisle, Pennsylvania, Joe Green is presently fulfilling his mission as the pastor and founder of the Antioch Assembly Church in Harrisburg, Pennsylvania and as founder of Josiah Generation Ministries, an international ministry providing public speaking, training, and Bible teaching.

Joe grew up in the church and was baptized at the age of nine. As a teenager, he was lured into a world of sex, drugs, and violence. This fast life came to a head when in the year 2000 he returned to Harrisburg homeless and broken. But in 2007, when he became the owner of his first radio station, he became a living testimony who proved that through God all things are possible regardless of any failures, setbacks, or disadvantages an individual has faced in life.

He was inspired to write his autobiography to show how God changed him from a law-breaking person who sold kilos of drugs to a law-abiding citizen who is now sold out to building God's kingdom.

Joe is married to Gwendolyn Green and together they have four children.

Made in the USA
Charleston, SC
13 January 2013